TEXAS RANGER SERVICE RECORDS

1847-1900

VOLUME 6
T - Z

Frances T. Ingmire

Heritage Books
2024

HERITAGE BOOKS

AN IMPRINT OF HERITAGE BOOKS, INC.

Books, CDs, and more—Worldwide

For our listing of thousands of titles see our website
at
www.HeritageBooks.com

Published 2024 by
HERITAGE BOOKS, INC.
Publishing Division
5810 Ruatan Street
Berwyn Heights, MD 20740

International Standard Book Number
Paperbound: 978-0-7884-7792-8

TABLE OF CONTENTS

FRONTIER BATTALIONS & COMPANIES
MINUTE MEN & COMPANIES
COUNTIES--MINUTE MEN--COMMANDING OFFICERS
COUNTIES--FRONTIER BATTALLIONS--COMMANDING OFFICERS
COUNTIES--MISC. UNITS--COMMANDING OFFICERS

NOTE: Place of Birth in this Ranger Index usually means place of Residence at time of enlistment.

TABER, Robert See TABOR, Robert.
TABOR, Robert, Pvt., Comm. Off: SUBLETT, David L., Capt., Organ: Co. of Texas Rangers, Enlist: Jan. 19,61 at Waco for 3 months, Mus. out May 14, 61 at Waco, Age: 24. R&F 57; En. Off: L.S. ROSS; Mus. Off: D.L. SUBLETT; Val. H. $90; HE. $15; Guns. $25; Pistols. $35; Serv. 3 mos. 26 days at $25-Amt. of pay $96.66, less stoppages of: $36.54 to F.C. DOWNS, J. THOMA-son by P/A $64.00 - Total stoppages $100.54; Mus. roll pays stoppages to J. THOMASON were $55.25; Called into serv. of state by Gov. Sam HOUSTON from Feb. 7-61 for 3 mos.; 1 Muster Roll & 1 Pay Roll; Ammunition stotes, pack mules, etc. turned over to Capt. J.M. KNIGHT's Co.. Men residing in vicinity of station may be discharged before marching.
TACKITT, A.C., Capt., Comm. Off: TACKITT, A.C., Organ: Young Co. Rangers, Enlist: Jan. 6, 1874, Disc: Feb. 14, 1874, Place of Birth: Young County, 39 days of service, Ranger Muster Roll. Girard, Kent Co., Texas.
TACKITT, A.C., 1st Sgt., Comm. Off: TACKITT, L.L., Organ: Co. I Minute Men, Enlist: Oct. 20, 1865, Disc: June 22, 1866, Place of Birth: Parker County, 58 days, Ranger Muster Roll.
TACKITT, L.L., Capt., Comm. Off: TACKITT, L.L., Organ: 1st Co. of Minute Men, Enlist: Oct. 20, 1865, Disc: June 22, 1866, Place of Birth: Parker County, 95 days service, Ranger Muster Roll.
TACKITT, L.L., Comm. Off: GILLILAND, J.C., Lt., Organ: Co. P, Texas Minute Men, Enlist: Aug. 22, 1872, Disc: Aug. 18, 1873, Place of Birth: Leedey, Dewey Co., Okla., Box 96, Dept. of the Interior--Pensions, N.H. NICHOLSON, Inspector.
TACKITT, M.D., Capt., Comm. Off: TACKITT, M.D., Capt., Organ: Jack Cty. Rangers or Minute Men, Enlist: Jy.17, 61. Total Service 114 days. R&F 51; 3 QR dated Jy.24-O.13-61, ex. call 7 days Au.5;O.16-D.31-61, ex. call 6 days; Ja.1-Feb.28-62, ex. call 10 days Feb. 10; H & HE $100; Arms 1 Shotgun $25; $1 deducted from wages & placed to order of Reuben HENDRICKS for furnishing beef for ex. calls, $55 for beef; Co. organized under act of F.7-61; 1 Muster Roll dated Jy.24-61, 3 QR & 1 Appraisal Roll; Oath with Roll; QR dated Jy.24-Oct.13-61 shows 42 days reg. scout, 8 days ex. call, total 50 days; QR dated Oct.16-D.31-61 shows 30 days reg. scout, 10 days ex. call, total 40 days; QR dated Jan. 1-Feb. 28-62 shows 19 days reg. scout, 5 days ex. call, total 24 days; $1.50 pd to HENDRICKS for beef.
TACKITT, P.A., 2nd Sgt., Comm. Off: TACKITT, A.C., Organ: Young Co. Rangers, Enlist: Jan. 6, 1874, Disc: Feb. 14, 1874, Place of Birth: Young County, 39 days of service, Ranger Muster Roll. Seymour, Baylor Co., TExas.
TACKITT, R.E., Pvt., Comm. Off: TACKITT, L.L., Organ: 1 Co. of Minute Men, Enlist: Oct. 20, 1865, Disc: June 22, 1866, Place of Birth: Parker County, 60 days, Ranger Muster Roll.
TACKITT, W.A., Pvt., Comm. Off: TACKITT, A.C., Organ: Young Co. Rangers, Enlist: Jan. 6, 1874, Disc: Feb. 14, 1874, Place of Birth: Young County, 39 days of service, Ranger Muster Roll. Graham, Young Co., Texas. Box 428.

TACKITT, W.A., Pvt., Comm. Off: TACKITT, L.L., Organ: 1 Company
    of Minute Men, Enlist: Oct. 20, 1865, Disc: June 22, 1866,
    Place of Birth: Parker County, 64 days service, RAnger Muster
    Roll.
TAFF, Nimrod J., Pvt., Comm. Off: CONNER, John H., Organ: Mounted
    Rangers, Enlist: Jan. 20, 1860, 12 months service, Age: 20,
    Place of Birth: Austin, Ranger Muster Roll.
TALAMANTES, Jose Ma., Comm. Off: MONTES, Telesforo, Lt.,
    Organ: Minute Men, Enlist: May 27, 1874, Disc: April 20, 1876,
    Place of Birth: San Elizario, El Paso, Texas, Dept. of the
    Interior--Pensions, N.H. NICHOLSON, Inspector.
TALAMENTES, Jose Maria, Pvt., Comm. Off: GARCIA, Gregorio,
    Organ: Co. N & D Frontier Forces, Enlist: Sept. 1, 1870,
    Disc: June 15, 1871, Place of Birth: El Paso County, Ranger
    Muster Roll.
TALBOT, Simons, Pvt., Comm. Off: WILLIAMS, Samuel J., Organ: Prov.
    State Troops, Co. A, Enlist: Oct. 9, 1871, Disc: Nov. 13, 1871,
    Place of Birth: Limestone County, Ranger Muster Roll.
TALIAFERRO, M.A., Pvt., Comm. Off: STEVENS, G.W., Organ: Wise Co.
    Rangers, Enlist: Nov. 26, 1873, Disc: March 26, 1874, Place
    of Birth: Wise County, 4 months service, Ranger Muster Roll.
    Sonara, Sutton Co., Texas.
TALLEY, G.W., Pvt., Comm. Off: HALL, J.L., Organ: Special State
    Troops, Enlist: Jan. 25, 1877, Disc: Feb. 28, 1878, Place of
    Birth: Clinton, Texas, 13 months, 5 days service, Ranger Mus-
    ter Roll.
TALLY, G.W., Pvt., Comm. Off: MCNELLY, L.H., Organ: Washington
    Co. Vol. Militia, Enlist: Aug. 1, 1876, Disc: Feb. 1, 1877,
    Place of Birth: Austin, Texas, 6 months service, Ranger Muster
    Roll.
TALLEY, Jacob R., Pvt., Comm. Off: BURLESON, Ed, Organ: Mounted
    Rangers, Enlist: Jan. 2o, 1860, Disc: Sept. 7, 1860, Age: 18,
    Place of Birth: San Marcos, Ranger Muster Roll.
TALLY, John W., Pvt., Comm. Off: JONES, John S., Organ: Texas Ran-
    gers, Enlist: June 9, 1858, Disc: Aug. 5, 1858, Age: 21, Place
    of Birth: Comanche County, 1 month, 26 days service, Ranger
    Muster Roll.
TANKERSELEY, Rich. F., Pvt., Comm. Off: WILLIAMS, John, Lt.,
    Organ: Rangers, Enlist: May 24, 1858, Disc: July 28, 1858, 2
    months service, Ranger Muster Roll.
TANKERSLY, George, Pvt., Comm. Off: WILLIAMS, John, Organ: Second
    Co. of Texas Rangers, Enlist: Nov. 2, 1858, 2 months, 25 days
    Ranger Muster Roll.
TANKERSLEY, James H., Lt., Comm. Off: FORD, John S., Organ: Texas
    Rangers, Enlist: Feb. 23, 1858, Disc: Aug. 5, 1858, Place of
    Birth: Comanche County, 5 months, 12 days service, Ranger Mus-
    ter Roll.
TANKSLEY (TANKASLEY), John S., Pvt., Comm. Off: FROST, Thomas C.,
    Lt., Organ: Mounted Rangers, Enlist: Dec. 21, 1857, Disc: Mar.
    21, 1858, 3 months service, Ranger Muster Roll.
TANKERSLEY, R.T., Pvt., Comm. Off: WILLIAMS, John, Organ: Second
    Co. of Texas Rangers, Enlist: Oct. 16, 1858, 6 months service,
    Ranger Muster Roll.
TANNER, Al, Pvt., Comm. Off: SIMS, W.H., Organ: CO. O., Minute

TANNER, Al, Pvt., (Continued)
    Men, Enlist: Jan. 10, 1873, Disc: Jan. 16, 1873, Place of
    Birth: Burnet County, No service recorded, Ranger Muster Roll.
TANNER, A.Y., Pvt., Comm. Off: LONG, Ira, Organ: Co. A, Frontier
    Battalion, Enlist: Sept. 2m 1875, Disc: Nov. 30, 1875, Age: 20,
    5'11", fair, blue eyes, dark hair, farmer, Place of Birth: Bur-
    net, Texas, 2 months, 29 days service, Ranger Muster Roll.
TANNER, Isaac, Pvt., Comm. Off: BURLESON, Ed, Organ: Mounted Ran-
    gers, Enlist: Jan. 20, 1860, Disc: Sept. 7, 1860, Age: 22,
    Place of Birth: San Marcos, Discharged July 6 at Camp Beaver,
    Ranger Muster Roll.
TANER, Isaac, Pvt., Comm. Off: GRAY, S.B., Organ: Minute Men,
    Enlist: April 1, 1873, Disc: Sept. 1, 1873, Place of Birth:
    Blanco County, 21 days service, Ranger Muster Roll.
TANNER, Samuel, Pvt., Comm. Off: BURLESON, Ed, Organ: Mounted Ran-
    gers, Enlist: May 20, 1860, Disc: Sept. 7, 1860, Age: 21,
    Place of Birth: Blanco, Ranger Muster Roll.
TANNER, Solomon, Pvt., Comm. Off: CALLAHAN, James H., Organ: Mtd.
    Rangers, Enlist: July 20, 1855, Disc: Oct. 19, 1855, Place of
    Birth: Rio Blanco, 2 months, 29 days service, Ranger Muster
    Roll.
TANNER, Sol., Sgt., Comm. Off: SANSOM, John W., Organ: Texas Mtd.
    Rangers, Enlist: April 16, 1856, Disc: July 16, 1856, Age: 21,
    Place of Birth: Comal County, 90 days service, Ranger Muster
    Roll.
TARBLE, Ed, Pvt., Comm. Off: TAY, J.B., Lt., Organ: Vol Battalion
    Co. C, Enlist: Feb. 14, 1878, Disc: Feb. 28, 1878, 15 days of
    service, Ranger Muster Roll.
TARBLE, Ed, PVt., Comm. Off: TAYS, J.B., Organ: Co. C, Vol.
    Battalion, Enlist: Feb. 14, 1878, Disc: Feb. 28, 1878, Place
    of Birth: El Paso, Texas, 1 month, 16 days service, Ranger
    MusterRoll.
TARDY, R.L., Pvt., Comm. Off: BAYLOR, G.W., Organ: Co. A, Frontier
    Battalion, Enlist: Dec. 1, 1882, Disc: Feb. 15, 1883, 2 months
    15 days service, Died with Pnemonia, Ranger Muster Roll.
TARTER, Wesley, Pvt., Comm. Off: MCADAMS, W.C., Organ: Palo Pinto
    County Rangers, Enlist: Dec. 13, 1873, Disc: April 13, 1874,
    Place of Birth: Palo Pinto County, 4 months service, Ranger
    Muster Roll.
TARTER, Wiley, Pvt., Comm. Off: MCADAMS, W.C., Organ: Palo Pinto
    County Rangers, Enlist: Dec. 13, 1873, Disc: April 13, 1874,
    Place of Birth: Palo Pinto County, 4 months service, Ranger
    Muster Roll.
TARVER, R.B., Pvt., Comm. Off: CONNELL, J.G., Organ: Brown and San
    Saba Co. Rangers, Enlist: Jan. 6, 1874, Disc: March 26, 1874,
    Place of Birth: Brown and San Saba Counties, 2 months, 20 days
    service, Ranger Muster Roll.
TATE, J.L., 1st Corp., Comm. Off: WOOD, W.R., Organ: Minute Men,
    Enlist: March 6, 1860, Disc: June 4, 1860, Age: 24, Place of
    Birth: San Saba, Ranger Muster Roll.
TATUM, S.H., Pvt., Comm. Off: COLDWELL, Neal, Organ: Co. F, Fron-
    tier Battalion, Enlist: June 4, 1874, Disc: Dec. 1, 1874, Place
    of Birth: Kerr County, 5 months, 27 days service, Ranger Muster
    Roll.

TATUM, Thomas, Pvt., Comm. Off: JONES, John S., Organ: Texas Rangers, Enlist: Feb. 23, 1858, Disc: Aug. 5, 1858, Age: 20, Place of Birth: Comanche County, 5 months, 12 days service, Ranger Muster Roll.

TATUM, Thomas, 2nd Corp., Comm. Off: BLEVINS, John H., Organ: Min. Men, Enlist: March 20, 1860, Disc: June 19, 1860, Age: 23, Place of Birth: Comanche County, Ranger Muster Roll.

TATUM, Walter, Pvt., Comm. Off: BLEVINS, John H., Organ: Minute Men, Enlist: March 20, 1860, Disc: June 19, 1860, Age: 19, Place of Birth: Comanche, Ranger Muster Roll.

TAY, J.B., 2nd Lt., Comm. Off: TAY, J.B., Lt., Organ: Vol. Battalion Co. C, Enlist: Nov. 10, 1877, Disc: Feb. 28, 1878, 3 mos. 21 days service, RAnger Muster Roll.

TAYLOR, A., Pvt., Comm. Off: TEAGUE, John, Organ: Minute Men, Enlist: Oct. 13, 1865, Disc: April 3, 1866, Age: 20, Place of Birth: Wise County, 20 days service, Ranger Muster Roll.

TAYLOR, A.L., Pvt., Comm. Off: WALLER, J.R., Organ: Co. A, Frontier Battalion, Enlist: May 25, 1874, Disc: April 30, 1874, Place of Birth: Erath County, 11 months, 11 days service, Ranger Muster Roll. Grimes, Okla., R.F.Q.3.

TAYLOR, A,T,, Corp., Comm. Off: ALEXANDER, John, Organ: Co. O, Minute Men, Burnet Co., Enlist: Sept. 11, 1872, Disc: Aug. 13, 1873, Place of Birth: Burnet County, 20 days of service, Ranger Muster Roll.

TAYLOR, Albert C., Pvt., Comm. Off: FORD, John S., Organ: 2nd Co. of Rangers, Enlist: Nov. 10, 1858, Disc: May 10, 1859, Age: 21, Place of Birth: Austin, Ranger Muster Roll.

TAYLOR, B.F., Pvt., Comm. Off: BAYLOR, G.W., Organ: Co. A, Frontier Battalion, Enlist: March 1884, Disc: Jan. 20, 1885, Place of Birth: Pecos City, 4 months, 20 days service, Ranger Muster Roll.

TAYLOR, B.W., Pvt., Comm. Off: HAMILTON, G.H., Organ: Co. B, Frontier Battalion, Enlist: Sept. 1, 1875, Disc: Nov. 30, 1875, Place of Birth: Flat Top Mountain, 3 months service, Ranger Muster Roll.

TAYLOR, C., Pvt., Comm. Off: HOFFAR, John, Lt., Organ: Frontier Battalion Co. C, Enlist: Mar. 1, 1883, Disc: Aug. 31, 1883, 5 months service, Photostat: Orig. in A.G. Office.

TAYLOR, Charley, Pvt., Comm. Off: CALLAHAN, James H., Organ: Mtd. Rangers, Enlist: July 20, 1855, Disc: Oct. 19, 1855, Place of Birth: San Marcos, 2 months, 29 days service, Ranger Muster Roll.

TAYLOR, Chas., Pvt., Comm. Off: CONNELL, J.G., Organ: Brown and San Saba Co. Rangers, Enlist: Jan. 6, 1874, Disc: March 26, 1874, Place of Birth: Brown and San Saba Counties, 2 months, 20 days service, Ranger Muster Roll. Brownwood, TExas, 608 Main St.

TAYLOR, Chas. L., Pvt., Comm. Off: WEEKES, Nicholas, Organ: Star Rifles Militia, Enlist: Sept. 21, 1874, Disc: Sept. 27, 1874, Place of Birth: Galveston County, 7 days service, Ranger Muster Roll.

TAYLOR, D.S., Pvt., Comm. Off: STEVENS, G.W., Organ: Co. B, Frontier Battalion, Enlist: Aug. 15, 1874, Disc: Dec. 10, 1874, Place of Birth: Lost Valley, 17 days and 3 months service, Ranger Muster Roll.

TAYLOR, D.H., Pvt., Comm. Off: STEVENS, G.W., Organ: Wise County
    Rangers, Enlist: Nov. 26, 1873, Disc: March 26, 1874, Place of
    Birth: Wise County, 4 months service, Ranger Muster Roll.
TAYLOR, Edward, Pvt., Comm. Off: HENRY, W.W., Organ: Rangers,
    Enlist: June 19, 1859, Place of Birth: Sabinal River, Ranger
    Muster Roll.
TAYLOR, E.D., Pvt., Comm. Off: BAKER, D.P., Organ: Frontier For-
    ces, Co. F., Enlist: Nov. 5, 1870, Disc: June 15, 1871, Place
    of Birth: Decatur, Wise County, Ranger Muster Roll.
TAYLOR, Francis C., Pvt., Comm. Off: FITZHUGH, Wm., Organ: Texas
    Militia, Mtd. Vol., Enlist: Nov. 2, 1854, Disc: Feb. 2, 1854,
    Age: 19, Place of Birth: McKinney, Texas, 3 months service,
    Ranger Muster Roll.
TAYLOR, R.W., Pvt., Comm. Off: MCCLURE, D.H., Organ: Co. T, Min.
    Men, Palo Pinto Co., Enlist: Sept. 5, 1872, Disc: Aug. 12,
    1873, Place of Birth: Palo Pinto County, 120 days of service,
    Ranger Muster Roll. Clarendon, Texas.
TAYLOR, G.A., Pvt., Comm. Off: CAMPBELL, G.W., Organ: Montague
    Co. Rangers, Enlist: Dec. 13, 1873, Disc: Feb. 13, 1874, Place
    of Birth: Montague County, 2 months service, Ranger Muster
    Roll.
TAYLOR, J.H., Pvt., Comm. Off: WALLER, J.H., Organ: Co. A, Fron-
    tier Battalion, Enlist: May 25, 1874, Disc: April 30, 1875,
    Place of Birth: Stevens County, 11 months, 11 days service,
    Ranger Muster Roll. Cheyenne, Okla., R.R. 3.
TAYLOR, J. Andrew, Pvt., Comm. Off: DARNELL, N.H., Organ: Mtd.
    Rangers, Enlist: April 14, 1860, Disc: Aug. 13, 1860, Place of
    Birth: Dallas, Ranger Muster Roll.
TAYLOR, Jacob A., Pvt., Comm. Off: WOODS, Wm. M., Organ: Mtd.
    Rangers, Enlist: April 10, 1860, Disc: Aug. 10, 1860, Age: 19,
    Place of Birth: Bonham, Ranger Muster Roll.
TAYLOR, James R., Pvt., Comm. Off: HERRON, Andrew, Organ: Mounted
    Vol. for Cortinas War, Enlist: Nov. 18, 1859, Disc: Jan. 1,
    1860, Age: 21, Place of Birth: Swguine, Ranger Muster Roll.
TAYLOR, John, Pvt., Comm. Off: ENGLISH, Levi, Organ: Mounted
    Volunteers, Enlist: Aug. 6, 1855, Disc: Nov. 13, 1855, Place
    of Birth: Bexar County, 3 months, 8 days service, Ranger Mus-
    ter Roll.
TAYLOR, John, Pvt., Comm. Off: ROGERS, P.H., Capt., Organ: Mtd.
    Vol., Enlist: Oct. 1854, Disc: Dec. 1854, 3 months service,
    Ranger Muster Roll. Ex. order of March 1856.
TAYLOR, John, Pvt., Comm. Off: MARLIN, W.N.P., Organ: Texas Mtd.
    Rangers, Enlist: July 15, 1858, Disc: Nov. 14, 1858, Place of
    Birth: Camp Runnels, 4 months service, Ranger Muster Roll.
TAYLOR, John A., Pvt., Comm. Off: ROGERS, P.H., Capt.,
    Organ: Mtd. Vol., Enlist: Oct. 1854, Disc: Dec. 1854, 3 months
    service, Ranger Muster Roll. Ex. order of March, 1856.
TAYLOR, John M., SEE S. MCMAHAN.
TAYLOR, Joseph, Pvt., Comm. Off: HENRY, William R., Organ: Co. C,
    Mounted Vol., Enlist: Dec. 14, 1854, Disc: March 14, 1855,
    Age: 21, Place of Birth: San Antonio, 3 months service, Ranger
    Muster Roll.
TAYLOR, Isaac N., Pvt., Comm. Off: FORD, John S., Organ: 3rd Co.
    of Rangers, Enlist: Feb. 1, 1860, Disc: May 17, 1860, Age: 26,
    Place of Birth: Brownsville, Detailed as Captain, Ranger Muster
    Roll.

TAYLOR, John, Pvt., Comm. Off: MARLIN, Wm. N.P., Organ: Rangers,
    Enlist: July 16, 1858, Disc: April 4, 1859, Age: 38, Place of
    Birth: Camp Runnel, Ranger Muster Roll.
TAYLOR, J.T., Pvt., Comm. Off: LACEY, Organ: Co. F, Minute Men of
    Gillispie Co., Enlist: April 18, 1872, Disc: April 23, 1874,
    Place of Birth: Gillispie County, 100 days of service, Ranger
    Muster Roll.
TAYLOR, John W., Pvt., Comm. Off: CASEY, B.P., Organ: Co. F, Min.
    Men of Gillispie Co., Enlist: Jan. 17, 1874, Disc: April 23,
    1874, Place of Birth: Gillispie County, 40 days of service,
    Ranger Muster Roll. Junction, Kimble Co., Texas.
TAYLOR, Lewis H., Pvt., Comm. Off: DARNELL, N.H., Organ: Unknown;
    Enlist: April 14, 1860, Disc: Aug. 13, 1860, Place of
    Birth: Dallas, Ranger Muster Roll.
TAYLOR, M.J., Pvt., Comm. Off: MOORE, D.D., Capt., Organ: Moscow
    Guards, Cav. Co., Polk Co., TST, Enlist: Nov. 1860, at Moscow,
    Tex. R&F 76; Co. org. with 64 volunteers who agreed to meet
    not less than 6 or more than 7 times a year; unless called out
    on special duty; 1 Muster Roll.
TAYLOR, Moses, Pvt., Comm. Off: CONNER, John H., Organ: Mounted
    Rangers, Enlist: Jan. 20, 1860, 12 months service, Age: 22,
    Place of Birth: Austin, Elected 4th Sgt. Feb. 7, 1860, Ranger
    Muster Roll.
TAYLOR, N.A., Pvt., Comm. Off: WILLIAMS, John, Organ: Second Co.
    of Texas Rangers, Enlist: Nov. 2, 1858, 6 months service,
    Ranger Muster Roll.
TAYLOR, Parker, Pvt., Comm. Off: SNOWBALL, James, Organ: Prov.
    State Troops, Enlist: Oct. 13, 1871, Disc: Oct. 20, 1871,
    Place of Birth: Groesbeck, Texas, Ranger Muster Roll.
TAYLOR, P.J., Pvt., Comm. Off: MCADAMS, W.C., Organ: Palo Pinto
    County Rangers, Enlist: Dec. 13, 1873, Disc: April 13, 1874,
    Place of Birth: Palo Pinto County, 4 months service, Ranger
    Muster Roll. Tipton Tillman Co., Okla.
TAYLOR, Robert B., Pvt., Comm. Off: HENRY, William R., Organ: Co.
    C, Mounted Vol., Enlist: Dec. 14, 1854, Disc: March 14, 1855,
    Age: 25, Place of Birth: San Antonio, 3 months service, Ranger
    Muster Roll.
TAYLOR, S.S., Pvt., Comm. Off: JONES, Stephen F., Organ: Minute
    Men, Detached, Enlist: Aug. 1, 1860, Disc: Aug. 29, 1860,
    Place of Birth: Palo Pinto, Ranger Muster Roll.
TAYLOR, T.Y., Pvt., Comm. Off: PATTON, C.A., Organ: Kendall Co.
    Min. Men Co. C, Enlist: Feb. 4, 1872, Disc: March 1, 1874,
    Place of Birth: Kendall County, No service recorded, Ranger
    Muster Roll.
TAYLOR, W.B., Pvt., Comm. Off: CAMPBELL, G.W., Organ: Montague
    Co. Rangers, Enlist: Dec. 13, 1873, Disc: Feb. 13, 1874, Place
    of Birth: Montague County, 2 months service, Ranger Muster
    Roll. Vinita, Craig Co., Okla.
TAYLOR, W.H., Pvt., Comm. Off: LACEY, J.C., Organ: Co. F, Minute
    Men of Gillispie Co., Enlist: April 18, 1872, Disc: April 23,
    1874, Place of Birth: Gillispie County, 110 days of service,
    Ranger Muster Roll.
TAYLOR, W.H., 1st Corp., Comm. Off: PEAK, June, Organ: Co. B,
    Frontier Battalion, Enlist: Sept. 1, 1878, Disc: Nov. 30, 1878,

TAYLOR, W.H., 1st Corp., (Continued)
Place of Birth: Runnels County, 3 months service, Ranger Muster Roll.

TAYLOR, W.H., Pvt., Comm. Off: ARRINGTON, G.W., Organ: Co. C, Frontier Battalion, Enlist: Aug. 31, 1877, Disc: Feb. 28, 1878, Place of Birth: Coleman County, 6 months service, Ranger Muster Roll.

TAYLOR, W.H.H., Pvt., Comm. Off: GREEN, M.R., Organ: Comanche Co. Rangers, Enlist: Jan. 17, 1874, Disc: Feb. 17, 1874, Place of Birth: Comanche County, 1 month service, Ranger Muster Roll.

TAYLOR, W.M., Pvt., Comm. Off: MCNELLY, L.H., Organ: Washington Co. Vol. Militia, Enlist: April 1, 1875, Disc: June 30, 1875, Place of Birth: Austin, Texas, 3 months service, Ranger Muster Roll.

TAYLOR, Wm., Pvt., Comm. Off: SNOWBALL, James, Organ: Prov. State Troops, Enlist: Oct. 13, 1871, Disc: Oct. 20, 1871, Place of Birth: Groesbeck, Texas, Ranger Muster Roll.

TAYS, J.B., 2nd Lt., Comm. Off: TAYS, J.B., Organ: Co. C, Vol. Battalion, Enlist: Nov. 10, 1877, Disc: Feb. 28, 1878, Place of Birth: El Paso County, 3 months 21 days service, Ranger Muster Roll.

TEAGUE, John, Capt., Comm. Off: TEAGUE, John, Organ: Minute Men, Enlist: Oct. 13, 1865, Disc: April 3, 1866, Age: 42, Place of Birth: Wise County, 17 days service, Ranger Muster Roll.

TEAGUE, John, Capt., Comm. Off: TEAGUE, John, Capt., Organ: Min. Men, Wise County, Enlist: Oct. 14, 1865, Age: 42. R&F 32; Arms: Rifle and Revolver; 1 Muster Roll.

TEAGUE, Malem, Pvt., Comm. Off: HUNTER, James M., Organ: Co. I, Frontier Forces, Enlist: Sept. 12, 1870, Disc: Dec. 1, 1870, Place of Birth: Austin, Texas, Deserted 2 months 18 days, Ranger Muster Roll.

TEAGUE, Thomas, Pvt., Comm. Off: SUBLETT, David L., Capt., Organ: Co. of Texas Rangers, Enlist: Feb. 15, 61 at McKinney for 3 mos., Mus. out May 14, 61 at Waco. R&F 57; En. Off: MCGARAH; Mus. Off: D.L. SUBLETT; Val. H. $135, HE. $10; Guns. $30; Serv. 3 mos. at $25.00 - Amt. of pay $75.00, less stoppages of $61.14 to F.C. DOWNS; Called into serv. of state by Gov. Sam HOUSTON from F.7-61 for 3 mos.; 1 Muster Roll & 1 Pay Roll; Ammunition stores, pack mules, etc. turned over to Capt. J.M. KNIGHT's Co.. Men residing in vicinity of station may be discharged before marching.

TEASMAN, Frederick, Pvt., Comm. Off: SANSOM, John W., Organ: Frontier Forces, Enlist: Aug. 25, 1870, Disc: May 31, 1871, Place of Birth: Shackleford County, Ranger MusterRoll.

TEBO, A.E., Pvt., Comm. Off: GREEN, M.R., Organ: Comanche County Rangers, Enlist: Jan. 17, 1874, Disc: Feb. 17, 1874, Place of Birth: Comanche County, 1 month service, Ranger Muster Roll.

TEBO, A.E., Pvt., Comm. Off: WALLER, J.E., Organ: Co. A., Frontier Battalion, Enlist: May 25, 1874, Disc: April 30, 1875, Place of Birth: Erath County, 11 months, 11 days, Ranger Muster Roll.

TEDFORD, R.O., Pvt., Comm. Off: SANSOM, John W., Organ: Frontier Forces, Enlist: Aug. 25, 1870, Disc: May 31, 1871, Place of Birth: Shackleford Co., Ranger Muster Roll. San Antonio, Tex. 122 Klein St.

TEETER, George T., Pvt., Comm. Off: FITZHUGH, Wm., Organ: Texas
    Militia, Mtd. Vol., Enlist: Nov. 2, 1854, Disc: Feb. 2, 1854,
    Age: 22, Place of Birth: McKinney, Texas, 3 months service,
    Ranger Muster Roll.
TEJARINO, Francisco, Pvt., Comm. Off: MCCULLOCH, Henry E., Capt.,
    Organ: Texas Mtd. Vols., Enlist: May 5, 1851, Disc: Nov. 5,
    1851, Age: 24, Enlisted at: Fort Merrill, 6 months service,
    Ranger Muster Roll.
TELOTTE, N.L., Pvt., Comm. Off: DOLAN, Pat, Organ: Co. F, Fron-
    tier Battalion, Enlist: Aug. 20, 1877, Disc: Feb. 28, 1878,
    Place of Birth: Kerr County, 6 months, 13 days service, Ranger
    Muster Roll.
TELGMAN, Charles, Pvt., Comm. Off: HENRY, William R., Organ: Co.
    C, Mounted Vol., Enlist: Dec. 14, 1854, Disc: Jan. 1, 1855,
    Age: 22, Place of Birth: San Antonio, Discharged with Disgrace,
    18 days service, Ranger Muster Roll. Pay Roll gives 2 months
    service.
TELLEGEMAN, Chas., Pvt., Comm. Off: COLDWELL, Neal, Organ: Co. F,
    Frontier Battalion, Enlist: Oct. 18, 1875, Disc: Dec. 31, 1875,
    Place of Birth: Kerr County, 2 months, 14 days--Deserted, Ran-
    ger Muster Roll.
TELGMAN, William, Pvt., Comm. Off: HENRY, William R., Organ: Co.
    C, Mounted Vol., Enlist: Dec. 14, 1854, Disc: Jan. 1, 1855,
    Age: 24, Place of Birth: San Antonio, Discharged with Disgrace,
    18 days service in U.S. Service, Ranger Muster Roll. Pay Roll
    gives 2 months service.
TEMPLE, B.L., Pvt., Comm. Off: DOLAN, Pat, Organ: Co. F, Frontier
    Battalion, Enlist: May 1, 1877, Disc: Nov. 30, 1877, Place of
    Birth: Kerr County, 4 months service, Ranger Muster Roll.
    Yoakum, Texas, 311 Montgomery St.
TEMPLE, James L., Pvt., Comm. Off: HARRELL, J.M., Organ: Co. K,
    Frontier Forces, Enlist: Sept. 16, 1870, Disc: Feb. 20, 1871,
    Place of Birth: Austin, Ranger Muster Roll.
TEMPLETON, W.R., Pvt., Comm. Off: MCNELLY, L.H., Organ: Washing-
    ton Co. Vol. Militia, Enlist: April 6, 1875, Disc: Oct. 1,
    1875, Place of Birth: Austin, Texas, 5 months, 25 days service,
    Ranger Muster Roll.
TENIS, Bazel, Pvt., Comm. Off: LOWE, John C., 1st Lt., Organ: Ran-
    ger Company, Enlist: Je. 19-60, Disc: Dec. 24, 60. R&F 43;
    Serv. 11 days at $25 per mo. - $9.16, plus $2.40 for travelling
    rations - $11.56 Total amt. paid; Due 8 days rations; 1 Pay
    Roll.
TENTROH, William, Pvt., Comm. Off: WALKER, John G., Capt.,
    Organ: Mtd. Vol., Enlist: Nov. 1854, Ranger Muster Roll.
TERCEY, L.W., Pvt., Comm. Off: JOHNSON, Thomas J., Organ: Mounted
    Rangers, Enlist: June 18, 1860, Disc: Nov. 10, 1860, Place of
    Birth: Fort Worth, Ranger Muster Roll.
TERO, Francisco, Pvt., Comm. Off: HARRISON, Thos., Capt.,
    Organ: Tex. Rangers, Enlist: Jan. 10, 61 at Waco for 6 months;
    unless sooner discharged, Age: 36. R&F 51; Thos. HARRISON, En.
    Off: J.C. NEWLON, Mus. Off: S.P. ROSS & D.R. LINSLEY, Apprs.
    H: $80; HE: $30; Gun: $25. Co. sta. at camp near Waco Ja. 8-
    61. Called into service of State by Gov. Sam HOUSTON. 1 Mus-
    ter Roll.

TERO, Guadalupe, Pvt., Comm. Off: HARRISON, Thos., Capt.,
    Organ: Tex. Rangers, Enlist: Ja. 10-61 at Waco for 6 months;
    unless sooner discharged. Age: 26. R&F 51; Thos. HARRISON;
    En. Off: J.C. NEWLON, Mus. Off: S.P. ROSS & D.R. LINSLEY,
    apprs. H: $100; HE: $30; Gun: $25. Co. sta. at camp near
    Waco Ja. 8-61. Called into service of State by Gov. HOUSTON.
    1 Muster Roll: Ja. 10, 61.
TERRELL, A.J., Pvt., Comm. Off: LONG, Ira & COLDWELL, Neal,
    Organ: Co. A, Frontier Battalion, Enlist: Sept. 16, 1875,
    Disc: Feb. 14, 1878, Age: 18, 5'6", dark hair, brown eyes,
    Student-later lawyer, Place of Birth: Austin, TExas, 7 months
    24 days service, Ranger Muster Roll.
TERRELL, Harry, Pvt., Comm. Off: WILLIAMS, Organ: Prov. State
    Troops, Co. A, Enlist: Oct. 9, 1871, Disc: Nov. 13, 1871,
    Place of Birth: Limestone County, Ranger Muster Roll.
TERRELL, J., Pvt., Comm. Off: IKARD, E.F., Organ: Co. C, Frontier
    Battalion, Enlist: May 20, 1874, Disc: Dec. 10, 1874, Place of
    Birth: Clay County, 6 months, 22 days service, Ranger Muster
    Roll.
TERRELL, John, Pvt., Comm. Off: CHAMBERLAIN, Bland, Organ: Fron-
    tier Forces, Co. H, Enlist: Nov. 15, 1870, Disc: Feb. 28, 1871,
    Place of Birth: San Antonio, Ranger Muster Roll.
TERRELL, John W., Pvt., Comm. Off: EASTIN, S.W., Organ: Jack Cty.
    Rangers, Enlist: Dec. 3, 1873, Disc: April 3, 1874, Place of
    Birth: Jack County, 4 months service, Ranger Muster Roll.
TERRELL, Saml. A., Pvt., Comm. Off: ROGERS, P.H., Capt.,
    Organ: Mtd. Vol., Enlist: Oct. 1854, Disc: Dec. 1854, 3 months
    service, Ranger Muster Roll. Ex. order of March 1856.
TERRELL, W.A., Pvt., Comm. Off: FOSTER, B.S., Organ: Co. E, Fron-
    tier Battalion, Enlist: June 1, 1875, Disc: Nov. 30, 1875,
    Age: 22, 5'5", dark, dark eyes, dark hair, farmer, Place of
    Birth: Ga., 6 months service, Ranger Muster Roll.
TERRY, Nathaniel, Pvt., Comm. Off: TOBIN, W.G., Capt., Organ: Mtd
    Rangers, Enlist: Oct. 12, 1855, Disc: Nov. 15, 1855, 1 month
    service, Ranger Muster Roll.
TERRY, William W., Pvt., Comm. Off: JONES, John S., Organ: Texas
    Rangers, Enlist: Feb. 5, 1858, Disc: Aug. 5, 1858, Age: 23,
    Place of Birth: Austin, Texas, 6 months service, Ranger Muster
    Roll.
TERRY, W.J., Pvt., Comm. Off: JOHNSON, Thomas J., Organ: Mounted
    Rangers, Enlist: May 15, 1860, Disc: Aug. 26, 1860, Place of
    Birth: Fort Worth, Ranger Muster Roll.
TERRY, W.J., Pvt., Comm. Off: JOHNSON, T.J., Capt., Organ: Ranger
    Company, Enlist: May 15, 1860, Disc: Aug. 26, 1860. R&F 99;
    1 Pay Roll; Serv. 3 mos. 12 days at $25 = Total $85; Less
    stoppages: J.M. GIBBINS $21.85, State $30 - Total $51.85; Bal.
    Paid $33.13; Capt. T.J. JOHNSON, Genl. P/A.
TEURKNETT, J.W., Pvt., Comm. Off: SCHWETHELM, H., Organ: Co. E,
    Minute Men, Kerr County, Enlist: April 10, 1873, Disc: April
    10, 1874, Place of Birth: Kerr County, 130 days of service,
    Ranger Muster Roll.
TEUKNETT, R., Pvt., Comm. Off: SCHWETHELM, H., Organ: Co. E, Min.
    Men, Enlist: April 7, 1872, Disc: March 15, 1873, Place of
    Birth: Kerr County, 110 days service, Ranger Muster Roll.

THALHEIMER, David, Pvt., Comm. Off: FORD, John S., Organ: 3rd Co. of Rangers, Enlist: Feb. 1, 1860, Disc: May 17, 1860, Age: 42, Place of Birth: Brownsville, Ranger Muster Roll.

THARP, J.W., Pvt., Comm. Off: MATLBY, W.J., Organ: Co. E, Frontier Battalion, Enlist: June 6, 1874, Disc: Dec. 13, 1874, Place of Birth: Coleman County, 6 months, 8 days service, Ranger Muster Roll.

THARSHER, James, Pvt., Comm. Off: MCCULLOCH, Henry E., Organ: Tex. Mounted Vol., Enlist: Oct. 25, 1847, Age: 35, Dark eyes, dark hair, 5'8", Place of Birth: Mississippi.

THOMAS, Auther, Teamster, Comm. Off: GILLESPIE, J.T., Organ: Co. E, Frontier Battalion, Enlist: March 12, 1886, Disc: Nov. 30, 1886, Place of Birth: Camp Johnson, Texas, 5 months, 19 days service, Ranger Muster Roll.

THOMAS, E.F., Pvt., Comm. Off: DALRYMPLE, W.C., Organ: Mounted Rangers, Enlist: Jan. 14, 1860, Disc: Oct. 13, 1860, Age: 18, Place of Birth: Liberty Hill, Ranger Muster Roll.

THOMAS, George, Pvt., Comm. Off: HARRELL, J.M., Organ: Co. K. Frontier Forces, Enlist: Sept. 16, 1870, Disc: Feb. 20, 1871, Place of Birth: Penal Ranch, Discharged Feb. 16, 1871, Ranger Muster Roll.

THOMAS, George, Pvt., Comm. Off: WOOD, J.D., Organ: Prov. Mtd. State Troops, Enlist: Oct. 9, 1871, Disc: Nov. 13, 1871, Place of Birth: Limestone County, Ranger Muster Roll.

THOMAS, G.W., Pvt., Comm. Off: EASTIN, S.W., Organ: Jack County Rangers, Enlist: Dec. 3, 1873, Disc: April 3, 1874, Place of Birth: Jack County, 4 months service, Ranger Muster Roll.

THOMAS, H.J., Pvt., Comm. Off: LONG, Ira, Organ: Co. A, Frontier Battalion, Enlist: Sept. 2, 1875, Age: 19, 5'9", dark, brown eyes, dark hair, farmer, Place of Birth: Burnet, Texas, 17 mos. 29 days service, Ranger Muster Roll.

THOMAS, H.J., Pvt., Comm. Off: MALTBY, W.J., Organ: Co. E, Frontier Battalion, Enlist: May 30, 1874, Disc: May 31, 1876, Place of Birth: Coleman County, 12 months, 1 day service, Ranger Muster Roll.

THOMAS, H.J., Pvt., Comm. Off: REYNOLDS, H.O., Organ: Co. E, Frontier Battalion, Enlist: Sept. 1, 1877, Disc: Feb. 28, 1878, Place of Birth: Coleman County, 6 months service, Ranger Muster Roll.

THOMAS, Henry, Pvt., Comm. Off: FOSTER, B.S., Organ: Co. E, Frontier Battalion, Enlist: Dec. 1, 1876, Disc: Aug. 31, 1877, Place of Birth: Coleman County, 9 months service, Ranger Muster Roll.

THOMAS, Ivy, Pvt., Comm. Off: JOHNSON, Thomas J., Organ: Mounted Rangers, Enlist: April 21, 1860, Disc: June 12, 1860, Place of Birth: Fort Worth, Ranger Muster Roll.

THOMAS, J.M., Pvt., Comm. Off: THOMPSON, H.J., Capt., Organ: Min. Men, Parker Cty., Enlist: May 25, 61 at Veal Sta., Parker Cty. 39 days regular scout. R&F 40; Co. organized under Act of the Legislature Feb. 7, 61; Election cert. with Roll; 1 Muster Roll dated May 27-61; 6 Scout Reports dated Je.8-Je.23-61, Je.24-Jy.7-61, Jy.8-Jy.26-61, Jy.27-Aug.4-61, Aug.4-Aug.14-61 & Aug.17-S.22-61.

THOMAS, J.W., Pvt., Comm. Off: THOMPSON, H.J., Capt., Organ: Min.

THOMAS, J.W., Pvt., (Continued)
   Men, Parker County, May 25, 1861 at Veal Sta. , Parker Cty.,
   10 days regular scout. R&F 40; Co. organized under Act. of
   the Legislature Feb. 7, 61; Election cert. with Roll; Muster
   Roll dated May 27-61; 6 Scout Reports dated Je.8-Je.23-61,
   Je.24-Jy.7,61, J7.6-Jy.26-61, Jy.27-Aug.4-61, Aug.4-Aug.14-61,
   & Aug.17-S.22-61.
THOMAS, James G., Corp., Comm. Off: CARMACK, Thos. K., Organ: Mtd
   Rangers, Enlist: Dec. 14, 1857, Disc: March 14, 1858, Place of
   Birth: Travis County, 3 months service, Ranger Muster Roll.
THOMAS, James P., Pvt., Comm. Off: SNOWBALL, James, Organ: Prov.
   State Troops, Enlist: Oct. 13, 1871, Disc: Oct. 20, 1871,
   Place of Birth: Groesbeck, Texas, Ranger Muster Roll.
THOMAS, James S., Pvt., Comm. Off: FITZHUGH, Wm., Organ: Texas
   Militia, Mtd. Vol., Enlist: Nov. 2, 1854, Disc: Feb. 2, 1854,
   Age: 20, Place of Birth: McKinney, Texas, 3 months service,
   Ranger Muster Roll.
THOMAS, Sidney, Pvt., Comm. Off: MOORE, F.M., Organ: Co. D, Fron-
   tier Battalion, Enlist: May 1, 1877, Disc: Aug. 31, 1877, 4
   months, Ranger Muster Roll. San Antonio, Texas, 734 Ruiz St.
THOMAS, W.A., 2nd Corp., Comm. Off: WALLACE, Warren, Organ: Fron-
   tier Company, Nueces County, Enlist: June 29, 1874, Place of
   Birth: Nueces County, Ranger Muster Roll.
THOMAS, Warren L., 1st Lt., Comm. Off: WEEKES, Nicholas,
   Organ: Star Rifles Militia, Enlist: Sept. 21, 1874, Disc: Sept
   27, 1874, Place of Birth: Galveston County, 7 days service,
   Ranger Muster Roll.
THOMASON, J.S., 2nd Corp., Comm. Off: MCNELLY, L.H., Organ: Wash-
   ington Co. Vol. Militia, Enlist: July 25, 1874, Disc: Mar. 31,
   1875, 8 months, 6 days service, Ranger Muster Roll.
THOMASON, Thomas, Pvt., Comm. Off: DALRYMPLE, W.C., Organ: Mounted
   Rangers, Enlist: Jan. 14, 1860, Disc: Oct. 13, 1860, Age: 19,
   Place of Birth: Liberty Hill, Ranger Muster Roll.
THOMPKINS, W.O., Pvt., Comm. Off: DENTON, J.M., Organ: Co. A, Fron-
   tier Battalion, Enlist: Sept. 1, 1876, Disc: Aug. 31, 1877,
   Age: 24, 5'7", light hair, grey eyes, fair, farmer, Place of
   Birth: Alabama, 12 months service, Ranger Muster Roll.
THOMPSON, A., Pvt., Comm. Off: HOLT, John T., Capt., Organ: Fort
   Bend Rifles, Mtd. Riflemen (Rangers), Enlist: Jan. 14, 60 at
   Richmond, R&F 64; 1 Muster Roll dated Jan. 16, 60.
THOMPSON, A.J., Pvt., Comm. Off: THOMPSON, H.J., Capt.,
   Organ: Minute Men, Parker County, Enlist: May 25, 61 at Veal
   Sta., Parker County, 24 days regular scout. R&F 40; Co. orga-
   nized under Act of the Legislature Feb. 7-61; Election cert.
   with Roll; 1 Muster Roll dated May 27-61; 6 Scout Reports dtd.
   Je.8-Je.23-61, Je.24-Jy.7-61, Jy.8-Jy.23-61, Jy.27-Aug.4-61,
   Aug. 4-Aug. 14-61, & Aug. 17-S.22-61.
THOMPSON, A.J., 1st Lt., Comm. Off: HUNTER, W.L., Organ: Co. Ran-
   gers, Parker County, Enlist: Dec. 24, 1873, Disc: March 29,
   1874, Place of Birth: Parker County, 96 days of service, Ranger
   Muster Roll.
THOMPSON, B.M., 4th Sgt., Comm. Off: THOMPSON, H.J., Capt.,
   Organ: Minute Men, Parker County, Enlist: May 25, 61 at Veal
   Sta. Parker County, 28 days regular scout. R&F 40; Co. orga-

THOMPSON, B.M., 4th Sgt., (Continued)
    nized under Act of the Legislature Feb. 7-61; Election cert.
    with Roll; 1 Muster Roll dated May 27-61; 6 Scout Reports dtd.
    Je.8=Je.23-61, Je.24-Jy.7-61, Jy.8-Jy.26-61, Jy.27-Aug.4-61,
    Aug.4-Aug.14-61 & Aug.17-S.22-61.
THOMPSON, Charles, Pvt., Comm. Off: JONES, John S., Organ: Texas
    Rangers, Enlist: Feb. 5, 1858, Disc: Aug. 5, 1858, Age: 26,
    Place of Birth: Austin, Texas, 6 months service, Ranger Muster
    Roll.
THOMPSON, Charles, Pvt., Comm. Off: MCCULLOCH, Henry E.,
    Organ: Texas Mounted Vol., Enlist: Oct. 25, 1847, Age: 21,
    Blue eyes, light hair, 5'6", Place of Birth: Red River.
THOMPSON, Charles, Pvt., Comm. Off: BURLESON, Ed, Organ: Mounted
    Rangers, Enlist: Jan. 20, 1860, Disc: Sept. 7, 1860, Age: 30,
    Place of Birth: San Marcos, Ranger Muster Roll.
THOMPSON, Charles, Pvt., Comm. Off: SHAW, Owen, Organ: Texas Mi-
    litia Volunteers, Enlist: Aug. 18, 1852, Disc: Feb. 17, 1853,
    Age: 22, Place of Birth: Austin, 6 months service, Ranger Mus-
    ter Roll.
THOMPSON, Charles, Pvt., Comm. Off: MCCULLOCH, Henry E., Capt.,
    Organ: Texas Mounted Volunteers, Enlist: Sept. 22, 1851,
    Disc: Nov. 5, 1851, Age: 21, Enlisted at: Fort M. Scott, 1
    month, 13 days service, Ranger Muster Roll.
THOMPSON, Charles, Pvt., Comm. Off: SHAW, Owen, Capt., Organ: Mtd.
    Vol., Enlist: Austin, Texas, 6 months service, Ranger Muster
    Roll.
THOMPSON, Charles, Pvt., Comm. Off: MCCULLOCH, Henry E., Capt.,
    Organ: Texas Vols., Enlist: Oct. 23, 1847, Disc: Dec. 8, 1847,
    Age: 21, Height: 5'6", fair Comp., Blue eyes, light hair, Place
    of Birth: Red River, Texas, 13 months, 15 days service, Ranger
    Muster Roll.
THOMPSON, G.W., Pvt., Comm. Off: GREEN, M.R., Organ: Comanche Co.
    Rangers, Enlist: Jan. 17, 1874, Disc: Feb. 17, 1874, Place of
    Birth: Comanche County, 1 month service, Ranger Muster Roll.
THOMPSON, Geo. W., Pvt., Comm. Off: HARRISON, Thos., Capt.,
    Organ: Tex. Rangers, Enlist: Ja. 10, 61 at Waco for 6 mos.;
    unless sooner discharged, Age: 25. R&F 51; Thos. HARRISON, En.
    Off: J.C. NEWLON, Mus. Off: S.P. ROSS & D.R. LINSLEY, apprs.
    H: $150; HE: $30; Gun: $25; Pistol: $30. Co. sta. at camp near
    Waco Jan. 8, 61. Called into service of State by Gov. Sam
    HOUSTON. 1 Muster Roll dated Jan. 10-61.
THOMPSON, Gideon, Pvt., Comm. Off: DAVENPORT, John M., Organ: Mtd
    Vol. Minute Men, Enlist: March 13, 1856, Disc: June 1, 1857,
    Place of Birth: Uvalde County, 3 months service, Ranger Muster
    Roll.
THOMPSON, H.J., Capt., Comm. Off: THOMPSON, H.J., Capt.,
    Organ: Minute Men, Parker County, Enlist: May 25, 61 at Veal
    Sta. Parker Cty., 43 days regular scout. R&F 40; Co. orga-
    nized under Act of the Legislature Feb. 7-61; Election cert.
    with Roll; 1 Muster Roll dated May 27-61, 6 Scout Reports dtd.
    Je.8-Je.23-61, Je.24-Jy.7-61, Jy.8-Jy.26-61, Jy.27-Aug.4-61,
    Aug.4-Aug.14-61 & Aug.17-S.22-61.
THOMPSON, J.W., Pvt., Comm. Off: MCNELLY, L.H., Organ: Washington
    Co. Vol. Militia, Enlist: July 25, 1874, Disc: Aug. 16, 1874,

THOMPSON, J.W., Pvt., (Continued)
Place of Birth: Austin, Texas, 22 days service, Dishonorably discharged, Ranger Muster Roll.

THOMPSON, Jas., Pvt., Comm. Off: HENRY, William R., Organ: Texas Mounted Vol., Enlist: Sept. 15, 1855, Disc: Oct. 15, 1855, Age: 27, Place of Birth: San Antonio, 1 month service, Ranger Muster Roll.

THOMPSON, Jasper, Pvt., Comm. Off: JONES, J.W., Organ: Co. No. 4, Minute Men, Callahan, Enlist: Oct. 30, 1873, Disc: Mar. 30, 1874, Place of Birth: Callahan County, 30 days of service, Ranger Muster Roll.

THOMPSON, Jno. N., Pvt., Comm. Off: DARNELL, N.H., Organ: April 14, 1860, Disc: Aug. 13, 1860, Place of Birth: Dallas, Ranger Muster Roll.

THOMPSON, Jonathon, Pvt., Comm. Off: BOURLAND, James, Capt., Organ: Mtd. Vol., Enlist: Dec. 22, 1858, Disc: Feb. 27, 1859, Died Feb. 27, 1859, Place of Birth: Station, Tex., 64 days of service, Ranger Muster Roll.

THOMPSON, John, Pvt., Comm. Off: EASTIN, S.W., Organ: Jack County Rangers, Enlist: Dec. 3, 1873, Disc: April 3, 1874, Place of Birth: Jack County, 4 months service, Ranger Muster Roll.

THOMPSON, Johnthan, Pvt., Comm. Off: BOURLAND, James, Organ: Tex. Mounted Rangers, Enlist: Oct. 28, 1858, Disc: Feb. 27, 1859, Place of Birth: Gainesville, Texas, 4 months service, Ranger Muster Roll.

THOMPSON, Joseph C., Pvt., Comm. Off: WALKER, Joseph, Organ: Rangers for Cortinas War, Enlist: Nov. 1, 1859, Disc: Jan. 20, 1860, Place of Birth: Banquete, Ranger Muster Roll.

THOMPSON, Joseph C., Pvt., Comm. Off: FORD, John S., Organ: 3rd Co. of Rangers, Enlist: Jan. 20, 1860, Disc: May 17, 1860, Age: 24, Place of Birth: Brownsville, Ranger Muster Roll.

THOMPSON, M., Pvt., Comm. Off: HALL, A.B., Organ: Prov. State Troops, Detached, Enlist: Oct. 13, 1871, Disc: Oct. 20, 1871, Place of Birth: Groesbeck, Texas, Ranger Muster Roll.

THOMPSON, M.U., Pvt., Comm. Off: DARNELL, N.H., Organ: Mounted Rangers, Enlist: April 14, 1860, Disc: Aug. 13, 1860, Place of Birth: Dallas, Ranger Muster Roll.

THOMPSON, M.W., Pvt., Comm. Off: CONNELL, J.G., Organ: Brown and San Saba Co., Rangers, Enlist: Jan. 6, 1874, Disc: March 26, 1874, Place of Birth: Brown and San Saba Counties, 2 months, 20 days service, Ranger Muster Roll.

THOMPSON, M.W., Pvt., Comm. Off: MALTBY, W.J., Organ: Co. E, Frontier Battalion, Enlist: May 30, 1874, Disc: Dec. 12, 1874, Place of Birth: Coleman County, 6 months, 13 days service, Ranger Muster Roll.

THOMPSON, Nathaniel, Pvt., Comm. Off: WALKER, John G., Capt., Organ: Mtd. Vol., Enlist: Nov. 1854, Ranger Muster Roll.

THOMPSON, Nathaniel H., Pvt., Comm. Off: FORD, John S., Organ: Texas Rangers, Enlist: June 10, 1858, Disc: July 10, 1858, Age: 27, Place of Birth: Bosque County, 6 months service, Ranger Muster Roll.

THOMPSON, Oliver, Pvt., Comm. Off: COX, A.H., Organ: Frontier Forces, Co. B, Enlist: Sept. 8, 1870, Disc: May 31, 1871, Place of Birth: Shackleford County, Ranger Muster Roll.

THOMPSON, Robert, Pvt., Comm. Off: WOOD, J.D., Organ: Prov. Mtd. State Troops, Enlist: Oct. 2, 1871, Disc: Nov. 13, 1871, Place of Birth: Limestone County, Ranger Muster Roll.

THOMPSON, S.G., Pvt., Comm. Off: THOMPSON, H.J., Capt., Organ: Minute Men, Parker County, Enlist: May 25, 61 at Veal Sta., Parker County, 20 days regular scout. R&F 40; Co. organized under Act of the Legislature Feb. 7-61; Election cert. with Roll; 1 Muster Roll dated May 27-61; 6 Scout reports dtd. Je.8-Je.23-61, Je.24-Jy.7-61, Jy.8-Jy.26-61, Jy.27-Aug.4-61, Aug.4-Aug.14-61 & Aug.17-S.22-61.

THOMPSON, T.A., Pvt., Comm. Off: FITZHUGH, G.S., Capt., Organ: Ranger Company, Enlist: April 14, 60, Disc: Oct. 25,60; served 6 mo. & 12 days at $25. Total: $160. R&F 83; Stoppages: $44.90; Balance Paid: $115.10. A.G. PATTERSON P/A, $25. 1 Pay Roll.

THOMPSON, W.A., Pvt., Comm. Off: CONNELL, J.G., Organ: Brown and San Saba County Rangers, Enlist: Jan. 6, 1874, Disc: March 26, 1874, Place of Birth: Brown and San Saba Counties, 2 months, 20 days service, Ranger Muster Roll.

THOMPSON, W.G., Pvt., Comm. Off: BAKER, D.P., Organ: Frontier Forces, Co. F, Enlist: Nov. 5, 1870, Disc: June 15, 1871, Place of Birth: Decatur, Wise County, Ranger Muster Roll.

THOMPSON, Whit, Pvt., Comm. Off: HOLT, John T., Capt., Organ: Ft. Bend Rifles, Mtd. Riflemen (Rangers), Enlist: Jan. 14, 60 at Richmond, R&F 64; 1 Muster Roll dated Jan. 16, 60.

THORMERS, William, Pvt., Comm. Off: HENRY, William R., Organ: Co. C, Mounted Vol., Enlist: Dec. 14, 1854, Disc: March 14, 1855, Age: 28, Place of Birth: San Antonio, 3 months service, Ranger Muster Roll.

THOMPSON, Wm., Pvt., Comm. Off: FITZHUGH, G.S., Capt., Organ: Ranger Company, Enlist: April 14, 60, Disc: Oct. 25, 60; Served 6 mo. & 12 days at $25-Total: $160. R&F 83; Stoppages: $10.50, Balance Pd: $149.50. G.W. FISHER, $10.50. 1 Pay Roll.

THOMSON, John, Pvt., Comm. Off: JONES, Franklin, Organ: Co. A, Frontier Forces, Enlist: Oct. 6, 1870, Disc: Nov. 11, 1870, Place of Birth: Ft. Mason, TExas, 1 month, 6 days service, Ranger Muster Roll.

THOMSON, John, Pvt., Comm. Off: JONES, Franklin, Organ: Co. A, Frontier Battalion, Enlist: Oct. 6, 1870, Disc: Oct. 31, 1870, Place of Birth: Mason, TExas, Ranger Muster Roll.

THOMSON, Stephen, Pvt., Comm. Off: JONES, Franklin, Organ: Co. A, Frontier Forces, Enlist: Oct. 6, 1870, Disc: Nov. 11, 1870, Place of Birth: Ft. Mason, Texas, 1 month, 6 days service, Ranger Muster Roll.

THOMSON, Stephen, Pvt., Comm. Off: JONES, Franklin, Pvt., Organ: Co. A, Frontier Battalion, Enlist: Oct. 6, 1870, Disc: Oct. 31, 1870, Place of Birth: Mason, Texas, Ranger Muster Roll.

THOMY, Conrad, Pvt., Comm. Off: TAY, J.B., Lt., Organ: Vol. Batt. Co. C, Enlist: Nov. 13, 1877, Disc: Nov. 30, 1877, 18 days of service, Ranger Muster Roll.

THORN, T.W., Sgt., Comm. Off: BAKER, D.P., Organ: Frontier Forces, Co. F, Enlist: Nov. 5, 1870, Disc: June 15, 1871, Place of Birth: Decatur, Wise County, Ranger Muster Roll.

THORNHILL, Wm., Pvt., Comm. Off: BOURLAND, James, Organ: Texas
    Mounted Rangers, Enlist: Oct. 28, 1858, Disc: Jan. 28, 1858,
    Place of Birth: Gainesville, Texas, 3 months service, Ranger
    Muster Roll.
THORNTON, S.B., Ensign, Comm. Off: MOORE, D.D., Capt., Organ: Mos-
    cow Guards, Cav. Co., Polk Co., TST, Enlist: Nov., 1860, at
    Moscow, Tex. R&F 76; Co. org. with 64 volunteers who agreed
    to meet not less than 6 or more than 7 times a year; unless
    called out on special duty; 1 Muster Roll.
THORNTON, William, Pvt., Comm. Off: WILLIAMS, Samuel J.,
    Organ: Prov. State Troops, Co. A, Enlist: Oct. 9, 1871,
    Disc: Nov. 13, 1871, Place of Birth: Limestone County, Ranger
    Muster Roll.
THORNTON, Wm. H., Pvt., Comm. Off: TOM, Wm., Capt., Organ: Texas
    Vol., Enlist: Oct. 18, 1855, Disc: Nov. 16, 1855, 1 month of
    service, Ranger Muster Roll.
THORP, J.L., Pvt., Comm. Off: WILLIAMS, John, Lt., Organ: Rangers,
    Enlist: May 24, 1858, Disc: July 24, 1858, 2 months of service,
    Ranger Muster Roll.
THORP, John T., Pvt., Comm. Off: TUMLINSON, Peter, Capt.,
    Organ: Mtd. Vols., Enlist: Dec. 2, 1859, Disc: Dec. 27, 1859,
    24 days service, Ranger Muster Roll.
THORPE, John W., Organ: Co. E., Frontier Battalion, Enlist: 1874,
    Place of Birth: Floydada, Texas, R.R. 4, Box 11, Dept. of the
    Interior--Pensions, N.H. NICHOLSON, Inspector.
THRALL, Frank, Pvt., Comm. Off: TAYS, J.B., Organ: Co. C, Vol.
    Battalion, Enlist: Nov. 11, 1877, Disc: Feb. 28, 1878, Place
    of Birth: El Paso County, 3 months, 20 days service, RAnger
    Muster Roll.
THRALL, Frank, Pvt., Comm. Off: TAY, J.B., Lt., Organ: Vol. Batt.
    Co. C, Enlist: Nov. 11, 1877, Disc: Feb. 28, 1878, 3 months of
    service, 20 days, Ranger Muster Roll.
THRASHER, James, Pvt., Comm. Off: MCCULLOCH, Henry E., Capt.,
    Organ: Texas Vols., Enlist: Oct. 25, 1847, Disc: Oct. 24, 1848,
    Age: 35; Height: 5'8", Dk. hair, Dk. eyes, Dk. Comp., Place of
    Birth: Mississippi, 12 months service, Ranger Muster Roll.
THRESHER, John, Pvt., Comm. Off: STEVENS, G.W., Organ: Wise County
    Rangers, Enlist: Nov. 26, 1873, Disc: March 26, 1874, Place of
    Birth: Wise County, 4 months service, Ranger Muster Roll.
THROURES, John, Pvt., Comm. Off: JOHNSON, Thomas J., Organ: Mtd.
    Rangers, Enlist: May 15, 1860, Disc: Nov. 3, 1860, Place of
    Birth: Belknap, Ranger Muster Roll.
THURMAN, A.J., Pvt., Comm. Off: COX, A.H., Organ: Frontier Forces,
    Co. B, Enlist: Sept. 8, 1870, Disc: May 31, 1871, Place of
    Birth: Shackleford County, Ranger Muster Roll. Harper, Gilles-
    pe Co., TEx.,
THURMAN, H.G.,Pvt., Comm. Off: COX, A.H., Organ: Frontier Forces,
    Co. B, Enlist: Sept. 8, 1870, Disc: May 31, 1871, Place of
    Birth: Shackleford County, Ranger Muster Roll. Austin, Travis
    Co., Texas, R.R. 3, Box. 60.
THURMAN, J.O., Pvt., Comm. Off: MCNELLY, L.H., Organ: Washington
    Co. Vol. Militia, Enlist: July 25, 1874, Disc: Sept. 12, 1874,
    Place of Birth: Austin, Texas, 1 month, 18 days service, Ranger
    Muster Roll.

THURMAN, M., Pvt., Comm. Off: WATKINS, W.C., Organ: Co. D, Min.
    Men, Comanche County, Enlist: Oct. 6, 1873, Disc: April 30,
    1874, Place of Birth: Comanche County, 15 days of service, Ran-
    ger Muster Roll.
THURMAN, T.E., Pvt., Comm. Off: COX, A.H., Organ: Frontier Forces,
    Co. B, Enlist: Sept. 8, 1870, Disc: May 31, 1871, Place of
    Birth: Shackleford County, Ranger Muster Roll.
THURMOND, Jasper, Pvt., Comm. Off: HOLT, John T., Capt.,
    Organ: Fort Bend Rifles, Mtd. Riflemen (Rangers), Enlist: Jan.
    14, 60 at Richmond. R&F 64; 1 Muster Roll dated Jan. 16, 60.
THWEATT, N.M., Pvt., Comm. Off: SWISHER, Jas. M., Organ: Co. P,
    Frontier Forces, Enlist: Sept. 6, 1870, Disc: Feb. 6, 1871,
    Place of Birth: Camp Colorado, Ranger Muster Roll.
TIBBETTS, Alen F., Lt., Comm. Off: BERRY, Henry W., Organ: Mtd.
    Vol. for Cortinas War, Enlist: Nov. 10, 1859, Disc: Dec. 20,
    1859, Age: 35, Place of Birth: Brownsville, Ranger Muster Roll.
TIBBS, Anderson, Pvt., Comm. Off: WOOD, J.D., Organ: Prov. Mtd.
    State Troops, Enlist: Oct. 9, 1871, Disc: Nov. 13, 1871, Place
    of Birth: Limestone County, Ranger Muster Roll.
TICKNOR, E.H., Comm. Off: GREEN, Sam, Capt., Organ: Minute Men,
    Clay County, Enlist: Sept. 5, 1861, 88 days service, Ranger
    Muster Roll.
TILMAN, Elias, Pvt., Comm. Off: WOOD, J.D., Organ: Prov. Mounted
    State Troops, Enlist: Oct. 9, 1871, Disc: Nov. 13, 1871, Place
    of Birth: Limestone County, Ranger Muster Roll.
TINDEL, Geo. G., 2nd Corp., Comm. Off: LEDBETTER, Wm. H.,
    Organ: Co. N, Minute Men, San Saba Co., Enlist: Sept. 13, 1872,
    Disc: April 5, 1874, Place of Birth: San Saba County, No ser-
    vice recorded, Ranger Muster Roll.
TINKER, W.C., Pvt., Comm. Off: STEVENS, G.W., Organ: Wise County
    Rangers, Enlist: Nov. 26, 1873, Disc: March 26, 1874, Place
    of Birth: Wise County, 4 months service, Ranger Muster Roll.
TINKER, W.C., Pvt., Comm.Off: STEVENS, G.W., Organ: Co. B, Fron-
    tier Battalion, Enlist: May 18, 1874, Disc: Dec. 10, 1874,
    Place of Birth: Lost Valley, 6 months, 26 days, Ranger Muster
    Roll.
TINNEY, Thomas M,, 4th Sgt., Comm. Off: LOVENSKIOLD, Charles,
    Organ: Walker Mtd. Rifles, Cortinas War, Enlist: Nov. 22, 1859,
    Place of Birth: Corpus Christi, Ranger Muster Roll.
TINNEY, Tom N., Pvt., Comm. Off: WALLACE, Warren, Organ: Frontier
    Company, Neuces Co., Enlist: June 29, 1874, Place of
    Birth: Nueces County, aanger Muster Roll.
TINNIN, William, Pvt., Comm. Off: FORD, John S., Organ: 2nd Co.
    of Rangers, Enlist: Nov. 10, 1858, Disc: May 10, 1859, Age: 18,
    Place of Birth: Austin, Ranger Muster Roll.
TIPTON, Benjamin, Pvt., Comm. Off: BURLESON, A.B., Capt.,
    Organ: Mounted Ranger Co., Enlist: Jan. 16, 61 at Cowhouse on
    April Muster Roll 7 in Coryell County on Dec. Muster Roll for
    12 months; unless sooner discharged., Age: 22. R&F 69; Enr.
    Off: Capt. A.B. BURLESON on Dec. Muster Roll & Lt. Sam DUNCAN
    on April Muster Roll; H. $60; HE. $15; Arms--guns $16, pistols
    $22, Apprs. David THOMASON & Jno. T. EVERETT; Co. called into
    service, by Gov. Samuel HOUSTON April 4, 60. 2 Muster Rolls;
    One giving date of HOUSTON's order as April 4, 60, the other

TIPTON, Benjamin, Pvt., (Continued)
Dec. 29-60. Deserted Feb. 23, 61. W.B. CLEMENT $3.75.
TIPTON, Isham, Pvt., Comm. Off: FORD, John S., Organ: 2nd Co. of
Rangers, Enlist: Nov. 10, 1858, Disc: May 10, 1859, Age: 25,
Place of Birth: Austin, Ranger Muster Roll.
TIPTON, John E., Pvt., Comm. Off: ROSS, L.S., Capt., Organ: Ran-
ger Company, Enlist: S. 22-60 at Waco for 12 mos., Serv. from
S.22-60 to F.5-61; 4 mos. & 14 days at $25--$111.66, Age: 17.
R&F 66; En. Off: Capt. ROSS: Mus. Off: J.M.W. HALL; Appraiser
Jas. H. SWINDELLS; Val. H: $90; HE: $20; Gun: $20; Pistol: $30;
Stoppage: $88.27; Elec. certif. with roll; Co. sta. at Ft.
Belknap O.17 & N.22-60; 1 Muster Roll & 1 Pay Roll. By order
of Giv. HOUSTON placed on duty at Ft. Belknap S.22-60.
TIPTON, John E., Pvt., Comm. Off: ROSS, L.S., Organ: Mounted Ran-
gers, Enlist: Sept. 22, 1860, Age: 27, Place of Birth: Waco,
Ranger Muster Roll.
TI-WNI-TEET, Spy, Comm. Off: ROSS, Peter F., Capt., Organ: Spy Co.,
Enlist: 1860, Serv. from July 1 to Aug. 12-60; 1 mo. & 12 days
at $25--$35, R&F 39; 1 Pay Roll.
TOBEY, Avery, Pvt., Comm. Off: JONES, John S., Organ: Texas Ran-
gers, Enlist: April 7, 1858, Disc: Aug. 5, 1858, Age: 24,
Place of Birth: Comanche County, 5 months, 12 days service,
Ranger Muster Roll.
TOBIAS, G.E., Pvt., Comm. Off: STEVENS, G.W., Organ: Wise County
Rangers, Enlist: Nov. 26, 1873, Disc: March 26, 1874, Place
of Birth: Wise County, RangerMuster Roll.
TOBIN, Wm. G., Capt., Organ: TOBIN, Wm. G., Organ: Mounted Volun-
teers, Enlist: Oct. 18, 1859, Disc: Nov. 3, 1859, Place of
Birth: San Antonio, Ranger Muster Roll.
TOBIN, William G., Capt., Comm. Off: TOBIN, W.G., Capt.,
Organ: Rangers, Enlist: Oct. 12, 1855, Disc: Nov. 15, 1855, 1
month service, Ranger Muster Roll.
TODD, George R.C. Surgeon, Comm. Off: CONNOR, John H., Organ: Mtd
Rangers, Enlist: Jan. 20, 1860, 12 months, Place of
Birth: Austin, Mustered in by order of HOUSTON, Ranger Muster
Roll.
TOEPPERWIEN, H.W., Corp., Comm. Off: NELSON, G.H., Capt.,
Organ: Tex. Mtd. Mil., Enlist: Oct. 10, 1857, Disc: De. 8, 57,
Place of Birth: Fredericksburg, 2 months service, Ranger Mus-
ter Roll.
TODD, G.W., Pvt., Comm. Off: HERSTER, Daniel, Organ: Co. R, Min.
Men, Macon Co., Enlist: Oct. 5, 1872, Disc: Feb. 24, 1874,
Place of Birth: Mason County, 50 days of service, Ranger Mus-
ter Roll.
TODD, Mebus, Pvt., Comm. Off: LONG, Ira, Organ: Co. A, Frontier
Battalion, Enlist: March 1, 1876, Disc: June 1, 1876, 3 months
service, Ranger Muster Roll.
TOLDERA, Ramon, Pvt., Comm. Off: FALCON, C.G., Organ: Co. G,
Frontier Forces, Enlist: Oct. 8, 1870, Disc: Dec. 31, 1870,
Place of Birth: Hidago County, Detached Service at Lomo Blanco
Ranger Muster Roll.
TOLER, John, Pvt., Comm. Off: NOWLIN, James C., Organ: Kendall
County Min. Men, Co. C, Enlist: March 9, 1873, Disc: March 1,
1874, Place of Birth: Kendall County, 53 days service, Ranger
Muster Roll.

TOLER, John T., Farrier, Comm. Off: SANSOM, John W., Organ: Frontier Forces, Enlist: Aug. 25, 1870, Disc: May 31, 1871, Place of Birth: Shackleford County, Ranger Muster Roll.

TOLER, W.J., Pvt., Comm. Off: COLDWELL, Neal, Organ: Co. F, Frontier Battalion, Enlist: June 30, 1875, Disc: Nov. 30, 1875, Age: 18, 5'8", light hair, gray eyes, fair, farmer, Place of Birth: Hays Co., Texas, 5 months, 6 days service, Ranger Muster Roll.

TOLER, W.J., Pvt., Comm. Off: DOLAN, Pat, Organ: Co. F, Frontier Battalion, Enlist: Sept. 1, 1876, Disc: Aug. 20, 1877, Age: 19, 5'8", light hair, grey eyes, fair, farmer, Place of Birth: Kenall Co. Texas, 11 months, 21 days service, Ranger Muster Roll.

TOLIVER, Andrew, Pvt., Comm. Off: JONES, John S., Organ: Texas Rangers, Enlist: Jan. 10, 1858, Disc: July 10, 1858, Age: 18, Place of Birth: Bosque County, 6 months service, Ranger Muster Roll.

TOM, Choctaw, Spy, Comm. Off: ROSS, Peter F., Capt., Organ: Spy Company, Enlist: 1860, Serv. from July 1 to Aug. 1, 60; 1 mo. & 1 day at $25--$25.83. R&F 39; 1 Pay Roll.

TOM, George W., Pvt., Comm. Off: CALLAHAN, James H., Organ: Mtd. Rangers, Enlist: July 20, 1855, Disc: Oct. 19, 1855, Place of Birth: Seguin, 2 months, 29 days service, Ranger Muster Roll.

TOM, Houston, 1st Lt., Comm. Off: HENRY, William R., Organ: Texas Mounted Vol., Enlist: Sept. 15, 1855, Disc: Oct. 15, 1855, Age: 30, Place of Birth: San Antonio, 1 month service, Ranger Muster Roll.

TOM, Simpson, Pvt., Comm. Off: CALLAHAN, James H., Organ: Mounted Rangers, Enlist: July 20, 1855, Disc: Oct. 19, 1855, Place of Birth: Seguin, 2 months, 29 days service, Ranger Muster Roll.

TOM, William, Pvt., Comm. Off: MCCULLOCH, Henry E., Capt., Organ: Texas Mtd. Vol., Enlist: Sept. 16, 1851, Disc: Nov. 5, 1851, Age: 19, Enlisted at: Seguin, Tex., 1 month, 19 days service, Ranger Muster Roll.

TOM, William, 2nd Lt., Comm. Off: HENRY, William R., Organ: Co. C, Mounted Volunteers, Enlist: Dec. 14, 1854, Disc: March 14, 1855, Age: 22, Place of Birth: San Antonio, 3 months service, Ranger Muster Roll.

TOM, William, Capt., Comm. Off: TOM, William, Capt., Organ: Tex. Vol., Enlist: Oct. 18, 1855, Disc: Nov. 16, 1855, 1 month of service, Ranger Muster Roll.

TOM, William, Pvt., Comm. Off: CALLAHAN, James H., Organ: Mounted Rangers, Enlist: July 20, 1855, Disc: Oct. 19, 1855, Place of Birth: Seguin, 2 months, 29 days service, Ranger Muster Roll.

TOMILSON, A.T., Pvt., Comm. Off: TOMLINSON, Peter, Organ: Mounted Vols., Enlist: Jan. 2, 1860, Ranger Muster Roll.

TOMLINSON, E.A., Pvt., Comm. Off: ARRINGTON, G.W., Capt., Organ: Frontier Battalion Co. C, Enlist: July 15, 1881, Disc: Aug. 31, 1882, Age: 27; Height: 6', Black, hair, brown eyes, dk. comp., Stockman, Place of Birth: Alabama, 12 months, 15 days service, Photostat: Orig. in A.G. Office.

TOMLINSON, Joseph, Comm. Off: TOMLINSON, Peter, Organ: Mounted Volunteers, Enlist: Jan. 2, 1860, Ranger Muster Roll.

TOMLINSON, Peter, Capt., Comm. Off: TOMLINSON, Peter, Organ: Mtd. Vols., Enlist: Jan. 2, 1860, Ranger Muster Roll.

TOMPKINS, W.O., Pvt., Comm. Off: ROBERTS, D.W., Organ: Co. D, Frontier Battalion, Enlist: June 22, 1876, Disc: Aug. 31, 1876, 2 months, 9 days service, Ranger Muster Roll.

TONEY, G.A., Pvt., Comm. Off: MCADAMS, W.C., Organ: Palo Pinto Co. Rangers, Enlist: Dec. 13, 1873, Disc: April 13, 1874, Place of Birth: Palo Pinto County, 4 months service, Ranger Muster Roll.

TONGATE, E., Pvt., Comm. Off: COX, A.H., Organ: Frontier Forces, Co. B, Enlist: Sept. 8, 1870, Disc: May 31, 1871, Place of Birth: Shackleford County, Ranger Muster Roll. Cedar Park, Texas, R.R. 1.

TOOK, J.W., Pvt., Comm. Off: MCNELLY, L.H., Organ: Washington Co. Vol. Militia, Enlist: June 22, 1875, Disc: Sept. 14, 1875, Place of Birth: Austin, Texas, 2 months, 23 days of service, Ranger Muster Roll.

TOPPERWEIN, H.N., Pvt., Comm. Off: HUNTER, James M., Organ: Co. I, Frontier Forces, Enlist: Sept. 12, 1870, Disc: Nov. 29, 1870, Place of Birth: Austin, Texas, 2 months, 11 days of service, Ranger Muster Roll.

TORRIS, Carmel, Pvt., Comm. Off: SUBLETT, David L., Capt., Organ: Co. of Texas Rangers, Enlist: Feb. 5, 61 at Elm Creek for 3 mos., Mus. out May 14, 61 at Waco. R&F 57; En. Off: D.L. SUBLETT; Mus. Off: D.L. SUBLETT; Val. H: $100; HE: $20; Guns: $15; Pistols: $35; Serv. 3 mos. 10 days at $25.00 - Amt. of pay $83.33; Bal. paid $83.33; Called into serv. of state by Gov. Sam HOUSTON from F.7-61 for 3 mos; 1 Muster Roll & 1 Pay Roll; Ammunition stores, pack mules, etc. turned over to Capt. J.M. KNIGHT's Co.. Men residing in vicinity of station may be discharged before marching.

TOSIT, Spy, Comm. Off: ROSS, Peter F., Capt., Organ: Spy Company, Enlist: 1860, Serv. from July 1 to Aug. 20, 60; 1 Mo. & 20 days at $25 - $41.66. R&F 39; 1 Pay Roll.

TOUMEY, A.C., Pvt., Comm. Off: MCNELLY, L.H., Organ: Washington Co. Vol. Militia, Enlist: July 25, 1874, Disc: March 31, 1875, 8 months, 6 days service, Ranger Muster Roll.

TOWEY, Hugh, Pvt., Comm. Off: BERRY, Henry W., Organ: Mounted Vol. for Cortinas War, Enlist: Nov. 10, 1859, Disc: Dec. 20, 1859, Age: 25, Place of Birth: Brownsville, Ranger Muster Roll.

TOWNS, D.H., Pvt., Comm. Off: MOORE, D.D., Capt., Organ: Moscow Guards, Cav. Co., Polk Co., TST, Enlist: Nov. 1860 at Moscow, Tex. R&F 76; Co. org. with 64 volunteers who agreed to meet not less than 6 or more than 7 times a year; unless called out on special duty; 1 Muster Roll.

TOWNS, William, 2nd Corp., Comm. Off: MOORE, D.D., Capt., Organ: Moscow Guards, Cav. Co., Polk Co., TST, Enlist: Nov., 1860 at Moscow, Tex. R&F 76; Co. org, with 64 volunteers who agreed to meet not less than 6 or more than 7 times a year; unless called out on special duty; 1 Muster Roll.

TOWNSEND, George, Pvt., Comm. Off: EASTIN, S.W., Organ: Jack Co. Rangers, Enlist: Dec. 3, 1873, Disc: April 3, 1874, Place of Birth: Jack County, 4 months service, Ranger Muster Roll.

TOYLE, Geo. F., 1st Sgt., Comm. Off: BALLANTYNE, Robert, Organ: Mounted Rangers, Enlist: March 29, 1860, Disc: July 3, 1860, Age: 24, Place of Birth: Bandera City, Ranger Muster Roll.

TOWLS, Churchill, Pvt., Comm. Off: WEEKES, Nicholas, Organ: Star Rifles Militia, Enlist: Sept. 21, 1874, Disc: Sept. 27, 1874, Place of Birth: Galveston County, 7 days service, Ranger Muster Roll.

TOWNSEND, Joseph, 2nd Sgt., Comm. Off: DAVENPORT, John M., Organ: Mounted Vol. Minute Men, Enlist: March 13, 1856, Disc: June 1, 1857, Place of Birth: Uvalde County, 3 months service, Ranger Muster Roll.

TOWNSEND, J.P., Pvt., Comm. Off: BAKER, D.P., Organ: Frontier Forces Co. P, Enlist: Nov. 5, 1870, Disc: June 15, 1871, Place of Birth: Decatur, Wise County, Ranger Muster Roll.

TOWNSON (TOWNSEND), G.L., Pvt., Comm. Off: IKARD, E.F., Organ: Co. C, Frontier Battalion, Enlist: May 20, 1874, Disc: Dec. 10, 1874, Place of Birth: Clay County, 6 months, 22 days service, Ranger Muster Roll.

TRAINER, S.E., Pvt., Comm. Off: GRAY, S.B., Organ: Minute Men, Enlist: April 1, 1873, Disc: Sept. 1, 1873, Place of Birth: Blanco County, 33 days service, Ranger Muster Roll.

TRAUGHBOR, Wm. R., Pvt., Comm. Off: DARNELL, N.H., Organ: Mtd. Rangers, Enlist: April 14, 1860, Disc: Aug. 13, 1860, Place of Birth: Dallas, Ranger Muster Roll.

TRAVINO, Ramon, Pvt., Comm. Off: BAU, Manuel, Organ: Co. A, Min. Men, Maverick Co., Enlist: Oct. 8, 1872, Disc: Oct. 8, 1873, Place of Birth: Maverick County, 34 days of service, Ranger Muster Roll.

TRAVIS, C.E., Capt., Comm. Off: TRAVIS, Charles E., Capt., Organ: Texas Volunteers, Company E, Enlist: 1854, Disc: 1855, 3 months service, Ranger Muster Roll.

TRAVIS, C.E., Capt., Comm. Off: TRAVIS, C.E., Organ: Texas Mtd. Vol. Co. E, Enlist: Nov. 1, 1854, Disc: Feb. 1, 1855, Place of Birth: Austin, 3 months service, Voucher Records.

TRAWEEK, W.B., Pvt., Comm. Off: PERRY, C.R., Organ: Co. D, Frontier Battalion, Enlist: May 25, 1874, Disc: Dec. 9, 1874, Place of Birth: Blanco County, 6 months, 20 days, Ranger Muster Roll. Snyder, Texas, R.R. A. Box 31.

TRAYNOR, John, Pvt., Comm. Off: COX, A.H., Organ: Frontier Forces Co. B, Enlist: Sept. 8, 1870, Disc: May 31, 1871, Place of Birth: Shackleford County, Ranger Muster Roll.

TRAWALDER, Nicholas, Pvt., Comm. Off: BROWN, James H., Organ: Min. Men, Enlist: April 15, 1860, Disc: June 6, 1860, Place of Birth: Bexar County, Ranger Muster Roll.

TREADWELL, Wm., Pvt., Comm. Off: SCOTT, Wm., Capt., Organ: Co. F, Frontier Battalion, Enlist: Nov. 1, 1886, Disc: Nov. 30, 1886, Place of Birth: Brownwood, 1 month service, Ranger Muster Roll.

TREMPIE, Jacob, Pvt., Comm. Off: CHAMBERLAIN, Bland, Organ: Frontier Forces, Co. H, Enlist: Nov. 15, 1870, Disc: Feb. 28, 1871, Place of Birth: San Antonio, Ranger Muster Roll.

TREMIER, Obediah, Pvt., Comm. Off: TRAVIS, C.E., Capt., Organ: Texas Volunteers, Company E, Enlist: 1854, Disc: 1855, 3 months service, Ranger Muster Roll.

TREMIER,(TRENIER), O., Pvt., Comm. Off: COVINGTON, Wm. B., and TRAVIS, C.E., Capt., Organ: Texas Mounted Vol. Co. E, Enlist: Nov. 1, 1854, Disc: Feb. 1, 1855, Place of Birth: Austin, 3 mos., RangerMuster Roll.

TRENTHAM, C.M., Pvt., Comm. Off: NEVILL, C.L., Organ: Co. E, Frontier Battalion, Enlist: Sept. 1, 1881, Disc: Aug. 31, 1882, Age: 26, 5'4", light, brown hair, brown eyes, farmer, Place of Birth: Rhea, Tenn., 12 months service, Ranger Muster Roll.

TRESSELL, Andrew J., 2nd Lt., Comm. Off: FITZHUGH, Wm., Organ: Tex. Militia, Enlist: Nov. 2, 1854, Disc: Feb. 2, 1854, Place of Birth: McKinney, Texas, 3 months service, Ranger Muster Roll.

TREVINO, Louis, Pvt., Comm. Off: DONELSON, John, Organ: Rangers for Cortinas War, Enlist: Nov. 5, 1859, Disc: Dec. 10, 1859, Age: 35, Place of Birth: Live Oak County, Ranger MusterRoll. Service: 1 mo. 6 days at $12--$14.40; $3 allowed for clothing & $14.40 for hire of horse--total pay $31.80.

TREVINO, Ramon, Pvt., Comm. Off: FALCON, C.G., Organ: Co. G, Frontier Forces, Enlist: Oct. 8, 1870, Disc: Dec. 21, 1870, Place of Birth: Hidalgo County, On detached service at Lomo Blanco, Ranger Muster Roll.

TRIBE, James E., Pvt., Comm. Off: TUMLINSON, Peter, Capt., Organ: Mtd. Vols., Enlist: Jan.1, 1860, Disc: Feb. 10, 1860, 1 month, 10 days service, Ranger Muster Roll.

TRIBE, James E., Corp., Comm. Off: WALKER, Joseph, Organ: Rangers for Cortinas War, Enlist: Nov. 25, 1859, Disc: Jan. 20, 1860, Place of Birth: Goliad, Ranger Muster Roll.

TRICE, W.R., Pvt., Comm. Off: JOHNSON, T.J., Capt., Organ: Ranger Company, Enlist: April 21, 1860, Serv. to Nov. 10-60, 6 mos. & 20 days at $25 - Total $166.66; Less stoppages: J.M. GIBBINS $22.40, State $30 - Total $52.40, Bal. paid $114.26; R&F 99; 1 Pay Roll; J.P. SMITH, Genl. Power of Attorney.

TRICE, William R., Pvt., Comm, Off: BARRY, James Buck, 1st Lt., Organ: Co. org. & fighting Indians interval before conv. of '61, Enlist: Jan. 10, 61, Expiration of service Feb. 25-61; Serv. 1 mo. 15 days at $25 -- $37.50. R&F 25; 1 Pay Roll; BARRY received commission from Governor; Convention assumed authority while in field and company not mustered out.

TRICE, W.H., Pvt., Comm. Off: JOHNSON, Thomas J., Organ: Mounted Rangers, Enlist: April 21, 1860, Disc: Nov. 10, 1860, Place of Birth: Fort Worth, Due B. MONROE 30. for pistol, Ranger Muster Roll.

TRIDLE, John, Pvt., Comm. Off: JONES, John S., Organ: Texas Rangers, Enlist: June 9, 1858, Disc: Aug. 5, 1858, Age: 20, Place of Birth: Comanche County, 1 month, 26 days service, Ranger Muster Roll.

TRIDLE, John, Pvt., Comm. Off: BLEVINS, John H., Organ: Minute Men, Enlist: March 20, 1860, Disc: June 19, 1860, Age: 21, Place of Birth: Comanche County, Ranger Muster Roll.

TRIMBLE, Fredrick W., 1st Corp., Comm. Off: BROWNE, James H., Organ: Minute Men, Enlist: April 5, 1860, Disc: June 6, 1860, Place of Birth: Bexar County, Ranger Muster Roll.

TRIPLETT, W.S., Pvt., Comm. Off: GREEN, M.R., Organ: Comanche County, 1 months service, Ranger Muster Roll.

TROTT, J.H., Pvt., Comm. Off: CONNELL, J.G., Organ: Brown and San Saba Co. Rangers, Enlist: Jan. 6, 1874, Disc: March 26, 1874, Place of Birth: Brown and San Saba Counties, 2 months, 20 days service, Ranger Muster Roll.

TROTTER, A., Pvt., Comm. Off: MALTBY, W.J., Organ: Co. E, Frontier
    Battalion, Enlist: June 6, 1874, Disc: Dec. 12, 1874, Place of
    Birth: Coleman County, 6 months, 7 days service, Ranger Muster
    Roll. Ingram, Texas.
TROTTER, J.B., Pvt., Comm. Off: MCADAMS, W.C., Organ: Palo Pinto
    County Rangers, Enlist: Dec. 13, 1873, Disc: April 13, 1874,
    Place of Birth: Palo Pinto County, 4 months service, Ranger
    Muster Roll.
TROUT, J.W., Pvt., Comm. Off: GREEN, M.R., Organ: Comanche County,
    Enlist: Jan. 17, 1874, Disc: Feb. 17, 1874, Place of Birth: Co
    manche County, 1 months service, Ranger Muster Roll.
TROUTT, Alfred, Pvt., Comm. Off: ROBERTS, D.W., Organ: Co. D, Fron-
    tier Battalion, Enlist: June 1, 1875, Disc: Nov. 30, 1875,
    Place of Birth: Jefferson, Ill., Age: 19, 5'5", fair, black
    eyes, black hair, farmer, Ranger Muster Roll.
TROUTT, James Pvt., Comm.Off: ROBERTS, D.W., Organ: Co. D, Fron-
    tier Battalion, Enlist: June 1, 1875, Disc: Aug. 31, 1876,
    Age: 30, 5'9", fair, brown eyes, dark hair, farmer, Place of
    Birth: Jefferson, Ill., 11 months service, Ranger Muster Roll.
TRUELOVE, J.R., Pvt., Comm. Off: BOURLAND, James, Organ: Texas
    Mtd. Rangers, Enlist: Oct. 28, 1858, Disc: Jan. 28, 1858, Place
    of Birth: Gainesville, Texas, 3 months service, Ranger Muster
    Roll.
TRUITT, A.J., Pvt., Comm. Off: JOHNSON, Thomas J., Organ: Mounted
    Rangers, Enlist: April 21, 1860, Disc: Nov. 10, 1860, Place of
    Birth: Fort Worth, Due B. MONROE 30. for pistol, Ranger Muster
    Roll.
TRUJILLO, Thomas, Pvt., Comm. Off: GARCIA, Gregorio, Organ: Co. N
    & D, Frontier Forces, Enlist: Sept. 1, 1870, Disc: June 15,
    1871, Place of Birth: El Paso County, Ranger Muster Roll.
TUBBS, John B., Corp., Comm. Off: RAGSDALE, D.H., Lt.,
    Organ: Ranger Co., Enlist: April 28, 60, Serv. from April 28,
    to Je. 8-60; 1 mo. & 12 days at $28 -- $39.20. R&F 14; allow-
    ances for trav. 65 miles $3.02; Total pay $42.22; 1 Pay Roll.
TUCKER, D.F., Pvt., Comm. Off: FITZHUGH, G.S., Capt., Organ: Ran-
    ger Co., Enlist: April 14, 60, Disc: Oct. 25, 60; served 6 mo.
    & 12 days at $25. Total: $160. R&F 83; Total pd: $160. 1
    Pay Roll.
TUCKER, D.F., Pvt., Comm. Off: BOURLAND, James, Organ: Texas Mtd.
    Rangers, Enlist: Jan. 28, 1859, Disc: April 29, 1859, Place of
    Birth: Gainesville, Texas, 3 months service, Ranger Muster Roll.
TUCKER, D.F., Pvt., Comm. Off: FITZHUGH, G.S., Organ: Mounted Ran-
    gers, Enlist: May 20, 1860, Disc: Oct. 25, 1860, Ranger Muster
    Roll.
TUCKER, (?), Pvt., Comm. Off: HUNTER, James M., Organ: Co. I, Fron-
    tier Forces, Enlist: Sept. 12, 1870, Place of Birth: Austin,
    served for Crocket COLLIER, Ranger Muster Roll.
TUCKER, James, Pvt., Comm. Off: MCADAMS, W.C., Organ: Palo Pinto
    County Rangers, Enlist: Dec. 13, 1873, Disc: April 13, 1874,
    Place of Birth: Palo Pinto County, 4 months service, Ranger
    Muster Roll. Sunset, Texas.
TUCKER, L.M., Pvt., Comm. Off: JOHNSON, T.J., Capt., Organ: Ranger
    Company, Enlist: April 21, 1860, Died July 6, 1860. R&F 99; 1
    Pay Roll; Serv. 2 mos. 16 days-Amt. of pay $63.33; Less stop-

TUCKER, L.M., Pvt., (Continued)
   pages of $2 to J.M. GIBBINS; Bal. paid $61.53.
TUCKER, L.M., Pvt., Comm. Off: JOHNSON, Thomas J., Organ: Mounted
   Rangers, Enlist: April 21, 1860, Disc: July 6, 1860, Place of
   Birth: Fort Worth, Due B. MONROE 30. for pistol, Ranger Muster
   Roll.
TUCKER, J.M., Pvt., Comm. Off: BOURLAND, James, Organ: Texas Mtd.
   Rangers, Enlist: Jan. 28, 1859, Disc: April 28, 1859, Place of
   Birth: Gainesville, Texas, 3 months service, Ranger Muster Roll.
TUCKER, Madison, Pvt., Comm. Off: LOWE, John C., 1st Lt.,
   Organ: Rangers Company, Enlist: Sept. 18, 60, Disc: Dec. 24, 60;
   R&F 43; Serv. 8 days at $25 per mo. - $6.66 total amount paid
   1 Pay Roll.
TUCKER, William, Pvt., Comm. Off: COVINGTON, Wm. B., and
   TRAVIS, C.E., Capt., Organ: Texas Mounted Vol. Co. E,
   Enlist: Nov. 1, 1854, Disc: Feb. 1, 1855, Place of Birth: Aus-
   tin, 3 months service in U.S. Service, Ranger Muster Roll.
TUCKER, William, Pvt., Comm. Off: TRAVIS, C.E., Capt.,
   Organ: Texas Volunteers, Company E, Enlist: 1854, Disc: 1855,
   3 months service, Ranger Muster Roll.
TUCKER, William, Pvt., Comm. Off: BOURLAND, James, Organ: Texas Mtd
   Rangers, Enlist: Oct. 28, 1858, Disc: April 28, 1859, Place of
   Birth: Gainesville, Texas, 6 months service, Ranger Muster Roll.
TUDAR, Thos., Pvt., Comm. Off: TACKITT, L.L., Organ: 1 Co. Minute
   Men, Enlist: Feb. 1, 1866, Disc: June 22, 1866, Place of
   Birth: Parker County, 30 days service, Ranger Muster Roll.
TUGGLE, Jas. C., Pvt., Comm. Off: MALTBY, W.J., Organ: Co. E,
   Frontier Battalion, Enlist: June 6, 1874, Disc: Nov. 13, 1874,
   Place of Birth: Coleman County, 5 months, 8 days service, Ran-
   ger Muster Roll. Kapperl, Texas, R.R. A. Box 150.
TULLOS, William H., Comm. Off: CONNELL, J.G., Capt., Organ: Co. C,
   Texas Rangers, Enlist: Jan. 6, 1874, Disc: March 6, 1874, Place
   of Birth: Strawn, Palo Pinto Co., Texas, Dept. of the Interior-
   Pensions, N.H. NICHOLSON, Inspector.
TULLY, M.D., Pvt., Comm. Off: BOURLAND, James, Organ: Texas Mtd.
   Rangers, Enlist: Oct. 28, 1858, Disc: Jan. 28, 1858, Place of
   Birth: Gainesville, Texas, 3 months service, Ranger Muster
   Roll.
TUMEY, Griffin, Pvt., Comm. Off: HENRY, William R., Organ: Co. C,
   Mounted Vol., Enlist: Dec. 14, 1854, Disc: March 14, 1855,
   Age: 21, Place of Birth: San Antonio, 3 months service in U.S.
   Service, Ranger Muster Roll.
TUMHAM, Robt. C., Pvt., Comm. Off: ROSS, L.S., Organ: Mounted Ran-
   gers, Enlist: Oct. 3, 1860, Age: 23, Place of Birth: Waco, Ran-
   ger Muster Roll.
TUMLINSON, J.J., Capt., Comm. Off: TUMLINSON, J.J., Organ: Tumlin-
   son's Spy, 1 Rgt. Mtd. Gunmen, Enlist: Oct. 13, 1839, Disc: Nov.
   22, 1839, 1 month, 11 days service, Transferred from
   Capt. HALLUMS Co., Ranger Muster Roll.
TUMLINSON, Joseph, Pvt., Comm. Off: TUMLINSON, Peter, Capt.,
   Organ: Mtd. Vols., Enlist: Nov. 12, 1850, Disc: Feb. 10, 1860,
   2 months, 29 days service, Ranger Muster Roll.
TUMLINSON, Peter, Pvt., Comm. Off: ENGLISH, Levi, Organ: Mounted
   Volunteers, Enlist: Aug. 5, 1855, Disc: Nov. 13, 1855, Place

TUMLINSON, Peter, Pvt., (Continued)
of Birth: Bexar County, 3 months, 8 days service, Ranger Muster Roll.

TUMLINSON, Peter, Capt., Comm. Off: TUMLINSON, Peter, Organ: Mtd. Vols., Enlist: Nov. 12, 1859, Disc: Feb. 10, 1860, 2 months, 29 days service, Ranger Muster Roll.

TUMLINSON, William O., Pvt., Comm. Off: TUMLINSON, Peter, Capt., Organ: Unknown, Enlist: Nov. 12, 1859, Disc: Feb. 10, 1860, 2 months, 29 days service, Ranger Muster Roll.

TUNNELL, Wm. C., Pvt., Comm. Off: DARNELL, N.H., Organ: Mounted Rangers, Enlist: April 14, 1860, Disc: Aug. 13, 1860, Place of Birth: Dallas, Ranger Muster Roll.

TURCE, T.W., Pvt., Comm. Off: JOHNSON, T.J., Capt., Organ: Ranger Company, Enlist: June 18, 1860, Serv. to Nov. 10-60, 4 mos. & 23 days at $25-Total $119.16; less stoppages: J.M. GIBBINS $3, Bal. Paid $116.16; R&F 99; 1 Pay Roll; TURNER & DAGGETT, Genl. Power of Attorney.

TURKNETT, James W., Comm. Off: SCHWETHELM, Henry, Lt., Organ: Co. E, Texas Minute Men, Enlist: April 7, 1872, Disc: April 10, 1874, Place of Birth: Artesia, Eddy Co., N. Mexico, Dept. of the Interior--Pensions, N.H. NICHOLSON, Inspector.

TURLEY, Elisha, Pvt., Comm. Off: MCCULLOCH, Henry E., Organ: Tex. Mounted Vol., Enlist: Oct. 25, 1847, Age: 23, grey eyes, dark hair, 5'6", Place of Birth: Red River.

TURLEY, Elisha, Pvt., Comm. Off: MCCULLOCH, Henry E., capt., Organ: Texas Vols., Enlist: Oct. 25, 1847, Died July 11, 1848, Age: 23; Height: 5'6", dk. comp., grey eyes, dk. hair, Place of Birth: Red River, Texas, 8 months, 15 days service, Ranger Muster Roll.

TURNBOW, A.E., Pvt., Comm. Off: ARRINGTON, G.W., Capt., Organ: Frontier Battalion, Co. C, Enlist: Mar. 1, 1881, Disc: Aug. 31, 1881, 6 months service, Photostat: Orig. in A.G. Office.

TURNBO, L.S., Sgt., Comm. Off: BAYLOR, G.W., Organ: CO. A, Frontier Batt., Enlist: Dec. 1, 1882, Disc: Feb. 28, 1885, Place of Birth: Pecos City, 12 months service, Ranger Muster Roll.

TURNBOW, L.S., Pvt., Comm. Off: SPARKS, J.C., Organ: Co. C, Frontier Battalion, Enlist: Oct. 1, 1876, Disc: Feb. 28, 1878, Place of Birth: Clay County, 17 months service, Ranger Muster Roll. Wagoner, Okla.

TURNBO, N., Pvt., Comm. Off: BAYLOR, G.W., Organ: Co. A, Frontier Battalion, Enlist: Dec. 1, 1882, Disc: Feb. 28 1883, 3 months service, Ranger Muster Roll.

TURNER, A., Pvt., Comm. Off: MOORE, D.D., Capt., Organ: Moscow Guards, Cav. Co., Polk Co., TST, Enlist: Nov. 1860 at Moscow, Tex. R&F 76; Co. org. with 64 volunteers who agreed to meet not less than 6 or more than 7 times a year, unless called out on special duty; 1 Muster Roll.

TURNER, Ben C., Pvt., Comm. Off: HAYNIE, Geo. E., Organ: Co. N, Minute Men, Lampasas Co., Enlist: Sept. 12, 1872, Disc: March 10, 1874, Place of Birth: Lampasas County, 17 days of service, Ranger Muster Roll.

TURNER, Calvin S., 2nd Lt., Comm. Off: MCCULLOCH, Henry E., Capt., Organ: Texas Vols., Enlist: Oct. 25, 1848, Disc: Dec. 8, 1848,

TURNER, Calvin, S., 2nd Lt., (Continued)
   Age: 22, 1 month, 13 days service, Ranger Muster Roll.
TURNER, Calvin S., Pvt., Comm. Off: MCCULLOCH, Henry E., Capt.,
   Organ: Texas Vols., Enlist: Oct. 25, 1847, Disc: Oct. 24, 1848,
   Age: 21, Height: 5'11", light Comp., Blue eyes, Light hair,
   Place of Birth: Seguin, Texas, 12 months service, Ranger Muster
   Roll.
TURNER, Calvin S., 2nd Lt., Comm. Off: MCCULLOCH, Henry E., Capt.,
   Organ: Texas Mtd. Volunteers, Enlist: Nov. 5, 1850, Disc: May
   5, 1851, Age: 25, Enlisted: Austin, Tex., 6 months service,
   Ranger Muster Roll.
TURNER, Calvin S., Pvt., Comm. Off: MCCULLOCH, Henry E.,
   Organ: Texas Mounted Vol., Enlist: Oct. 25, 1847, Age: 21,
   Blue eyes, light hair, 5'11", Place of Birth: Seguin.
TURNER, Cornelius, Pvt., Comm. Off: FISHER, J.C., Organ: Prov.
   State Troops, Co. C, 3 Regt., Enlist: Oct. 9, 1871, Disc: Nov.
   18, 1871, Place of Birth: Springfield, Texas, Ranger Muster
   Roll.
TURNER, Edwin W., Corp., Comm. Off: MCCULLOCH, H.E., Capt.,
   Organ: Tex Mtd. Volunteers, Enlist: Nov. 5, 1850, Disc: May 5,
   1851, Age: 30, Enlisted at: Austin, TExas, 6 months service,
   Ranger Muster Roll.
TURNER, E.P., Discharged, Pvt., Comm. Off: WILLIAMS, John,
   Organ: Second Co. of Texas Rangers, Enlist: Oct. 15, 1858, 9
   months, 5 days, Ranger Muster Roll.
TURNER, Isaac N., Pvt., Comm. Off: MCCULLOCH, Henry E., Capt.,
   Organ: Texas Mounted Volunteers, Enlist: Nov. 5, 1850,
   Disc: May 5, 1851, Age: 30, Enlisted at: Austin, Texas, 6 mos.
   service, Ranger Muster Roll.
TURNER, J.C., Pvt., Comm. Off: CAMPBELL, G.W., Organ: Co. B, Fron-
   tier Battalion, Enlist: June 1, 1877, Disc: Nov. 30, 1877,
   Place of Birth: Camp Throckmorton, 6 months, Ranger Muster Roll.
TURNER, J.F., Pvt., Comm. Off: MCNELLY, L.H., Organ: Washington
   Co. Vol. Militia, Enlist: July 25, 1874, Disc: Oct. 4, 1874,
   Place of Birth: Austin, TExas, 2 months, 10 days service, Ran-
   ger Muster Roll.
TURNER, Monroe, Pvt., Comm. Off: HALL, A.B., Organ: Prov. State
   Troops, Detached, Enlist: Oct. 13, 1871, Disc: Oct. 20, 1871,
   Place of Birth: Groesbeck, Texas, Ranger Muster Roll.
TURNER, P., Pvt., Comm. Off: MOORE, D.D., Capt., Organ: Moscow
   Guards, Cav. Co., Polk Co., TST, Enlist: Nov. 1860, at Moscow,
   Tex. R&F 76; Co. org. with 64 volunteers who agreed to meet
   not less than 6 or more than 7 times a year; unless called out
   on special duty; 1 Muster Roll.
TURNER, R., Pvt., Comm. Off: MOORE, D.D., Capt., Organ: Moscow
   Guards, Cav. Co., Polk Co., TST, Enlist; Nov. 1860, at Moscow,
   Tex. R&F 76; Co. org. with 64 volunteers who agreed to meet
   not less than 6 or more than 7 times a year; unless called out
   on special duty; 1 Muster Roll.
TURNER, Robt. A., Pvt., Comm. Off: HAYNIE, Geo. E., Organ: Co. N,
   Minute Men, Lampasas Co., Enlist: March 9, 1873, Disc: March
   10, 1874, Place of Birth: Lampasas County, Ranger Muster Roll.
TURNER, R.O., Pvt., Comm. Off: HAYNIE, Geo. E., Organ: Co. M,
   Minute Men, Lampasas Co., Enlist: Dec. 3, 1873, Disc: Dec. 12,

TURNER, R.O., Pvt., (Continued)
1873, Place of Birth: Lampasas County, 18 days of service, Ranger Muster Roll.

TURNER, W.H., Pvt., Comm. Off: COLDWELL, Neal, Organ: Co. A, Frontier Battalion, Enlist: April 1, 1876, Disc: June 30, 1877, Place of Birth: Frio County, 3 months service, Ranger Muster Roll.

TWONSKY, A., Pvt., Comm. Off: SANSOM, John W., Organ: Texas Mtd. Rangers, Enlist: April 16, 1856, Disc: July 8, 1856, Age: 24, Place of Birth: Comal County, 82 days service, Ranger Muster Roll.

TURNEY, Daniel, Pvt., Comm. Off: HENRY, W.R., Organ: Rangers, Enlist: June 19, 1859, Place of Birth: Frio Canyon, Ranger Muster Roll.

TURNEY, John, Pvt., Comm. Off: COVINGTON, Wm. B., and TRAVIS, C.E., Capt., Organ: Texas Mounted Volunteers, Co. E, Enlist: Nov. 1, 1854, Disc: Feb. 1, 1855, Place of Birth: Austin, 3 months, Ranger Muster Roll.

TURNEY, John, Pvt., Comm. Off: TRAVIS, C.E., Capt., Organ: Texas Volunteers, Company E, Enlist: 1854, Disc: 1855, 3 months of service, Ranger Muster Roll.

TURNHAM, Robert C., Pvt., Comm. Off: ROSS, L.S., Capt., Organ: Ranger Company, Enlist: Oct. 3, 60 at Waco for 12 mos., Serv. from Oct. 3, 60 to Feb. 5, 61: 4 mos. & 3 days at $25-$102.50, Age: 23. R&F 66; En. Off: Capt. ROSS; Mus. Off: J.M.W. HALL; Appraiser Jas. H. SWINDELLS; Val. H: $175, HE. $35; Gun: $30, Pistol $40; Stoppage $78.31; elec. certif. with roll Co. sta. at Ft. Belknap Oct. 17 & Nov. 22, 60; 1 Muster Roll & 1 Pay Roll.

TUSCHINSKY, Theodore, Capt., Comm. Off: TUSCHINSKY, Theodore, Organ: Co. K, Mounted Militia, Enlist: Aug. 2, 1873, Disc: Dec. 9, 1873, Place of Birth: Travis County, Copied Roster, 4 months, 7 days, Ranger Muster Roll.

TUTT, Hansford, Lt., Comm. Off: YOUNT, Andrew J., Capt., Organ: Ranger Company, Enlist: Nov. 26, 66 at Denton, Texas. R&F 71; Co. org. in conformity to instructions from Governor THROCKMORTON. 1 Muster Roll.

TWADDELL, Jacob, Pvt., Comm. Off: HARRISON, Thos., Capt., Organ: Tex. Rangers, Enlist: Jan. 10, 61 at Waco for 6 mos.; unless sooner discharged, Age: 25. R&F 51; Thos. HARRISON, En. Off; J.C. NEWLON, Mus. Off; S.P. ROSS & D.R. LINSLEY, apprs. H: $140; HE: $30; Gun: $25; Pistol: $30. Co. sta. at camp near Waco Jan. 8, 61. Called into service of State by Gov. Sam HOUSTON. 1 Muster Roll: Jan. 10, 61.

TYLER, B.H., Pvt., Comm. Off: MOORE, D.D., Capt., Organ: Moscow Guards, Cav. Co., Polk Co., TST, Enlist: Nov. 1860, at Moscow, Tex. R&F 76; Co. org. with 64 volunteers who agreed to meet not less than 6 or more than 7 times a year; unless called out on special duty; 1 Muster Roll.

TYLER, E.B., Pvt., Comm. Off: BAKER, D.P., Organ: Frontier Forces, Co. F, Enlist: Nov. 5, 1870, Disc: June 15, 1871, Place of Birth: Decatur, Wise County, Ranger Muster Roll.

TYLER, James, Pvt., Comm. Off: BAKER, D.P., Organ: Frontier Forces, Co. F, Enlist: Nov. 5, 1870, Disc: June 15, 1871, Place

TYLER, James, Pvt., (Continued)
of Birth: Decatur, Wise County, Ranger Muster Roll.

UHR, August, Pvt., Comm. Off: KLEID, Peter, Organ: Co. G, Frontier Forces, Enlist: Oct. 31, 1870, Disc: May 31, 1871, Place of Birth: Camp Rio Frio, Ranger Muster Roll.

UNDERHILL, John W., Pvt., Comm. Off: REED, Henry, Organ: 1 Rgt., Mtd. Gunmen, Enlist: Oct. 10, 1839, Disc: Nov. 22, 1839, 1 month, 14 days service, Ranger Muster Roll.

UNDERWOOD, Edmond, Pvt., Comm. Off: FISHER, J.C., Organ: Prov. State Troops, Co. C, 3 Regt., Enlist: Oct. 9, 1871, Disc: Nov. 18, 1871, Place of Birth: Springfield, Texas, Ranger Muster Roll.

UNDERWOOD, Wm. B., 4th Sgt., Comm. Off: WOODS, Wm. M., Organ: Mtd Rangers, Enlist: April 10, 1860, Disc: Oct. 16, 1860, Age: 25, Place of Birth: Bonham, Ranger Muster Roll.

UNDERWOOD, William, Pvt., Comm. Off: YOUNT, Andrew J., Capt., Organ: Ranger Company, Enlist: Nov. 26, 66 at Denton, TExas, R&F 71; Co. org. in conformity to instructions from Governor THROCKMORTON. 1 Muster Roll.

UNDERWOOD, William D., Pvt., Comm. Off: HAMNER, H.A., Capt., Organ: Rangers, Enlist: Jan. 14, 60 at Jacksboro for 12 months, R&F 86; citizens of Wise, Parker, Montague, Young & Jack counties in public meeting at Jacksboro org. Co. for protection of frontier; 1 Muster Roll.

UPTON, W.T., Pvt., Comm. Off: MCADAMS, W.C., Organ: Palo Pinto County Rangers, Enlist: Dec. 13, 1873, Disc: April 13, 1874, Place of Birth: Palo Pinto County, 4 months service, Ranger Muster Roll. Taft, Kern Co., California.

UTTER, S.A., Pvt., Comm. Off: WALLER, J.R., Organ: Co. A, Frontier Battalion, Enlist: May 25, 1874, Disc: April 30, 1875, Place of Birth: Erath County, 11 months and 11 days service, Ranger Muster Roll.

UTTLEY, D.J., Pvt., Comm. Off: IKARD, E.F., Organ: Co. C, Frontier Battalion, Enlist: July 20, 1874, Disc: Aug. 31, 1874, Place of Birth: Clay County, 1 month, 7 days service, Ranger Muster Roll.

UTLY, D.S., Pvt., Comm. Off: CAMPBELL, G.W., Organ: Montague Co. Rangers, Enlist: Dec. 13, 1873, Disc: Feb. 13, 1874, Place of Birth: Montague County, 2 months service, Ranger Muster Roll.

U-WS-NEE, Spy, Comm. Off: ROSS, Peter F., Capt., Organ: Spy Company, Enlist: 1860, Serv. from July 1 to Aug. 20, 60; 1 mo. & 20 days at $25 - $41.66. R&F 39; 1 Pay Roll.

VACA, Hilario, Pvt., Comm. Off: SHAW, Owen, Organ: Texas Militia Volunteers, Enlist: Oct. 4, 1852, Disc: Feb. 17, 1853, Age: 18, Place of Birth: Laredo, 6 months service, Ranger Muster Roll.

VACA, Hilario, Pvt., Comm. Off: SHAW, Owen, Capt., Organ: Mtd. Volunteers, Enlist: Oct. 4, 1852, Disc: Feb. 17, 1853, Age: 18, Enlisted at: Laredo, Texas, Recruited by order of Sept. 30/52, 4 months, 14 days service, Ranger Muster Roll.

VACA, Senobio, Pvt., Comm. Off: SHAW, Owen, Organ: Texas Militia Volunteers, Enlist: NOv. 11, 1852, Disc: Feb. 17, 1853, Age: 32, Place of Birth: Laredo, 4 months, 14 days service, Ranger Muster Roll.

VACA, Senobio, Pvt., Comm. Off: SHAW, Owen, Capt., Organ: Mounted
    Volunteers, Enlist: Nov. 11, 1852, Disc: Feb. 17, 1853, Age: 32,
    Enlisted at: Laredo, Texas, Recruited in lieu of
BARRY, Jasper, 3 months, 7 days service, Ranger Muster Roll.
VADEN, W.J., Pvt., Comm. Off: MOORE, F.M., Organ: Co. D, Frontier
    Battalion, Enlist: April 29, 1877, Disc: Aug. 31, 1877, 4 mos.
    2 days, Ranger Muster Roll.
VALDEZ, M.J., Farrier, Comm. Off: KLEID, Peter, Organ: Co. O,
    Frontier Forces, Enlist: Oct. 31, 1870, Disc: May 31, 1870,
    Place of Birth: Camp Rio Frio, Promoted to Farrier Nov. 15,
    Ranger Muster Roll.
VALENTINE, John, Pvt., Comm. Off: HUNTER, James M., Organ: Co. I,
    Frontier Forces, Enlist: Sept. 27, 1870, Disc: Jan. 24, 1871,
    Place of Birth: Austin, Texas, 3 months, 27 days service, Ran-
    ger Muster Roll.
VALENTINE, Dr. I.P., Pvt., Comm. Off: CURETON,J.J., Capt.,
    Organ: Rangers, Enlist: Dec. 5, 1860, See Newspaper Clippings,
    Ranger Muster Roll.
VALLI, Francisco, Pvt., Comm. Off: LEWIS, G.K., Capt.,
    Organ: Texas Mtd. Volunteers, Enlist: Sept. 16, 1852,
    Disc: Mar. 13, 1853, Age: 18, Place of Birth: Salt Lake, Tex.,
    Ranger Muster Roll.
VAN, Risser, 1st Sgt., Comm. Off: PEAK, June, Organ: Co. B, Fron-
    tier Battalion, Enlist: Setp. 1, 1878, Disc: Nov. 30, 1878,
    Place of Birth: Runnels County, 3 months service, Ranger Mus-
    ter Roll.
VANCE, John, Pvt., Comm. Off: WILLINGHAM, John, Organ: Co. U,
    Minute Men, Montague Co., Enlist: April 20, 1872, Disc: Aug.
    20, 1872, Place of Birth: Montague County, 8 days of service,
    Ranger Muster Roll.
VANCLEAVE, E.M., Pvt., Comm. Off: HAMNER, H.A., Capt., Organ: Ran-
    gers, Enlist: Jan. 14, 60 at Jacksboro for 12 months. R&F 86;
    citizens of Wise, Parker, Montague, Young & Jack counties in
    public meeting at Jacksboro org. Co. for protection of fron-
    tier; 1 Muster Roll.
VANCLEAVE, J.M., 1st Corp., Comm. Off: HAMNER, H.A., Capt.,
    Organ: Rangers, Enlist: Jan. 14, 60 at Jacksboro for 12 months.
    R&F 86; citizens of Wise, Parker, Montague, Young & Jack
    counties in public meeting at Jacksboro org. co. for protec-
    tion of frontier; 1 Muster Roll. Name does not appear on roll
    except in statement of election.
VANCLEAVE, Joel B., Pvt., Comm. Off: CONNER, John H., Organ: Mtd.
    Rangers, hnlist: Jan. 20, 1860, 12 months service, Age: 35,
    Place of Birth: Austin, Honorably discharged May 3, 60, Ranger
    Muster Roll.
VANCLEAVE, M.M., Pvt., Comm. Off: HAMNER, H.A., Capt.,
    Organ: Rangers, Enlist: Jan. 14, 60 at Jacksboro for 12 months.
    R&F 86; citizens of Wise, Parker, Montague, Young & Jack
    counties in public meeting at Jacksboro org. Co. for protec-
    tion of frontier; 1 Muster Roll.
VANCLEAVE, S.J., Pvt., Comm. Off: HAMNER, H.A., Capt.,
    Organ: Rangers, Enlist: Jan. 14, 60 at Jacksboro for 12 months.
    R&F 86; citizens of Wise, Parker, Montague, Young & Jack
    counties in public meeting at Jacksboro org. Co. for protection
    of Frontier; 1 Muster Roll.

VANDENBUGH, David S., 2nd Corp., Comm. Off: LEWIS, G.K., Capt., Organ: Texas Mtd. Vol., Enlist: Sept. 10, 1852, Disc: March 13, 1853, Age: 21, Place of Birth: Brownsville, Texas, Ranger Muster Roll.

VANDERBURY, George W., Pvt., Comm. Off: HAMNER, H.A., Capt., Organ: Rangers, Enlist: Jan. 14, 60 at Jacksboro for 12 months. R&F 86; citizens of Wise, Parker, Montague, Young & Jack counties in public meeting at Jacksboro org. Co. for protection of frontier; 1 Muster Roll..

VANDERGRIFF, T.L., Pvt., Comm. Off: STEVENS, G.W., Organ: Co. B, Frontier Battalion, Enlist: May 16, 1874, Disc: Oct. 2, 1874, Place of Birth: Lost Valley, 4 months, 12 days, Ranger Muster Roll.

VANGRIFFT, William, Pvt., Comm. Off: MCCULLOCH, Henry E., Organ: Texas Mounted Vol., Enlist: Oct. 25, 1847, Age: 24, Blue eyes, dark hair, 6¦ Place of Birth: Fannin.

VANDERGRIFT, William, Pvt., Comm. Off: MCCULLOCH, Henry E., Capt., Organ: Texas Volunteers, Enlist: Oct. 25, 1847, Disc: Dec. 8, 1848, Age: 24, Height: 6', Dk. comp., Blue eyes, Dk. hair, Place of Birth: Fannin County, 13 months, 15 days service, Ranger Muster Roll.

VANDERPOOL, Abraham, Pvt., Comm. Off: MCCULLOCH, Henry E., Capt., Organ: Texas Mounted Volunteers, Enlist: Nov. 5, 1850, Disc: Nov. 5, 1851, Age: 27, Enlisted at: Austin, TExas, 12 months service, Ranger Muster Roll.

VANDERVER, Logan, Pvt., Comm. Off: MCCULLOCH, Henry E., Capt., Organ: Texas Volunteers, Enlist: Oct. 25, 1848, Disc: Dec. 8, 1848, Age: 33, 1 month, 13 days service, Ranger Muster Roll.

VAN DORN, S.J., Pvt., Comm. Off: WALLACE, Warren, Organ: Frontier Company, Nueces Co., Enlist: June 29, 1874, Place of Birth: Nueces County, Ranger Muster Roll.

VANDUESEN, Wm., Pvt., Comm. Off: MCADAMS, W.C., Organ: Palo Pinto County Rangers, Enlist: Dec. 13, 1873, Disc: April 13, 1874, Place of Birth: Palo Pinto County, 4 months service, Ranger Muster Roll.

VANFLEER, H., Teamster, Comm. Off: PEAK, June, Organ: Co. B, Frontier Battalion, Enlist: Sept. 1.

VANFLEER, H., Teamster, Comm. Off: PEAK, June, Organ: Co. B, Frontier Battalion, Enlist: Nov. 16, 1878, Disc: Nov. 30, 1878, Place of Birth: Runnels County, 16 days service, Ranger Muster Roll.

VANHOOSER, W.B., Pvt., Comm. Off: PERRY, C.R., Organ: Co. D, Frontier Battalion, Enlist: May 25, 1874, Disc: May 25, 1875, Place of Birth: Blanco County, 12 months service, Ranger Muster Roll.

VAN LIEN, Jas., Pvt., Comm. Off: FORSHEY, J.M., Organ: Washington Guards, Enlist: Sept. 21, 1874, Disc: Sept. 27, 1874, Place of Birth: Galveston County, 7 days service, Ranger Muster Roll.

VANLITSER, J.E., 1st Sgt., Comm. Off: CAMPBELL, G.W., Organ: Co. B, Frontier Battalion, Enlist: Dec. 1, 1877, Disc: Feb. 28, 1876, Place of Birth: Throckmartin County, 3 months service, Ranger Muster Roll.

VAN RIPER, J.E., Pvt., Comm. Off: CAMPBELL, G.W., Organ: Co. B, Frontier Battalion, Enlist: June 5, 1877, Disc: Feb. 28, 1878,

VAN RIPER, J.E., Pvt., (Continued)
Place of Birth: Camp Throckmorton, 8 months, 26 days service, Ranger Muster Roll.

VAN RIPER, Jas. M., 2nd Corp., Comm. Off: HABY, George, Organ: Co. V, Minute Men, Medina Co., Enlist: Sept. 1, 1872, Disc: Aug. 15, 1873, Place of Birth: Medina County, 120 days of service, Ranger Muster Roll.

VAN RIPER, W.H., Pvt., Comm. Off: HABY, George, Organ: Co. V, Min. Men, Medina County, Enlist: Sept. 1, 1872, Disc: Aug. 15, 1873, Place of Birth: Medina County, 120 days of service, Ranger Muster Roll. San Bernandino, California, 165 5th St.

VANA, James, Pvt., Comm. Off: WOOD, J.D., Organ: Prov. Mounted State Troops, Enlist: Oct. 9, 1871, Disc: Nov. 13, 1871, Place of Birth: Limestone County, Ranger Muster Roll.

VANTINE, T., Pvt., Comm. Off: FITZHUGH, G.S., Capt., Organ: Ranger Co., Enlist: April 14, 60, Disc: Oct. 25, 60; Served 6 mo. & 12 days at $25. Total: $160. R&F 83; Stoppages: .90. Balance Pd: $159.10. 1 Pay Roll.

VANTINE, Thomas, Pvt., Comm. Off: FITZHUGH, G.S., Organ: Mounted Rangers, Enlist: May 20, 1860, Disc: Oct. 25, 1860, Ranger Muster Roll.

VANWINKLE, B.A., Pvt., Comm. Off: FITZHUGH, G.S., Capt., Organ: Ranger Co., Enlist: April 14, 60, Disc: Oct. 25, 60; Served 6 mo. & 12 days at $25. Total: $160. R&F 83; stoppages: $24.60. Balance Pd: $135.40. 1 Pay Roll.

VAN WINKLE, T.H., Pvt., Comm. Off: STEVENS, G.W., Organ: Wise County Rangers, Enlist: Nov. 26, 1873, Disc: March 26, 1874, Place of Birth: Wise County, 4 months service, Ranger Muster Roll.

VARDIMAN, E.P., Pvt., Comm. Off: BOURLAND, J., Capt., Organ: Mtd. Vol. TR, Enlist: Feb. 13, 59, Place of Birth: Gainesville, Tex., Disc: April 28, 59, $&F 43, April 28, 59, 1 Muster Rolls.

VARGAS, Clemente, Pvt., Comm. Off: BAU, Manuel, Organ: Co. A, Min. Men, Maverick County, Enlist: Oct. 8, 1872, Disc: Oct. 8, 1873, Place of Birth: Maverick County, 29 days of service, Ranger Muster Roll.

VARNAM, Hervey, Pvt., Comm. Off: MCCULLOCH, Henry E., Organ: Tex. Mounted Vol., Enlist: Oct. 25, 1847, Age: 27, Dark eyes, dark hair, 5'10", Place of Birth: Fannin County.

VARNAM, Henry, Pvt., Comm. Off: MCCULLOCH, Henry E., Capt., Organ: Texas Vols., Enlist: Oct. 25, 1847, Disc: Oct. 24, 1848, Age: 27, Height: 5'10", dk. comp., dk. eyes, dk. hair, Place of Birth: Fannin County, 12 months service, Ranger Muster Roll.

VARNELL, Russell, Pvt., Comm. Off: BLACK, R.W., Capt., Organ: Minute Men, Enlist: Jan. 1, 1856, Disc: Dec. 31, 1856, 2 months service, Ranger Muster Roll.

VASQUES, Antonio, Pvt., Comm. Off: HILL, A.C., Organ: Mounted Vol. for Cortinas War, Enlist: Jan. 11, 1860, Disc: Feb. 1, 1860, Ranger Muster Roll.

VASQUES, Gil, Pvt., Comm. Off: HILL, A.C., Organ: Mounted Vol. for Cortinas War, Enlist: Jan. 11, 1860, Disc: Feb. 1, 1860, Ranger Muster Roll.

VASQUEZ, Antonio, Pvt., Comm. Off: HILL, A.C., Sgt., Organ: Min. Men, Enlist: Jan. 11, 60 at Goliad for 12 mos., unless sooner

VASQUEZ, Antonio, Pvt., (Continued)
    discharged, Age: 24. R&F 21; A.C. HILL, En. & Mus. Off:
    W.B. WRATHER, & Louis COWEN, Apprs. H: $100; HE: $30; Gun: $25;
    Pistol: $30. Co. sta. at Asutin Dec. 30, 59; at Brownsville
    Feb. 1, 60. Co. called into service of State by Gov. HOUSTON
    Dec. 30, 59. 1 Muster Roll.
VASQUEZ, Gil, Pvt., Comm. Off: HILL, A.C., Sgt., Organ: Minute
    Men, Enlist: Jan. 11, 60 at Goliad for 12 mos.; unless sooner
    discharged, Age: 40. R&F 21; A.C. HILL, En. & Mus. off;
    W.B. WRATHER, & Louis COWEN, Apprs. H: $180; HE: $35; Gun: $40;
    Pistol: $40. Co. sta. at Austin Dec. 30, 59; at Brownsville
    Feb. 1, 60. Co. called into service of state by Gov. HOUSTON
    Dec. 30, 59. 1 Muster Roll.
VAUGHAN, J., Pvt., Comm. Off: HALL, A.B., Organ: Prov. State
    Troops, Detached, Enlist: Oct. 13, 1871, Disc: Oct. 20, 1871,
    Place of Birth: Groesbeck, Texas, Ranger Muster Roll.
VAUGHAN, John H., Pvt., Comm. Off: COX, A.H., Organ: Frontier
    Forces, Co. B, Enlist: Sept. 8, 1870, Disc: May 31, 1871,
    Place of Birth: SHackleford County, Ranger Muster Roll.
VAUGHAN, S., Pvt., Comm. Off: MCADAMS, W.C., Organ: Palo Pinto
    County Rangers, Enlist: Dec. 13, 1873, Disc: April 13, 1874,
    Place of Birth: Palo Pinto County, 4 months service, Ranger
    Muster Roll.
VAUGHN, Roma, 1st Corp., Comm. Off: WILLIAMS, John, Organ: Second
    Co. of Texas Rangers, Enlist: Oct. 30, 1858, 8 months, 8 days,
    Ranger Muster Roll.
VAUGHN, Wm. M., Comm. Off: ROSS, L.S., Capt., Organ: Mounted
    Rangers, Enlist: April 2, 1860 to Sept. 7, 1860, Disc: Oct. 5,
    1860 to Feb. 5, 1861, Place of Birth: Silverton, Brisco Co.,
    Texas, Dept. of the Interior, Pensions, N.H. NICHOLSON, In-
    spector.
VAULKER, Jackson, Pvt., Comm. Off: ENGLISH, Levi, Organ: Mounted
    Volunteers, Enlist: Aug. 6, 1855, Disc: Nov. 13, 1855, Place
    of Birth: Bexar County, 3 months, 8 days service, Ranger Mus-
    ter Roll.
VAUMEITER, W.C., Corp., Comm. Off: DONELSON, John, Organ: Rangers
    for Cortinas War, Enlist: Nov. 5, 1859, Disc: Dec. 10, 1859,
    Age: 27, Place of Birth: Live Oak County, Ranger Muster Roll.
    Service: 1 mo. & 6 days at $14--$16; $3 allowed for clothing
    & $14.40 for hire of horse--Total pay $34.20.
VEARREN, Peter, Pvt., Comm. Off: SNOWBALL, James, Organ: Prov.
    State Troops, Enlist: Oct. 13, 1871, Disc: Oct. 20, 1871,
    Place of Birth: Groesbeck, Texas, Ranger Muster Roll.
VELA, Peyus, Pvt., Comm. Off: MCNELLY, L.H., Organ: Washington Co.
    Vol. Militia, Enlist: July 1, 1875, Disc: May 22, 1876, Place
    of Birth: Austin, Texas, 10 months, 22 days service, Ranger
    Muster Roll.
VENABLE, Wm. J., Pvt., Comm. Off: WHITE, Robert M., 1st Lt.,
    Organ: Bell Cty. Rangers, Enlist: Feb. 18, 60 at Belton for 12
    mos.; Enrolled for duty Feb. 20, 60, Disbanded at Belton Je.
    29, 60, Age: 19, R&F 26; Enr. Off: Dr. John EMBREE; Mus.
    Off; J.M.W. HALL; Apprs.: John S. BLAIR, John W. SCOTT; Val.
    of: H: $75, HE: $25; Gun: $20; Gov. Pistol; Service 4 mos. 10
    days at $25, tot. $108,33; Co. stationed at Belton Feb. 20, 60,

VENABLE, Wm. J., Pvt., (Continued)
Co. Called into service by Gov. HOUSTON; state arms returned upon disbandment; 2 Muster Rolls dated Feb. 20, 60 each; 1 Pay Roll.

VENABLE, Wm. J., Pvt., Comm. Off: WHITE, Robt. M., Organ: Mounted Rangers, Enlist: Feb. 18, 1860, Disc: June 29, 1860, Age: 19, Place of Birth: Belton, Ranger Muster Roll.

VENDEMAN, E.P., Pvt., Comm. Off: BOURLAND, James, Organ: Texas Mounted Rangers, Enlist: Feb. 13, 1859, Disc: April 28, 1859, Place of Birth: Gainesville, Texas, 2 months, 15 days service, Ranger Muster Roll.

VERCOS, James, Pvt., Comm. Off: HARRELL, J.M., Organ: Co. K, Frontier Forces, Enlist: Sept. 16, 1870, Disc: Feb. 20, 1871, Place of Birth: Penal Ranch, Discharged Feb. 16, 1870, Ranger Muster Roll.

VERMILLION, J.H., Pvt., Comm. Off: FITZHUGH, G.S., Capt., Organ: Ranger Co., Enlist: April 14, 60, Disc: Oct. 25, 60; served 6 mo. & 12 days at $25. Total: $160. R&F 83; Stoppages $16.30. Balance Pd: $143.70. 1 Pay Roll.

VERMILLION, Wm., Pvt., Comm. Off: TACKITT, A.C., Organ: Young County Rangers, Enlist: Jan. 12, 1874, Disc: Feb. 14, 1874, Place of Birth: Young County, 33 days of service, Ranger Muster Roll.

VICARS (VICKERS), C., 2nd Corp., Comm. Off: STEWART, F.C., Organ: Co. Q, Minute Men, Llano County, Enlist: Sept. 8, 1872, Disc: Aug. 9, 1873, Place of Birth: Llano County, 49 days of service, Ranger Muster Roll.

VILLEREAL, Juan, Pvt., Comm. Off: LEWIS, G.K., Capt., Organ: Tex. Mtd. Vol., Enlist: Sept. 16, 1852, Disc: Mar. 13, 1853, Age: 38, Place of Birth: Brownsville, Texas, Ranger Muster Roll.

VINTON, John, Pvt., Comm. Off: RAGSDALE, D.H., Lt., Organ: Ranger Co., Enlist: April 28, 60, Serv. from April 26 to Je. 8, 60; 1 mo. & 12 days at $25 - $35. R&F 14; allowance for trav. 65 miles $2.70; Total pay $37.70; 1 Pay Roll.

VON BIBERSTEIN, H.R., Capt., Comm. Off: VON BIBERSTEIN, H.R., Organ: Frontier Forces, Co. L, Enlist: Aug. 12, 1870, Disc: May 31, 1871, Place of Birth: Gillespie County, became Co. G, Jan. 1, 71, Ranger Muster Roll.

VON GERMAN, Albert, Pvt., Comm. Off: SHAW, Owen, Organ: Texas Militia Volunteers, Enlist: Aug. 18, 1852, Disc: Feb. 17, 1853, Age: 30, Place of Birth: Austin, 6 months service, 6 months service, Ranger Muster Roll.

VON GERMAN, Albert, Pvt., Comm. Off: SHAW, Owen, Capt., Organ: Mtd. Vol., Enlist: Aug. 18, 1852, Disc: Feb. 17, 1853, Age: 30, Enlisted at: Austin, Texas, 6 months service, Ranger Muster Roll.

VOSBURG, A.W.A., Pvt., Comm. Off: EASTIN, S.W., Organ: Jack Co. Rangers, Enlist: Dec. 3, 1873, Disc: April 3, 1874, Place of Birth: Jack County, 4 months service, Ranger Muster Roll.

WACHTER, Robert, Pvt., Comm. Off: BURLESON, Edward, Capt., Organ: State Guards, Enlist: July 15, 65 at Austin. Mustd. in July 15, 65 at Austin. Disc: Aug. 4, 65, 21 days service, - $16.00. R&F 41; Mus. Off: Capt. Ed BURLESON; Amt. of pay

WACHTER, Robert, Pvt., (Continued)
    $11.20 plus subsistence $15.75, forage $5.60 & use of horse
    $8.40--total $40.95. Co. org. for protection of prop. belong-
    ing to state in Travis County under authority from Gen.
    G. GRANGER. Co. stationed at Austin, Aug. 4, 65. 1 Muster
    & Pay Roll dated Aug. 4, 65.
WACHTER, Bernard, Pvt., Comm. Off: BURLESON, Edward, Capt.,
    Organ: State Guards, Enlist: July 15, 65 at Austin. Mustd. in
    July 15, 65 at Austin, Disc: Aug. 4, 65, 21 days service, -
    $16.00. R&F 41; Mus. Off: Capt. Ed BURLESON; Amt. of pay
    $11.20 plus subsistence $15.75, forage $5.60 & use of horse
    $8.40--total $40.95. Co. org. for protection of prop. belong-
    ing to state in Travis Cty under authority from Gen.
    G. GRANGER. Co. stationed at Austin, Aug. 4, 1865. 1 Muster
    & Pay Roll dated Aug. 4, 65.
WADDELL, William A., Pvt., Comm. Off: HENRY, William R., Organ: Co.
    C, Mounted Vol., Enlist: Dec. 14, 1854, Disc: March 14, 1855,
    Age: 19, Place of Birth: San Antonio, 3 months service, Ranger
    Muster Roll.
WADDOCK, Bryan, Pvt., Comm. Off: LEWIS, G.K., Capt., Organ: Texas
    Mtd. Vol., Enlist: Sept. 1, 1852, Disc: Mar. 13, 1853, Age: 23,
    Place of Birth: Corpus Christi, Texas, Ranger Muster Roll.
WADDILL, H.B., Pvt., Comm. Off: SPARKS, J.C., Organ: Co. C, Fron-
    tier Battalion, Enlist: Oct. 1, 1876, Disc: Feb. 28, 1878,
    Place of Birth: Clay County, 17 months service, Ranger Muster
    Roll.
WADE, E.B., Farrier, Comm. Off: COVINGTON, Wm. B., and
    TRAVIS, C.E., Capt., Organ: Texas Mounted Volunteer Co. E,
    Enlist: Nov. 1, 1854, Disc: Feb. 1, 1855, Place of Birth: Aus-
    tin, 3 months service, Ranger Muster Roll.
WADE, George, Pvt., Comm. Off: JONES, Franklin, Organ: Co. A,
    Frontier Battalion, Enlist: Aug. 25, 1870, Disc: Nov. 11, 1870,
    Place of Birth: Ft. Mason, Texas, 2 months, 17 days service,
    Ranger Muster Roll.
WADE, George, Pvt., Comm. Off: JONES, Franklin, Organ: Co. A,
    Frontier Battalion, Enlist: Aug. 25, 1870, Disc: Oct. 31, 1870,
    Place of Birth: Mason, Texas, Ranger Muster Roll.
WADE, Edward B., Blacksmith and Farrier, Comm. Off: TRAVIS, C.E.,
    Capt., Organ: Texas Volunteers, Company E, Enlist: 1854,
    Disc: 1855, 3 months service, Ranger Muster Roll.
WADE, James H., Pvt., Comm. Off: TRAVIS, C.E., Capt., Organ: Tex.
    Volunteers, Company E, Enlist: 1854, Disc: 1855, 3 months of
    service, Ranger Muster Roll.
WADE, James H., Comm. Off: COVINGTON, Wm. B., and
    TRAVIS, C.E., Capt., Organ: Texas Mounted Volunteers, Co. E,
    Enlist: Nov. 1, 1854, Disc: Feb. 1, 1855, Place of Birth: Aus-
    tin, 3 months service, Ranger Muster Roll.
WADE, James H., Blacksmith, Comm. Off: CONNER, John H., Organ: Mtd
    Rangers, Enlist: Jan. 20, 1860, Place of Birth: Austin, On duty
    to 1860, Ranger Muster Roll.
WADE, J.J., Pvt., Comm. Off: HUNTER, James M., Organ: Co. I, Fron-
    tier Forces, Enlist: Sept. 12, 1870, Disc: Jan. 24, 1871,
    Place of Birth: Austin, Texas, 4 months, 12 days service, Ran-
    ger Muster Roll.

WADE, J.M., Lt., Comm. Off: WADE, J.M., Organ: Co. I, Minute Men, Cook County, Enlist: June 26, 1872, Disc: July 6, 1873, Place of Birth: Cook County, 15 days of service, Ranger Muster Roll.

WADE, S.H., Pvt., Comm. Off: MOORE, P.M., Organ: Co. D, Frontier Battalion, Enlist: April 1, 1877, Disc: Aug. 22, 1877, 4 mos. 22 days service, dishonorably discharged, Ranger Muster Roll.

WADE, T.A., Pvt., Comm. Off: HARRELL, J.M., Organ: Co. K, Frontier Forces, Enlist: Sept. 16, 1870, Disc: Feb. 20, 1871, Place of Birth: Penal Ranch, Discharged Feb. 16, 1872, Ranger Muster Roll.

WADKINS, Leroy, Pvt., Comm. Off: ALEXANDER, John, Organ: Co. O, Minute Men, Burnet Co., Enlist: Sept. 11, 1872, Disc: Aug. 13, 1873, Place of Birth: Burnet County, 20 days of service, Ranger Muster Roll.

WADKINS, W.W., Pvt., Comm. Off: FITZHUGH, G.S., Organ: Mounted Rangers, Enlist: May 20, 1860, Disc: Oct. 25, 1860, Ranger Muster Roll.

WAECHTER See WACHTER.

WAGGONER, Elias, Pvt., Comm. Off: BLACK, R.W., Capt., Organ: Min. Men, Enlist: Jan. 1, 1856, Disc: Dec. 31, 1856, 2 months of service, Ranger Muster Roll.

WAGNER, Charles, Pvt., Comm. Off: SANSOM, John W., Organ: Frontier Forces, Enlist: Aug. 25, 1870, Disc: May 31, 1871, Place of Birth: Shackleford County, Ranger Muster Roll.

WAGNER, John A., Comm. Off: ROSS, L.S., Capt., Organ: Mounted Rangers, Enlist: April 2, 1860 to Sept. 7, 1860, Disc: Oct. 5, 1860 to Feb. 5, 1861, Place of Birth: Cross Plains, Callhan Co., Texas, Box 157, Dept. of the Interior-Pensions, N.H. NICHOLSON, Inspector.

WAGNER, Powell, Pvt., Comm. Off: SHAW, Owen, Organ: Texas Militia Volunteer, Enlist: Aug. 18, 1852, Disc: Feb. 17, 1853, Age: 30, Place of Birth: New Braunfels, 6 months service, Ranger Muster Roll.

WAGNER, Powell, Pvt., Comm. Off: SHAW, Owen, Capt., Organ: Mtd. Vol., Enlist: Aug. 18, 1852, Disc: Feb. 17, 1853, Age: 30, Enlisted at: New Braunfels, Texas, 6 months service, Ranger Muster Roll.

WAGNER, William, Pvt., Comm. Off: WALLACE, Warren, Organ: Frontier Company, Nueces Co., Enlist: June 29, 1874, Place of Birth: Nueces County, Ranger Muster Roll.

WAGONER, A., Pvt., Comm. Off: IKARD, E.F., Organ: Co. C, Frontier Battalion, Enlist: May 20, 1874, Disc: Dec. 29, 1874, Place of Birth: Clay County, 7 months, 11 days service, Ranger Muster Roll.

WAGONER, Chas., Pvt., Comm. Off: KLEID, Peter, Organ: Co. O, Frontier Forces, Enlist: Oct. 31, 1870, Disc: May 31, 1871, Place of Birth: Camp Rio Frio, Discharged Nov. 30, Ranger Muster Roll.

WAID, J.W., Pvt., Comm. Off: MCADAMS, W.C., Organ: Palo Pinto County Rangers, Enlist: Dec. 13, 1873, Disc: April 13, 1874, Place of Birth: Palo Pinto County, 4 months service, Ranger Muster Roll. Stanfield, Amatilla, Oregon.

WAIDE, D.H., Pvt., Comm. Off: WADE, J.M., Organ: Co. I, Minute Men, Cook County, Enlist: July 24, 1872, Disc: July 5, 1873,

WAIDE, D.H., Pvt., (Continued)
   Place of Birth: Cook County, 10 days of service, Ranger Muster
   Roll.
WAINSCOTT, Cashaus, Pvt., Comm. Off: WILLINGHAM, John, Organ: Co.
   U, Minute Men, Montague Co., Enlist: Aug. 26, 1872, Disc: Dec.
   21, 1873, Place of Birth: Montague County, 76 days of service,
   Ranger Muster Roll.
WAINSCOTT, Hiram, Pvt., Comm. Off: WILLINGHAM, John, Organ: Co.
   U, Minute Men, Montague Co., Enlist: Aug. 26, 1872, Disc: Dec.
   21, 1873, Place of Birth: Montague County, 76 days of service,
   Ranger Muster Roll.
WAINSCOTT, Isaac, 2nd Sgt., Comm. Off: WILLINGHAM, John, Organ: Co.
   U, Minute Men, Montague County, Enlist: April 20, 1872,
   Disc: Dec. 21, 1873, Place of Birth: Montague County, 97 days
   of service, Ranger Muster Roll. Manitou, Tillman Co., Okla.,
   R.R. 1, Box 34.
WAIR (WARE), R.M., Pvt., Comm. Off: BLACK, R.W., Capt., Organ: Min.
   Men, Enlist: Jan. 1, 1856, Disc: Dec. 31, 1856, 2 months of
   service, Ranger MusterRoll.
WAITES, F.L., Pvt., Comm. Off: WALKER, John G., Capt., Organ: Mtd
   Vol., Enlist: Nov. 1854, Ranger Muster Roll.
WAITS, J.M., Pvt., Comm. Off: JOHNSON, Thomas J., Organ: Mounted
   Rangers, Enlist: April 21, 1860, Disc: Nov. 10, 1860, Place
   of Birth: Fort Worth, Due B. MONROE 30. for pistol, Ranger
   Muster Roll.
WAITS, L., 3rd Sgt., Comm. Off: EASTIN, S.W., Organ: Dec. 3, 1873,
   Disc: April 3, 1874, Place of Birth: Jack County, 4 months of
   service, Ranger Muster Roll.
WAITS, L., Pvt., Comm. Off: IKARD, E.F., Organ: Co. C, Frontier
   Battalion, Enlist: May 20, 1874, Disc: Dec. 10, 1874, Place of
   Birth: Clay County, 6 months, 22 days service, Ranger Muster
   Roll.
WAITS, W., Pvt., Comm. Off: IKARD, E.F., Organ: Co. C, Frontier
   Battalion, Enlist: May 20, 1874, Disc: Dec. 29, 1874, Place of
   Birth: Clay County, 7 months, 11 days service, Ranger Muster
   Roll.
WAKEFIELD, W.A., Pvt., Comm. Off: CAMPBELL, G.W., Organ: Montague
   Co. Rangers, Enlist: Dec. 13, 1873, Disc: Feb. 13, 1874,
   Place of Birth: Montague County, 2 months service, Ranger Mus-
   ter Roll.
WALDE, C.H., Pvt., Comm. Off: BARRY, James Buck, 1st Lt.,
   Organ: Co. org. & fighting Indians interval before conv. of
   '61, Expiration of service Feb. 25-61; Serv. 1 mo. 15 days at
   $25 - $37.50. R&F 25; 1 payroll; BARRY received commission
   from Governor; Convention assumed authority while in field and
   company not mustered out.
WALDE, C.H., Sgt., Comm. Off: GENTRY, F.B., Lt., Organ: Ranger
   Co., Enlist: Mar. 20, 60, Disc: Je. 21, 60; served 3 mo. & 1
   day at $29--$87.96. R&F 14; 2 Pay Rolls.
WALDE, C.E., Pvt., Comm. Off: GENTRY, F.B., Organ: Minute Men,
   Enlist: March 20, 1860, Disc: June 20, 1860, Age: 35, Place of
   Birth: Hamilton, Ranger Muster Roll.
WALDES, M.J., Pvt., Comm. Off: KLEID, Peter, Organ: Co. G, Fron-
   tier Forces, Enlist: Oct. 31, 1870, Disc: May 31, 1871, Place

WALDES, M.J., Pvt., (Continued)
  Of Birth: Camp Rio Frio, Ranger Muster Roll.
WALDROPE, F.S., Pvt., Comm. Off: INGRAM, James, and GRAY, S.B.,
  Organ: Minute Men, Enlist: Feb. 19, 1872, Disc: Nov. 17, 1872,
  Place of Birth: Blanco County, 71 days service, Ranger Muster
  Roll.
WALKER, Alfred, Pvt., Comm. Off: FITZHUGH, G.S., Capt.,
  Organ: Ranger Co., Enlist: April 14, 60, Disc: Oct. 25, 60;
  served 6 mo. & 12 days at $25. Total: $160. R&F 83; Stop-
  pages: $6.90. Balance Pd: $153.10. 1 Pay Roll.
WALKER, Alfred, Pvt., Comm. Off: MCNELLY, L.H., Organ: Washing-
  ton Co. Vol. Militia, Enlist: March 1, 1876, Disc: May 31,
  1876, Place of Birth: Austin, Texas, 3 months service, Ranger
  Muster Roll.
WALKER, A., Pvt., Comm. Off: FITZHUGH, G.S., Organ: Mounted Ran-
  gers, Enlist: May 20, 1860, Disc: Oct. 25, 1860, Ranger Mus-
  ter Roll.
WALKER, Alfred, Pvt., Comm. Off: HALL, J.L., Organ: Special State
  Troops, Enlist: Jan. 25, 1877, Disc: Feb. 28, 1878, Place of
  Birth: Clinton, Texas, 12 months, 18 days service, Ranger Mus-
  ter Roll.
WALKER, D.B., Pvt., Comm. Off: FOSTER, B.S., Organ: Co. E, Fron-
  tier Battalion, Enlist: Dec. 1, 1875, Disc: Feb. 29, 1876,
  Place of Birth: Coleman County, No service recorded, Ranger
  Muster Roll.
WALKER, Ben, Pvt., Comm. Off: TUSCHINSKY, Theodore, Organ: Co. K,
  Mounted Militia, Enlist: Aug. 2, 1873, Disc: Dec. 9, 1873,
  Place of Birth: Travis County, Copied Roster: 4 months, 7 days
  Ranger Muster Roll.
WALKER, C., Pvt., Comm. Off: HAMPTON, G.J., Capt., Organ: Mtd.
  Ranger Volunteers, Enlist: Nov. 12, 59, Disc: Jan. 1, 60;
  served 1 mo. & 20 days at $12, Total: $20. R&F 34; Allowances
  on: clothing: $4.17; use of horse: $20; Rations: $4.50;
  Forage: $8.25. Total: $56.92. Co. called into State service
  for suppression of CortinaRebellion on Rio Grande frontier by
  Gov. H.R. RUNNELS. 1 Pay Roll. This name is deleted on roll.
  NOTE: Paid on LITTLETON's 1st Copy.
WALKER, Cornelius, Pvt., Comm. Off: TUMLINSON, Peter, Capt.,
  Organ: Mtd. Vols., Enlist: Jan. 1, 1860, Disc: Feb. 10, 1860,
  1 month, 10 days service, Ranger Muster Roll.
WALKER, Dixon, Pvt., Comm. Off: WOOD, Hanna, Capt., Organ: Ranger
  Co., Enlist: Jan. 18, 1861, Disc: Feb. 29, 1861; 6 days at
  $1.50-$9.00. R&F 15; One Pay Roll.
WALKER, Dixon, Lt., Comm. Off: WALKER, Dixon, Lt., Organ: Mtd.
  Volunteers (?), Enlist: Feb. 25, 1860, Disc: May 18, 1860, 2
  months, 24 days service, Ranger Muster Roll.
WALKER, E.M., Pvt., Comm. Off: STEWART, F.C., Organ: Co. Q, Min.
  Men, Llano County, Enlist: Aug. 1, 1873, Disc: Aug. 9, 1873,
  Place of Birth: Llano County, 9 days of service A.W.O.L., Ran-
  ger Muster Roll.
WALKER, Edward, Pvt., Comm. Off: ROBERTS, D.W., Organ: Co. D,
  Frontier Battalion, Enlist: June 1, 1875, Disc: Nov. 30, 1875,
  Age: 24, 5'10", fair, blue eyes, dark hair, farmer, Place of
  Birth: Houston, Tex., 6 months service, Ranger Muster Roll.

WALKER, Geo., Pvt., Comm. Off: STEVENS, G.W., Organ: Wise County
    Rangers, Enlist: Nov. 26, 1873, Disc: March 26, 1874, Place of
    Birth: Wise County, 4 months service, RangerMuster Roll.
WALKER, Geo. F., 2nd Corp., Comm. Off: REYNOLDS, H.O., Organ: Co.
    E, Frontier Battalion, Enlist: Sept. 1, 1877, Disc: Oct. 15,
    1877, Place of Birth: Coleman County, 1 month, 15 days service,
    Ranger Muster Roll.
WALKER, G.F., Pvt., Comm. Off: FOSTER, B.S., Organ: Co. E, Fron-
    tier Battalion, Enlist: Sept. 1, 1876, Disc: Aug. 31, 1877,
    Place of Birth: Coleman County, 12 months service, Ranger Mus-
    ter Roll.
WALKER, G.W., Pvt., Comm. Off: STEVENS, G.W., Organ: Co. B, Fron-
    tier Battalion, Enlist: May 16, 1874, Disc: Aug. 31, 1875,
    Place of Birth: Lost Valley, 15 months, 16 days service, Ran-
    ger Muster Roll. Aluard, Texas, R.R. 4, Box 2.
WALKER, H., Pvt., Comm. Off: JONES, Stephen F., Organ: Minute Men,
    Detached, Enlist: July 1, 1860, Disc: Aug. 29, 1860, Place of
    Birth: Palo Pinto, Ranger Muster Roll.
WALKER, Howell, Pvt., Comm. Off: BROWN, John Henry, Organ: Texas
    State Troops, Enlist: July 7, 1849, Disc: Aug. 23, 1859,
    Place of Birth: Travis County, 1 month, 16 days service, Ran-
    ger Muster Roll.
WALKER, James, Pvt., Comm. Off: REED, Henry, Organ: 1 Rgt., Mtd.
    Gunmen, Enlist: Oct. 10, 1839, Disc: Nov. 22, 1839, 1 month,
    14 days service, Ranger Muster Roll.
WALKER, Joe, Pvt., Comm. Off: TUSCHINSKY, Theodore, Organ: Co. K,
    Mounted Militia, Enlist: Aug. 2, 1873, Disc: Dec. 9, 1873,
    Place of Birth: Travis County, Copied Roster: 4 months, 7 days
    service, Ranger Muster Roll.
WALKER, Joel M., 1st Sgt., Comm. Off: TUMLINSON, P., Capt.,
    Organ: Nov. 12, 1859, Disc: Feb. 10, 1860, 2 months, 29 days
    service, Ranger Muster Roll.
WALKER, John L., Pvt., Comm. Off: WALKER, D., Lt., Organ: Mtd.
    Vol., Enlist: Feb. 25, 1860, Disc: May 18, 1860, 2 months, 24
    days service, Ranger Muster Roll.
WALKER, Jereome B., Pvt., Comm. Off: TRAVIS, C.E., Capt.,
    Organ: Texas Volunteers, Company E, Enlist: 1854, Disc: 1855,
    3 months service, Ranger Muster Roll.
WALKER, Joel M., 1st Lt., Comm. Off: ENGLISH, Levi, Organ: Mounted
    Volunteers, Enlist: Aug. 6, 1855, Disc: Nov. 13, 1855, Place
    of Birth: Bexar County, 3 months, 8 days service, Ranger Mus-
    ter Roll.
WALKER, Joseph, Lt., Comm. Off: WALKER, Joseph, Organ: Rangers
    for Cortinas War, Enlist: Nov. 30, 1859, Disc: Jan. 20, 1860,
    Age: 32, Place of Birth: Austin, Ranger Muster Roll.
WALKER, Joseph, Quarter Master, Comm. Off: DALRYMPLE, William C.,
    Colonel, Organ: Field & Staff, Mounted Rangers, Enlist: Jan. 7,
    1861, Disc: June 22, 1861--serving 5 months & 16 days. F&S 5;
    Companies in his regiment, Capt. C. MAYS's, Thos. HARRISON's.
    D.L. SUBLETT's, E.W. ROGER'S after E.H. MOORE's Co.,
    J.M. WRIGHT's and A.B. BURLESON's Co. 1 Discharge roll dated
    July 3, 61.
WALKER, Joseph, Qr. Master, Comm. Off: DALRYMPLE, Wm. C., Col.,
    Organ: Regt., Col. DALRYMPLE's Front. Troops, TST,

WALKER, Joseph, Qr. Master (Continued)
Enlist: Jan. 7, 61, Disc: Je. 22- 61; served 5 mos. & 16 days
at $95 per month. Staff Payroll of Col. DALRYMPLE's Regt.,
Total amt. pay rec'd. $525.66; 1 Roll.

WALKER, J.A., Pvt., Comm. Off: HALL, J.L., Organ: Special State
Troops, Enlist: Aug. 31, 1877, Disc: Feb. 28, 1878, Place of
Birth: Clinton, Texas, 6 months service, Ranger Muster Roll.

WALKER, J.B., Pvt., Comm. Off: COVINGTON, Wm. B., and
TRAVIS, C.E., Capt., Organ: Texas Mounted Volunteers, Co. E,
Enlist: Nov. 1, 1854, Disc: Feb. 1, 1855, Place of Birth: Aus-
tin, 3 months service, Ranger Muster Roll.

WALKER, J.C., Pvt., Comm. Off: CAMPBELL, G.W., Organ: Co. B, Fron-
tier Battalion, Enlist: May 1, 1877, Disc: Feb. 28, 1878,
Place of Birth: Camp Throckmorton, 10 months, Ranger Muster
Roll.

WALKER, James H., Pvt., Comm. Off: FORD, John S., Organ: 3 Co.
of Rangers, Enlist: Jan. 20, 1860, Disc: May 17, 1860, Age: 23,
Place of Birth: Brownsville, Ranger Muster Roll.

WALKER, John M., Pvt., Comm. Off: WALKER, Joseph, Organ: Rangers
for Cortinas War, Enlist: Nov. 10, 1859, Disc: Jan. 20, 1860,
Age: 24, Place of Birth: Banquete, Ranger Muster Roll.

WALKER, J.N., Pvt., Comm. Off: BROWN, John Henry, Organ: Texas
State Troops, Enlist: July 7, 1849, Disc: Aug. 23, 1859, Place
of Birth: Travis County, 1 month, 16 days service, Ranger Muster Roll.

WALKER, J.P., Pvt., Comm. Off: CAMPBELL, G.W., Organ: Co. B, Fron-
tier Battalion, Enlist: Dec. 1, 1877, Disc: Feb. 28, 1878,
Place of Birth: Throckmartin County, 3 months service, Ranger
Muster Roll.

WALKER, John G., Capt., Comm. Off: WALKER, John G., Capt.,
Organ: Mtd. Vol., Enlist: Nov. 1854, Ranger Muster Roll.

WALKER, M.L., Pvt., Comm. Off: BROWN, John Henry, Organ: Texas
State Troops, Enlist: July 1, 1859, Disc: Sept. 4, 1859, Place
of Birth: Travis County, 2 months, 4 days service, Ranger Muster Roll.

WALKER, Nathaniel H., Pvt., Comm. Off: ENGLISH, Levi, Organ: Mtd.
Volunteers, Enlist: Aug. 6, 1855, Disc: Nov. 13, 1855, Place
of Birth: Bexar County, 3 months, 8 days service, Ranger Muster Roll.

WALKER, P.A., Pvt., Comm. Off: WALKER, John G., Capt., Organ: Mtd.
Vol., Enlist: Nov. 1854, Ranger Muster Roll.

WALKER, P., Pvt., Comm. Off: TOMLINSON, Peter, Organ: Mounted
Volunteers, Enlist: Jan. 2, 1860, Ranger Muster Roll.

WALKER, S.H., Pvt., Comm. Off: TJOMPSON, H.J., Capt., Organ: Min.
Men, Parker Cty., Enlist: May 25, 1861 at Veal Station, Parker
County, 20 days regular scout. R&F 40; Co. organized under
Act of the Legislature Feb. 7, 61; Election cert. with Roll; 1
Muster Roll dated May 27-61; 6 Scout Reports dated Je.8-Je.23-
61, Je.24-Jy.7-61, Jy.8-Jy.26-61, Jy.27-Aug.4-61, Aug.4-Aug.
14-61 & Aug.17-S.22-61.

WALKER, Stephen W., Pvt., Comm. Off: TUMLINSON, Peter, Capt.,
Organ: Mtd. Vols., Enlist: Nov. 12, 1859, Disc: Feb. 10, 1860,
2 months, 29 days service, Ranger Muster Roll.

WALKER, S.W., Pvt., Comm. Off: TOMLINSON, Peter, Organ: Mtd. Vol.,
Enlist: Jan. 2, 1860, Ranger Muster Roll.

WALKER, Wm. H., Pvt., Comm. Off: FITZHUGH, Wm., Organ: Texas Militia, Mtd. Vol., Enlist: Nov. 2, 1854, Disc: Feb. 2, 1854, Age: 21, Place of Birth: McKinney, Texas, 3 months service, Ranger Muster Roll.

WALL, O.F., Pvt., Comm. Off: ROBERTS, D.W., Organ: Co. D, Frontier Battalion, Enlist: May 3, 1878, Disc: May 31, 1878, 28 days, Transfer, Ranger MusterRoll.

WALL, George W., Pvt., Comm. Off: HENRY, W.R., Organ: Rangers, Enlist: June 19, 1859, Place of Birth: Frio Canyon, Ranger Muster Roll.

WALL, Phillip, Pvt., Comm. Off: SHAW, Owen, Organ: Texas Militia Volunteers, Enlist: Aug. 18, 1852, Dsic: Feb. 17, 1853, Age: 24, Place of Birth: New Braunfels, 6 months service, Ranger Muster Roll.

WALL, W.T., Pvt., Comm. Off: BENTON, Nat, Capt., Organ: Rangers, Enlist: Sept. 15, 1855, Disc: Oct. 15, 1855, Age: 33, Enlistted at: Leona River, 1 month service, Ranger Muster Roll.

WALL, Phillip, Pvt., Comm. Off: SHAW, Owen, Capt., Organ: Mtd. Volunteers, Enlist: Aug. 18, 1852, Disc: Feb. 17, 1853, Age 24, Enlisted at: New Braunfels, Texas, 6 months service, Ranger MusterRoll.

WALLACE, Benj., Rush, Pvt., Comm. Off: HILL, A.C., Sgt., Organ: Minute Men, Enlist: Dec. 30, 59, at Austin for 12 mos.; unless sooner discharged, Age: 19. R&F 21; A.C. HILL, En. & Mus. Off: W.B. WRATHER & Louis COWEN, Apprs. H: $150; HE: $35; Gun: $25; Pistol: $40; 1 Minnie Rifle; $16. Co. sta. at Austin Dec. 30, 59; at Brownsville, Feb. 1, 60. Co. called into service of state by Gov. HOUSTON Dec. 30, 59. 1 Muster Roll.

WALLACE, Benj. Rush, Pvt., Comm. Off: HILL, A.C., Organ: Mounted Vol. for Cortinas War, Enlist: Dec. 30, 1859 Disc: Feb. 1, 60, Ranger Muster Roll.

WALLACE, enjamin R., Pvt., Comm. Off: FORD, John S., Organ: 3 Co. of Rangers, Enlist: Feb. 1, 1860, Disc: May 17, 1860, Age: 22, Place of Birth: Brownsville, Ranger Muster Roll.

WALLACE, Clayton P., Pvt., Comm. Off: WALKER, D., Lt., Organ: Mtd Vol., Enlist: Feb. 25, 1860, Disc: May 18, 1860, 2 months, 24 days service, Ranger Muster Roll.

WALLACE, D. Wm., Corp., Comm. Off: FONTLEROY, F.W., Organ: Minute Men, Enlist: Minute Men, Enlist: March 16, 1860, Disc: June 16, 1860, Place of Birth: Coryell County, Ranger Muster Roll.

WALLACE, John R., Pvt., Comm. Off: STEVENS, G.W., Organ: Co. B, Frontier Battalion, Enlist: Aug. 15, 1874, Disc: Dec. 10, 1874, Place of Birth: Lost Valley, 3 months, 27 days service, Ranger Muster Roll.

WALLACE, J.H., 2nd Sgt., Comm. Off: STEVENS, G.W., Organ: Wise County Rangers, Enlist: Nov. 26, 1873, Disc: March 26, 1874, Place of Birth: Wise County, 4 months service, Ranger Muster Roll.

WALLACE, R.R., Pvt., Comm. Off: CAMPBELL, G.W., Organ: Montague Co. Rangers, Enlist: Dec. 13, 1873, Disc: Feb. 13, 1874, Place of Birth: Montague County, 2 months service, Ranger Muster Roll.

WALLACE, Warren, Capt., Comm. Off: WALLACE, Warren, Organ: FrontierCompany, Nueces Co., Enlist: June 29, 1874, Place of Birth: Nueces County, Ranger Muster Roll.

WALLAS, Scott, Pvt., Comm. Off: SNOWBALL, James, Organ: Prov.
State Troops, Enlist: Oct. 13, 1871, Disc: Oct. 20, 1871,
Place of Birth: Groesbeck, Texas, Ranger Muster Roll.

WALLER, J.R., Capt., Comm. Off: WALLER, J.R., Organ: Co. A, Frontier Battalion, Enlist: May 5, 1874, Disc: Oct. 4, 1874, Place
of Birth: Stevens County, 5 months service, Ranger Muster Roll.

WALLING, H.H., Pvt., Comm. Off: GILLESPIE, J.T., Organ: Co. A,
Frontier Battalion, Enlist: Nov. 23, 1886, Disc: Nov. 30, 1886,
Place of Birth: Camp Johnson, 8 days service, Ranger Muster
Roll.

WALLIS, J.H., Pvt., Comm. Off: JOHNSON, T.J., Capt., Organ: Ranger Company, Enlist: April 21, 1860, Serv. to Nov. 10, 60, 6
mos. & 20 days at $25-Total $166.66; Less stoppages:
J.M. GIBBINS $29.55, State $30 - Total $59.55; Bal paid $107.11.
R&F 99; 1 Pay Roll; J.P. SMITH, General Power of Attorney.

WALLIS, T.H., 1st Corp., Comm. Off: JOHNSON, Thomas J.,
Organ: Mounted Rangers, Enlist: April 22, 1860, Disc: Nov. 10,
1860, Place of Birth: Fort Worth, Due B. MONORE 30. for pistol
Ranger Muster Roll.

WALLOR, John, Pvt., Comm. Off: LOWE, John C., 1st Lt.,
Organ: Ranger Company, Enlist: Sept. 18, 60, Disc: Dec. 24, 60,
R&F 43; Serv. 8 days at $25 per mo. -$6.66 total amount paid;
1 Pay Roll.

WALSH, C.D., Pvt., Comm. Off: LONG, Ira & COLDWELL, Neal,
Organ: Co. A, Frontier Battalion, Enlist: Sept. 16, 1875,
Disc: Feb. 28, 1878, Age: 21, 6', dark, blue eyes, dark hair,
farmer, Place of Birth: Austin, Texas, 11 months service, Ranger Muster Roll.

WALSHE, N., Pvt., Comm. Off: FORSHEY, J.M., Organ: Washington
Guards, Enlist: Sept. 21, 1874, Disc: Sept. 27, 1874, Place
of Birth: Galveston County, 7 days service, Ranger Muster Roll.

WALTER, H., 3rd Corp., (2nd Corp. on dup. roll),
Comm. Off: CAMERON, Ewen, Capt., Organ: Co. of Texas Rangers,
Enlist: Mar. 20, 61 at Fredericksburg for 3 months, Mus. out
Je. 5-61 at Camp Mason by Lt. S.G. RAGSDALE, Age: 23. R&F 31;
En. & Mus. Off: W. WAHRMMUND; Appraisers F.V.D. STUCKEN &
Louis WEISS; Val. H: $75; HE: $20; Gun: $30; Pistol: $25;
$8.58 deducted from pay; no corn or forage issued, Co. Entitled
to commutation in money; 45 miles travelled from place of dis-
charge home; Co. called into service by Gov. HOUSTON; Co. sta.
on South Fork of Llano River Mar. 20, 61; 1 Muster Roll.

WALTER, Karl, Pvt., Comm. Off: MCCULLOCH, Henry E., Capt.,
Organ: Texas Mtd. Vols., Enlist: Nov. 5, 1850, Disc: Nov. 5,
1851, Age: 23, Enlisted at: Austin, Texas, 12 months service,
Ranger Muster Roll.

WALTER, Jno. SEE WOLTER, Jno.

WALTER, Peter, Pvt., Comm. Off: BURLESON, Ed, Organ: Mounted Rangers, Enlist: Jan. 20, 1860, Disc: Sept. 7, 1860, Age: 25,
Place of Birth: San Marcos, Ranger Muster Roll.

WALTERMIRE, W.J., Pvt., Comm. Off: ATKINSON, N., Organ: Co. S,
Min. Men, Jack County, Enlist: Oct. 8, 1872, Disc: Oct. 12, 72,
Place of Birth: Jack County, 5 days of service, Ranger Muster
Roll.

WALTON, Alexander, 1st Corp., Comm. Off: WOOD, J.D., Organ: Prov.

WALTON, Alexander, 1st Corp., (Continued)
Mounted State Troops, Enlist: Oct. 9, 1871, Disc: Nov. 13,
1871, Place of Birth: Limestone County, Ranger Muster Roll.
WALTON, David, Pvt., Comm. Off: CALLAHAN, James H., Organ: Mtd.
Rangers, Enlist: July 20, 1855, Disc: Oct. 19, 1855, Place of
Birth: Seguin, 2 months, 29 days service, Ranger Muster Roll.
WALTON, J.A., Pvt., Comm. Off: CAMPBELL, G.W., Organ: Montague
Co. Rangers, Enlist: Dec. 13, 1873, Disc: Feb. 13, 1874, Place
of Birth: Montague County, 2 months service, Ranger Muster Roll.
WALTON, J.S., Pvt., Comm. Off: STEVENS, G.W., Organ: Wise County
Rangers, Enlist: Nov. 26, 1873, Disc: March 26, 1874, Place of
Birth: Wise County, 4 months service, Ranger Muster Roll.
WAMACK, William, Pvt., Comm. Off: COVINGTON, Wm. B., and
TRAVIS, C.E., Organ: Texas Mounted Volunteers Co. E,
Enlist: Nov. 1, 1854, Disc: Feb. 1, 1855, Place of Birth: Aus-
tin, 3 months service, Ranger Muster Roll.
WANSLOW, David, Pvt., Comm. Off: COX, A.H., Organ: Frontier For-
ces Co. B, Enlist: Sept. 16, 1870, Disc: May 31, 1871, Place
of Birth: Shackleford County, Ranger Muster Roll.
WANZ, Haver, Lt., Comm. Off: RICHARZ, H.J., Organ: Co. E, Fron-
tier Forces, Enlist: Sept. 9, 1870, Disc: June 15, 1871, Place
of Birth: Uvalde County, Ranger Muster Roll.
WARBINGTON, William, Pvt., Comm. Off: MCCULLOCH, Henry E., Capt.,
Organ: Texas Mounted Volunteers, Enlist: Nov. 5, 1850,
Disc: May 5, 1851, Age: 22, Enlisted at: Austin, Texas, 6 mos.
service, Ranger Muster Roll.
WARD, Lawrence, Pvt., Comm. Off: HALL, A.B., Organ: Prov. State
Troops, Detached, Enlist: oct. 13, 1871, Disc: oct. 20, 1871,
Place of Birth: Groesbeck, Texas, Ranger Muster Roll.
WARD, John, 1st Sgt., Comm. Off: TUMLINSON, J.J., Organ: Tumlin-
son's Spy, 1 Rgt. Mtd. Gunmen, Enlist: Oct. 13, 1839,
Disc: Nov. 22, 1839, 1 month, 11 days service, Transferred
from Capt. CARROLLS Co., Ranger Muster Roll of the Republic.
WARD, J.L., Pvt., Comm. Off: WRIGHT, J.A., Organ: Co. D, Minute
Men, Comanche Co., Enlist: May 25, 1872, Disc: June 1, 1873,
Place of Birth: Comanche County, 60 days service, Ranger Mus-
ter Roll.
WARD, H.L., Pvt., Comm. Off: HAMILTON, C.H., Organ: Co. B, Fron=
tier Battalion, Enlist: Sept. 30, 1875, Disc: Nov. 30, 1875,
Place of Birth: Flat Top Mountain, 3 months service, Ranger
Muster Roll.. Decatur, Texas.
WARD, J.K., Pvt., Comm. Off: REIGER, R.T., Organ: Minute Men,
Enlist: March 19, 1872, Disc: Nov. 1872, Place of Birth: Wise
County, 17 days service, Ranger Muster Roll.
WARD, J.J., Pvt., Comm. Off: EASTIN, S.W., Organ: Jack County
Rangers, Enlist: Dec. 3, 1873, Disc: April 3, 1874, Place of
Birth: Jack County, 4 months service, Ranger Muster Roll.
WARD, J.A., Pvt., Comm. Off: HOLT, John T., Capt., Organ: Fort
Bend Rifles, Mtd. Riflemen (Rangers), Enlist: Jan. 14, 60 at
Richmond. R&F 64; 1 Muster Roll dated Jan. 16, 60.
WARD, Dan, Pvt., Comm. Off: FISHER, J.C., Organ: Prov. State
Troops, Co. C, 3 Reg., Enlist: Oct. 9, 1871, Disc: Nov. 18,
1871, Place of Birth: Springfield, Texas, Ranger Muster Roll.
WARD, Charles W., 1st Sgt., Comm. Off: JONES, Franklin, Organ: Co.

WARD, Charles W., 1st Sgt., (Continued)
A, Frontier Battalion, Enlist: Aug. 25, 1870, Disc: Oct. 31, 1870, Place of Birth: Fort Mason, Texas, Ranger Muster Roll.

WARD, Chas. W., 1st Sgt., Comm. Off: JONES, Franklin, Organ: Co. A, Frontier Forces, Enlist: Aug. 25, 1870, Disc: Nov. 11, 1870, Place of Birth: Fort Mason, Texas, 2 months, 17 days service, Ranger Muster Roll.

WARD, A.B., Pvt., Comm. Off: COLDWELL, Neal, Organ: Co. A, Frontier Battalion, Enlist: July 11, 1877, Disc: Aug. 31, 1877, Place of Birth: Frio County, 1 month, 1 day service, Ranger Muster Roll.

WARD, Guisamus, Pvt., Comm. Off: DALRYMPLE, W.C., Organ: Mounted Rangers, Enlist: Jan. 14, 1860, Disc: Oct. 13, 1860, Age: 17, Place of Birth: Liberty Hill, Ranger Muster Roll.

WARD, Pat, Pvt., Comm. Off: HALL, A.B., Organ: Prov. State Troops Detached, Enlist: Oct. 13, 1871, Disc: Oct. 20, 1871, Place of Birth: Groesbeck, Ranger Muster Roll.

WARD, Richard, Aid, Comm. Off: JOHNSON, Middleton T., Organ: Mtd. Rangers, Enlist: May 1, 1860, Disc: Aug. 20, 1860, Place of Birth: Fort Worth, Discharged Aug. 20, 1860 at Camp Wichita, Ranger Muster Roll.

WARD, Robert, Pvt., Comm. Off: SNOWBALL, James, Organ: Prov. State Troops, Enlist: Oct. 13, 1871, Disc: Oct. 20, 1871, Place of Birth: Groesbeck, Texas, Ranger Muster Roll.

WARD, William, Pvt., Comm. Off: NELSON, Allison, Organ: Minute Men, Enlist: March 12, 1860, Place of Birth: Bosque County, Ranger Muster Roll.

WARE, J.C., Pvt., Comm. Off: DAVENPORT, John M., Organ: Mounted Vol. Minute Men, Enlist: March 13, 1856, Disc: June 1, 1857, Place of Birth: Uvalde County, 3 months service, Ranger Muster Roll.

WARE, James B., Pvt., Comm. Off: REED, Henry, Organ: 1 Rgt., Mtd. Gunmen, Enlist: Oct. 10, 1839, Disc: Nov. 22, 1839, 1 month, 14 days service, Ranger Muster Roll.

WARE, Jas. A., Pvt., Comm. Off: LOVENSKIOLD, Charles, Organ: Walker Mtd. Rifles, Cortinas War, Enlist: Nov. 22, 1859, Place of Birth: Corpus Christi, Ranger Muster Roll.

WARE, N., Pvt., Comm.Off: MOORE, F.M., Organ: Co. D, Frontier Battalion, Enlist: Sept. 1, 1876, Disc: May 31, 1877, 5'5", black hair, blue eyes, farmer, Place of Birth: Monroe, Miss., 9 months service, Ranger Muster Roll.

WARE, N., Pvt., Comm. Off: PERRY, C.R., Organ: Co. D, Frontier Battalion, Enlist: May 25, 1874, Disc: May 31, 1875, Place of Birth: Blanco County, 12 months, 6 days service, Ranger Muster Roll.

WARE, N., Pvt., Comm. Off: ROBERTS, D.W., Organ: Co. D, Frontier Battalion, Enlist: April 1, 1876, Disc: Aug. 31, 1876, 7 months service, Ranger Muster Roll.

WARE, M.C., Pvt., Comm. Off: BAYLOR, G.W., Organ: Co. A, Frontier Battalion, Enlist: Dec. 1, 1882, Disc: Feb. 28, 1883, 3 mos. service, Ranger Muster Roll.

WARE, R.C., Pvt., Comm. Off: FOSTER, B.S., Organ: Co. E, Frontier Battalion, Enlist: April 1, 1876, Disc: Aug. 31, 1876, Place of Birth: Arkansas, 5 months service, Ranger Muster Roll.

WARE, R.C., Pvt., Comm. Off: FOSTER, B.S., Organ: Co. E, Frontier
    Battalion, Enlist: Sept. 1, 1876, Disc: Aug. 31, 1877, Place
    of Birth: Coleman County, 12 months service, Ranger Muster
    Roll.
WARE, R.C., Pvt., Comm. Off: REYNOLDS, H.O., Organ: Co. E, Fron-
    tier Battalion, Enlist: Sept. 1, 1877, Disc: Feb. 28, 1878,
    Place of Birth: Arkansas, 6 months service, Ranger Muster
    Roll.
WARE, Richard M., Pvt., Comm. Off: HENRY, W.R., Organ: Rangers,
    Enlist: June 19, 1859, Place of Birth: Frio Canyon, Ranger
    Muster Roll.
WARE, W.M., Pvt., Comm. Off: DOLAN, Pat, Organ: Co. F, Frontier
    Battalion, Enlist: Sept. 10, 1876, Disc: Nov. 30, 1877,
    Age: 21, 6'1", light hair, blue eyes, fair, stockman, Place
    of Birth: Medina Co., Texas, 11 months, 21 days service, Ran-
    ger Muster Roll. El Paso, Texas, Box 654.
WARE, William, Pvt., Comm. Off: COLDWELL, Neal, Organ: Co. A,
    Frontier Battalion, Enlist: Nov. 20, 1877, Disc: Feb. 14,
    1878, Place of Birth: Frio Canyon, 2 months, 14 days service,
    Ranger Muster Roll.
WARING, F.M., Pvt., Comm. Off: MCMURRY, S.A., Organ: Co. B, Fron-
    tier Battalion, Enlist: June 1, 1882, Disc: Aug. 31, 1882,
    Place of Birth: Colorado, Texas, 3 months service, Ranger Mus-
    ter Roll.
WARING, Frank W., Pvt., Comm. Off: ARRINGTON, G.W., Capt.,
    Organ: Frontier Battalion Co. C, Enlist: Mar. 1, 1881,
    Disc: April 15, 1881, Honorably discharged, 1 month, 10 days
    service, Photostat: Orog. in A.G. Office.
WARMAN, W.E., Pvt., Comm. Off: GILLESPIE, J.T., Organ: Co. E,
    Frontier Battalion, Enlist: Sept. 25, 1883, Disc: Nov. 30,
    1883, Place of Birth: Camp King, Texas, 2 months, 6 days ser-
    vice, Ranger Muster Roll.
WARNER, C., Pvt., Comm. Off: IKARD, E.F., Organ: Co. C, Frontier
    Battalion, Enlist: Sept. 26, 1874, Disc: Dec. 10, 1874, Place
    of Birth: Clay County, 2 months, 14 days service, Ranger Mus-
    ter Roll.
WARNICK (WARNOCK), W.A., Pvt., Comm. Off: HARRELL, J.M.,
    Organ: Co. K, Frontier Forces, Enlist: Sept. 16, 1870,
    Disc: Feb. 20, 1871, Place of Birth: Penal Ranch, Discharged
    Feb. 16, 1871, Ranger Muster Roll.
WARNOCK, Benjamin F., Pvt., Comm. Off: MCCULLOCH, Henry E., Capt.,
    Organ: Texas Vols., Enlist: Oct. 25, 1848, Disc: Dec. 8, 1848,
    Age: 36, 1 month, 13 days service, Ranger Muster Roll.
WARREN, G.W., Pvt., Comm. Off: BROWN, John Henry, Organ: Texas
    State Troops, Enlist: July 1, 1859, Disc: Sept. 4, 1859, 2
    months, 4 days service, Ranger Muster Roll.
WARREN, George W., Pvt., Comm. Off: WHITE, Robert M., 1st Lt.,
    Organ: Bell County Rangers, Enlist: Feb. 18, 60 at Belton for
    12 months; Enrolled for duty Feb. 20, 60. Disbanded at Belton
    Je.29,60, Age: 23. R&F 26; Enr. Off: Dr. John EMBREE; Mus.
    Off: J.M.W. HALL; Apprs.: John S. BLAIR, John W. SCOTT; Val.
    of: H: $125; HE: $25; Gun: $40; Gov. Pistol: Service 4 mos. 10
    days at $25, total $108.33; Co. std. at Belton Feb. 20, 60.
    Co. called into service by Gov. HOUSTON; State arms returned

WARREN, George W., Pvt., (Continued)
upon disbandment; 2 Muster Rolls dated Feb. 20, 60 each; 1 Pay
Roll.
WARREN, George W., Pvt., Comm. Off: WHITE, Robt. M., Organ: Mtd.
Rangers, Enlist: Feb. 18, 1860, Disc: June 29, 1860, Age: 23,
Place of Birth: Belton, Ranger Muster Roll.
WARREN, Henry C., Pvt., Comm. Off: WILLIAMS, John, Organ: Second
Co. of Texas Rangers, Enlist: April 27, 1859, 1 month, 19 days,
Ranger Muster Roll. Snyder, Oklahoma, R.R. 1.
WARREN, Jas. H., Pvt., Comm. Off: HUNTER, H.L., Organ: Rangers,
Parker County, Enlist: Dec. 24, 1873, Disc: March 29, 1874,
Place of Birth: Parker County, 96 days of service, Ranger Mus-
ter Roll.
WARREN, Josh. N., Pvt., Comm. Off: ROGERS, P.H., Capt.,
Organ: Mtd. Vol., Enlist: Oct. 1854, Disc: Dec. 1854, 3 mos.
service, Ranger Muster Rolls. Ex. order of March, 1856.
WARREN, Jno., Pvt., Comm. Off: LOVENSKIOLD, Charles, Organ: Wal-
ker Mtd. Rifles, Cortinas War, Enlist: Nov. 22, 1859, Place of
Birth: Corpus Christi, Ranger Muster Roll.
WARREN, J.G., 2nd Corp., Comm. Off: LOVENSKIOLD, Charles,
Organ: Walker Mtd. Rifles, Cortinas War, Enlist: Nov. 22, 1859,
Place of Birth: Corpus Christi, Ranger Muster Roll.
WARREN, J.W., 1st Corp., Comm. Off: REYNOLDS, N.O., Organ: Co. E,
Frontier Battalion, Enlist: Sept. 1, 1877, Disc: Feb. 28, 1878,
Place of Birth: Coleman County, 6 months service, Ranger Mus-
ter Roll.
WARREN, J.W., Pvt., Comm. Off: COLDWELL, Neal, Organ: Co. A,
Frontier Battalion, Enlist: April 1, 1877, Disc: Aug. 31, 1877,
Place of Birth: Frio County, 5 months service, Ranger Muster
Roll.
WARREN, Thaddeus, 1st Bugler, Comm. Off: SHAW, Owen, Organ: Texas
Militia Volunteers, Enlist: Aug. 18, 1852, Disc: Feb. 17, 1853,
Age: 21, Place of Birth: York Creek, 6 months service, Ranger
Muster Roll.
WARREN, Thomas, Pvt., Comm. Off: BURLESON, Edward, Capt.,
Organ: State Guards, Enlist: July 15, 65 at Austin. Mustd. in
July 15, 65 at Austin. Disc: Aug. 4, 65, 21 days service
$16.00. R&F 41; Mus. Off: Capt. Ed BURLESON; Amt. of pay
$11.20 plus subsistence $15.75, forage $5.60 & use of horse
$8.40--total $40.95. Co. org. for protection of prop. belong-
ing to state in Travis Cty. under authority from
Gen. G. GRANGER. Co. stationed at Austin, Aug. 4, 65. 1 Mus-
ter & Pay Roll dated Aug. 4, 65.
WARREN, Thaddeus, 1st Bugler, Comm. Off: SHAW. Owen, Capt.,
Organ: Mtd. Vol., Enlist: Aug. 18, 1852, Disc: Feb. 17, 1853,
Age: 21, Enlisted at: Yorks Creek, 6 months service, Ranger
Muster Roll.
WARREN, Titus, Pvt., Comm. Off: SNOWBALL, James, Organ: Prov.
State Troops, Enlist: Oct. 13, 1871, Disc: Oct. 20, 1871, Place
of Birth: Groesbeck, Texas, Ranger Muster Roll.
WARRENBURG, Wm., Pvt., Comm. Off: WOODS, Wm. M., Organ: Mounted
Rangers, Enlist: April 10, 1860, Disc: Aug. 10, 1860, Age: 19,
Place of Birth: Bonham, Ranger Muster Roll.
WASH, David, Pvt., Comm. Off: FITZHUGH, G.S., Organ: Mounted

WASH, David, Pvt., (Continued)
Rangers, Enlist: May 20, 1860, Disc: Oct. 25, 1860, Ranger
Muster Roll.

WASH, D.C.S., Pvt., Comm. Off: FITZHUGH, G.S., Capt., Organ: Ranger Company, Enlist: May 20, 60, Disc: Oct. 25, 60; served 5 mo. & 6 days at $25-Total: $130. R&F 83; Stoppages: $24.15. Balance Pd: $105.85. 1 Pay Roll.

WASHBURN, Israel G., Pvt., Comm. Off: FITZHUGH, Wm., Organ: Tex. Militia, Mtd. Vol., Enlist: Nov. 2, 1854, Disc: Feb. 2, 1854, Age: 23, Place of Birth: McKinney, Texas, 3 months service, Ranger Muster Roll.

WASHINGTON, Clark, Pvt., Comm. Off: SNOWBALL, James, Organ: Prov. State Troops, Enlist: Oct. 13, 1871, Disc: Oct. 20, 1871, Place of Birth: Groesbeck, Texas, Ranger Muster Roll.

WASHINGTON, George, 4th Corp., Comm. Off: FISHER, J.C., Organ: Prov. State Troops, Co. C, 3 Regt., Enlist: Oct. 9, 1871, Disc: Nov. 18, 1871, Place of Birth: Springfield, Texas, Ranger Muster Roll.

WASHINGTON, George, Pvt., Comm. Off: FISHER, J.C., Organ: Prov. State Troops, Co. C, 3rd Regt., Enlist: Oct. 9, 1871, Disc: Nov. 18, 1871, Place of Birth: Springfield, Texas, Ranger Muster Roll.

WASHINGTON, Geo., Pvt., Comm. Off: HALL, A.B., Organ: Prov. State Troops, Detached, Enlist: Oct. 13, 1871, Disc: Oct. 20, 1871, Place of Birth: Groesbeck, Texas, Ranger Muster Roll.

WASHINGTON, George, Pvt., Comm. Off: WILLIAMS, Samuel J., Organ: Prov. State Troops, Co. A, Enlist: Oct. 9, 1871, Disc: Nov. 13, 1871, Place of Birth: Limestone County, Ranger Muster Roll.

WASHINGTON, George, Pvt., Comm. Off: WOOD, J.D., Organ: Prov. Mounted State Troops, Enlist: Oct. 9, 1871, Disc: Nov. 16, 1871, Place of Birth: Limestone County, Ranger Muster Roll.

WASHINGTON, George, Pvt., Comm. Off: WOOD, J.D., Organ: Prov. Mtd. State Troops, Enlist: Oct. 9, 1871, Disc: Nov. 13, 1871, Place of Birth: Limestone County, Ranger Muster Roll.

WASHINGTON, Geo., Pvt., Comm. Off: SNOWBALL, James, Organ: Prov. State Troops, Enlist: Oct. 13, 1871, Disc: Oct. 20, 1871, Place of Birth: Groesbeck, Texas, Ranger Muster Roll.

WASHINGTON, Wm., Pvt., Comm. Off: SNOWBALL, James, Organ: Prov. State Troops, Enlist: Oct. 13, 1871, Disc: Oct. 20, 1871, Place of Birth: Groesbeck, Texas, Ranger Muster Roll.

WASHMAN, Israel G., Pvt., Comm. Off: MCCULLOCH, Henry E., Capt., Organ: Tex. Mtd. Vols., Enlist: April 5, 1851, Disc: Nov. 5, 1851, Age: 20, Enlisted at: Camp Oaks, 7 months service, Ranger Muster Roll.

WASSON, M., Pvt., Comm. Off: BOURLAND, James, Organ: Texas Mtd. Rangers, Enlist: Jan. 28, 1859, Disc: April 28, 1859, Place of Birth: Gainesville, Texas, 3 months service, Ranger Muster Roll.

WATERHOUSE, Jack, Pvt., Comm. Off: HILL, A.C., Sgt., Organ: Min. Men, Enlist: Dec. 30, 59 at Austin for 12 mos.; unless sooner discharged, Age: 24. R&F 21; A.C. HILL, En. & Mus. Off; W.B. WRATHER & Louis COWEN, Apprs. H: $175; HE: $35; Gun: $25;

WATERHOUSE, Jack, Pvt., (Continued)
Pistol: $45; Co. sta. at Austin Dec. 30, 59; at Brownsville Feb. 1, 60. Co. called into service of state by Governor HOUSTON Dec. 30, 59. 1 Muster Roll.

WATERHOUSE, Jack, Pvt., Comm. Off: HILL, A.C., Organ: Mounted Vol. for Cortinas War, Enlist: Dec. 30, 1859, Disc: Feb. 1, 1860, Ranger Muster Roll.

WATERHOUSE, Jack, 4th Lt., Comm. Off: FORD, John J., Organ: 3rd Company of Rangers, Enlist: Feb. 10, 1860, Disc: May 17, 1860, Age: 28, Place of Birth: Brownsville, Promoted April 21, 1860, Ranger Muster Roll.

WATERHOUSE, Jack, Pvt., Comm. Off: FORD, John S., Organ: 3rd Co. of Rangers, Enlist: Feb. 1, 1860, Disc: May 17, 1860, Age: 29, Place of Birth: Brownsville, Ranger Muster Roll.

WATERHOUSE, Jas., Pvt., Comm. Off: HILL, A.C., Sgt., Organ: Min. Men, Enlist: Dec. 30, 59 at Austin for 12 mos.; unless sooner discharged, Age: 19. R&F 21; A.C. HILL, En. & Mus. Off; W.B. WRATHER & Louis COWEN, Apprs. H: $80; HE: $25; Gun: $25; Pistol: $30. Co. sta. at Austin Dec. 30, 59; at Brownsville, Feb. 1, 60. Co. called into service of state by Governor HOUSTON Dec. 30, 59. 1 Muster Roll.

WATERHOUSE, James, Pvt., Comm. Off: HILL, A.C., Organ: Mounted Vol. for Cortinas War, Enlist: Dec. 30, 1859, Disc: Feb. 1, 1860, Ranger Muster Roll.

WATERHOUSE, James, Pvt., Comm. Off: FORD, John S., Organ: 3rd Co. of Rangers, Enlist: Feb. 1, 1860, Disc: May 17, 1860, Age: 23, Place of Birth: Brownsville, Promoted to 2nd Lt. April 21, Ranger Muster Roll.

WATERMAN, Jas. W., 3rd Corp., Comm. Off: SNOWBALL, James, Organ: Prov. State Troops, Enlist: Oct. 13, 1871, Disc: Oct. 20, 1871, Place of Birth: Groesbeck, Texas, Ranger Muster Roll.

WATERS, James S., 4th Corp., Comm. Off: WEEKES, Nicholas, Organ: Star Rifles Militia, Enlist: Sept. 21, 1874, Disc: Sept. 27, 1874, Place of Birth: Galveston County, 7 days service, Ranger Muster Roll.

WATERS, W.M., Pvt., Comm. Off: WEEKES, Nicholas, Organ: Star Rifles Militia, Enlist: Sept. 21, 1874, Disc: Sept. 27, 1874, Place of Birth: Galveston County, 7 days service, Ranger Muster Roll.

WATFORD, J.T., Pvt., Comm. Off: MOORE, D.D., Capt., Organ: Moscow Guards, Cav. Co., Polk Co., TST, Enlist: Nov. 1860 at Moscow, Tex. R&F 76; Co. org. with 64 volunteers who agreed to meet not less than 6 or more than 7 times a year; unless called out on special duty, 1 Muster Roll.

WATKINS, Calvert, Pvt., Comm. Off: BURLESON, Edward, Capt., Organ: State Guards, Enlist: July 15, 65 at Austin. Mustd. in July 15, 65 at Austin, Disc: Aug. 4, 65, 21 days service, $16.00. R&F 41; Mus. Off: Capt. Ed BURLESON; Amt. of pay $11.20; plus subsistence $15.75; Forage $5.60 & use of horse $8.40--total $40.95. Co. org. for protection of prop. belonging to state in Travis County under authority from Gen. G. GRANGER. Co. stationed at Asutin Aug. 4, 65. 1 Muster & Pay Roll dated Aug. 4, 65.

WATKINS, Edmond, Pvt., Comm. Off: HARRINGTON, James, Organ: Co. A,

WATKINS, Edmond, Pvt., (Continued)
Detached, Prov. State Troops, Enlist: Oct. 9, 1871, Disc: Nov. 13, 1871, Place of Birth: Springfield, Texas, Ranger Muster Roll.

WATKINS, Henry, Pvt., Comm. Off: CHAMBERLAIN, Bland, Organ: Frontier Forces, Co. H, Enlist: Nov. 15, 1870, Disc: Feb. 28, 1871, Place of Birth: San Antonio, Ranger Muster Roll.

WATKINS, Leroy, Comm. Off: ALEXANDER, John & SIMS, W.H., Lt., Organ: Minute Men, Enlist: Sept. 11, 1872, Disc: Aug. 13, 1873, Place of Birth: Goldthwaite, Texas, R.R. 2, Dept. of the Interior--Pensions, N.H. NICHOLSON, Inspector.

WATKINS, Tadoe B., Pvt., Comm. Off: TUMLINSON, Peter, Capt., Organ: Mtd. Vols., knlist: Jan. 1, 1860, Disc: Feb. 10, 1860, 1 month, 10 days service, Ranger Muster Roll.

WATKINS, W.C., Lt., Comm. Off: WATKINS, W.C., Organ: Co. D, Min. Men, ComancheCo., Enlist: Sept. 19, 1873, Disc: April 30, 1874, Place of Birth: Comanche County, 45 days of service, Ranger Muster Roll.

WATKINS, W.W., Pvt., Comm. Off: FITZHUGH, G.S., Capt., Organ: Ranger Company, Enlist: April 14, 60, Disc: Oct. 25, 60; Served 6 mo. & 12 days at $25 - Total $160. R&F 83; Stoppages: $14.90. Balance Pd: $145.10. 1 Pay Roll.

WATKINS, William W., Comm. Off: FITZHUGH, G.S., Capt., Organ: Mtd Rangers, Enlist: April 14, 1860, Disc: Oct. 25, 1860, Place of Birth: Brownwood, Brown Co., Texas, R.R. 3, Dept. of the Interior--Pensions, N.H. NICHOLSON, Inspector.

WATKINS, Tadoe B., Pvt., Comm. Off: HERRON, Andrew, Organ: Mtd. Vol. for Cortinas War, Enlist: Nov. 18, 1859, Disc: Jan. 1, 1860, Place of Birth: Sulphur Springs, Ranger Muster Roll.

WATKINS, T., Pvt., Comm. Off: ALEXANDER, John, Organ: Co. O, Min. Men, Burnet Co., Enlist: Jan. 10, 1873, Disc: Aug. 13, 1873, Place of Birth: Burnet County, 5 days of service, Ranger Muster Roll.

WATSON, Alex., Pvt., Comm. Off: MCADAMS, W.C., Organ: Palo Pinto County Rangers, Enlist: Dec. 13, 1873, Disc: April 13, 1874, Place of Birth: Palo Pinto County, 4 months service, Ranger Muster Roll. Weiser, Washington Co., Idaho, R.R. 1.

WATSON, A.W., Pvt., Comm. Off: STEVENS, G.W., Organ: Co. B, Frontier Battalion, Enlist: Aug. 15, 1874, Disc: Nov. 30, 1875, Place of Birth: Flat Top Mountain, 18 months, 17 days service, Ranger Muster Roll.

WATSON, A.W., Pvt., Comm. Off: REIGER, R.T., Organ: Minute Men, Enlist: April 1, 1872, Disc: Oct. 31, 1873, Place of Birth: Wise County, 37 days service, Ranger Muster Roll.

WATSON, A.W., 5th Corp., Comm. Off: STEVENS, G.W., Organ: Wise County, Enlist: Nov. 26, 1873, Disc: March 26, 1874, Place of Birth: Wise County, 4 months service, Ranger Muster Roll.

WATSON, Edward, 2nd Sgt., Comm. Off: FISHER, J.C., Organ: Prov. State Troops, Co. C, 3 Regt., Enlist: Oct. 9, 1871, Disc: Nov. 18, 1871, Place of Birth: Springfield, Texas, Ranger Muster Roll.

WATSON, Jacob, Pvt., Comm. Off: MCCULLOCH, Henry E., Organ: Tex. Mounted Vol., Enlist: Oct. 25, 1847, Age: 42, Blue eyes, light hair, 6', Place of Birth: Bastrop.

WATSON, Jacob, Pvt., Comm. Off: MCCULLOCH, Henry E., Capt., Organ: Texas Volunteers, Enlist: Oct. 25, 1847, Disc: Oct. 24, 1848, Age: 42; Height: 6', Dk. Comp., Blue eyes, light hair, Place of Birth: Bastrop, Texas, 12 months service, Ranger Muster Roll.

WATSON, Jas. A., Pvt., Comm.Off: FITZHUGH, G.S., Capt., Organ: Ranger Company, Enlist: April 14, 60 Disc: oct. 25, 60; Served 6 mo. & 12 days at $25. Total: $160. R&F 83; Stoppages: $21.10. Balance Pd: $138. 1 Pay Roll.

WATSON, Jno., Pvt., Comm. Off: SCHWETHELM, H., Organ: Co. E, Min. Men, Enlist: April 7, 1872, Disc: March 15, 1873, Place of Birth: Kerr County, 110 days service, Ranger Muster Roll.

WATSON, John, Pvt., Comm. Off: SANSOM, John W., Organ: Frontier Forces, Enlist: Aug. 25, 1870, Disc: May 31, 1871, Place of Birth: Shackleford County, Ranger Muster Roll.

WATSON, J.A., Pvt., Comm. Off: WALLER, J.R., Organ: Co. A, Frontier Battalion, Enlist: May 25, 1874, Disc: April 30, 1875, Place of Birth: Erath County, 11 months, 11 days of service, Ranger Muster Roll.

WATSON, J.L., Pvt., Comm. Off: SCHWETHELM, H., Organ: Co. E, Min. Men, Enlist: April 7, 1872, Disc: March 15, 1873, Place of Birth: Kerr County, 240 days of service, Ranger Muster Roll.

WATSON, J.A.W., Pvt., Comm.Off: STEVENS, G.W., Organ: Wise County Rangers, Enlist: Nov. 26, 1873, Disc: March 26, 1874, Place of Birth: Wise County, 4 months service, Ranger Muster Roll.

WATSON, J.W., Pvt., Comm. Off: COLDWELL, Neal, Organ: Co. F, Frontier Battalion, Enlist: June 4, 1874, Disc: Dec. 1, 1874, Place of Birth: Kerr County, 5 months, 27 days service, Ranger Muster Roll.

WATSON, O.S., 2nd Sgt., Comm. Off: HALL, J.L., Organ: Special State Troops, Enlist: Jan. 25, 1877, Disc: Oct. 30, 1877, Place of Birth: Clinton, Texas, 9 months, 6 days service, Ranger Muster Roll.

WATSON, O.S., Pvt., Comm. Off: MCNELLY, L.H., Organ: Washington Co. Vol. Militia, Enlist: Aug. 6, 1876, Disc: Feb. 1, 1877, Place of Birth: Austin, Texas, 5 months, 25 days service, Ranger Muster Roll.

WATSON, Robt., Pvt., Comm. Off: WILLIAMS, John, Lt., Organ: Rangers, Enlist: May 24, 1858, Disc: July 24, 1858, 2 months of service, Ranger Muster Roll.

WATSON, Robert, Pvt., Comm. Off: WEEKES, Nicholas, Organ: Star Rifles Militia, Enlist: Sept. 21, 1874, Disc: Sept. 27, 1874, Place of Birth: Galveston County, 7 days service, Ranger Muster Roll.

WATSON, Robert, Discharged, Pvt., Comm. Off: WILLIAMS, John, Organ: Second Co. of Texas Rangers, Enlist: Oct. 25, 1858, 7 months, 20 days service, Ranger Muster Roll.

WATSON, W.A., Pvt., Comm. Off: SCHWETHELM, H., Organ: Co. E, Min. Men, Kerr County, Enlist: April 10, 1873, Disc: April 10, 1874, Place of Birth: Kerr County, 130 days of service, Ranger Muster Roll.

WATSON, William C., Pvt., Comm. Off: HENRY, W.R., Organ: Rangers, Enlist: June 19, 1859, Place of Birth: Sabinal Canyon, Ranger Muster Roll.

WATSON, W.M., Pvt., Comm. Off: COX, A.H., Organ: Frontier Forces, Co. B, Enlist: Sept. 8, 1870, Disc: May 31, 1871, Ranger Muster Roll.

WATSON, Wm. M., Pvt., Comm. Off: COX, A.H., Organ: Frontier Forces, Co. B, Enlist: Sept. 8, 1870, Disc: May 31, 1871, Place of Birth: Shackleford County, Ranger Muster Roll.

WATTLES, Z.T., Pvt., Comm. Off: WALLER, J.R., Organ: Co. A, Frontier Battalion, Enlist: May 19, 1874, Disc: Sept. 1, 1875, Place of Birth: Erath County, 18 months, 17 days service, Ranger Muster Roll.

WATTS, Perry, Pvt., Comm. Off: WILLIAMS, Samuel J., Organ: Prov. State Troops, Co. A, Enlist: Oct. 9, 1871, Disc: Nov. 13, 1871, Place of Birth: Limestone County, Ranger Muster Roll.

WAYBURN(URN), W.D., Pvt., Comm. Off: IKARD, E.F., Organ: Co. C, Frontier Battalion, Enlist: May 20, 1874, Disc: Dec. 10, 1874, Place of Birth: Clay County, 6 months, 22 days service, Ranger Muster Roll. Pryor, Oklahoma.

WAYBORN, W.L., Pvt., Comm. Off: IKARD, E.F., Organ: Co. C, Frontier Battalion, Enlist: May 20, 1874, Disc: Dec. 10, 1874, Place of Birth: Clay County, 6 months, 22 days service, Ranger Muster Roll.

WAYBOURNE, J.W., Comm. Off: GREEN, Sam, Capt., Organ: Minute Men, Clay County, Enlist: Sept. 5, 1861, 88 days of service, Ranger Muster Roll.

WAYBOURNE, W.T., Comm. Off: GREEN, Sam, Capt., Organ: Minute Men, Clay County, Enlist: Sept. 5, 1861, 88 days service, Ranger Muster Roll.

WAYBOURNE, W.W., Comm. Off: GREEN, Sam, Capt., Organ: Minute Men, Clay County, Enlist: Sept. 5, 1861, 88 days service, Ranger Muster Roll.

WAYLAND, Edward, Pvt., Comm. Off: CALLAHAN, James H., Organ: Mtd. Rangers, Enlist: July 20, 1855, Disc: Oct. 19, 1855, Place of Birth: Curry Creek, 2 months, 29 days service, Ranger Muster Roll.

WEALCH, Jas., Pvt., Comm. Off: WOODS, Wm. M., Organ: Mounted Rangers, Enlist: April 10, 1860, Disc: Oct. 16, 1860, Age: 22, Place of Birth: Bonham, Ranger Muster Roll.

WEATHERSBY, W.W., Pvt., Comm. Off: HOFFAR, John, Lt., Organ: Frontier Battalion, Co. C, Enlist: Sept. 1, 1882, Disc: Dec. 27, 1882, Age: 21, Hazel Eyes, Dk. hair, Dk. Comp., Farmer, Place of Birth: Texas, 3 months, 27 days service, Photostat: Orig. in A.G. Office.

WEATHERFORD, T.H.B., Pvt., Comm. Off: DARNELL, N.H., Organ: Mtd. Rangers, Enlist: April 14, 1860, Disc: Aug. 13, 1860, Place of Birth: Dallas, Ranger Muster Roll.

WEAVER, Franklin, Pvt., Comm. Off: DARNELL, N.H., Organ: Mounted Rangers, Enlist: April 14, 1860, Disc: Aug. 13, 1860, Place of Birth: Dallas, Ranger Muster Roll.

WEAVER, J.W., Pvt., Comm. Off: CAMPBELL, G.W., Organ: Montague Co. Rangers, Enlist: Dec. 13, 1873, Disc: Feb. 13, 1874, Place of Birth: Montague County, 2 months service, Ranger Muster Roll.

WEAVER, Jesse W., Pvt., Comm. Off: FORD, John S., Organ: 2nd Co. of Rangers, Enlist: Nov. 10, 1858, Disc: May 10, 1859, Age: 23, Place of Birth: Austin, Ranger Muster Roll.

WEAVER, M.Z., Pvt., Comm. Off: COLDWELL, Neal, Organ: Co. F,
    Frontier Battalion, Enlist: June 4, 1874, Disc: Dec. 1874,
    Place of Birth: Kerr County, 5 months, 27 days of service,
    Ranger Muster Roll.
WEAVER, W.G.L., Pvt., Comm. Off: SANSOM, John W., Organ: Texas
    Mounted Rangers, Enlist: April 16, 1856, Disc: July 16, 1856,
    Age: 29, Place of Birth: Comal County, 90 days service, Ranger
    Muster Roll.
WEBB, Alex, 2nd Sgt., Comm. Off: DARNELL, N.H., Organ: Mounted
    Rangers, Enlist: April 14, 1860, Disc: Aug. 13, 1860, Place of
    Birth: Dallas, Discharged by order Lt. J.M. SMITH July 7, Ran-
    ger Muster Roll.
WEBB, A.H., 2nd Lt., Comm. Off: MCADAMS, W.C., Organ: Palo Pinto
    Co. Rangers, Enlist: Dec. 13, 1873, Disc: April 13, 1874,
    Place of Birth: Palo Pinto County, 4 months service, Ranger
    Muster Roll.
WEBB, A.H., Pvt., Comm. Off: ALEXANDER, John, Organ: Co. O, Min-
    Men, Burnet Co., Enlist: Sept. 11, 1872, Disc: Aug. 13, 1873,
    Place of Birth: Burnet County, 26 days of service, Ranger Mus-
    ter Roll.
WEBB, C.M., 1st Lt., Comm. Off: CONNELL, J.G., Organ: Brown and
    San Saba Co. Rangers, Enlist: Jan. 6, 1874, Disc: March 26,
    1874, Place of Birth: Brown and San Saba Counties, 2 months,
    20 days service, Ranger Muster Roll.
WEBB, Edmund, Pvt., Comm. Off: REED, Henry, Organ: 1st Rgt., Mtd.
    Gunmen, Enlist: Oct. 10, 1839, Disc: Nov. 22, 1839, 1 month
    14 days service, Ranger Muster Roll.
WEBB, J.C., Pvt., Comm. Off: BOURLAND, James, Organ: Texas Mtd.
    Rangers, Enlist: Oct. 28, 1858, Disc: April 28, 1859, Place
    of Birth: Gainesville, Texas, 6 months service, Ranger Muster
    Roll.
WEBB, Morris, Pvt., Comm. Off: REED, Henry, Organ: 1st Rgt., Mtd.
    Gunmen, Enlist: Oct. 10, 1839, Disc: Nov. 22, 1839, 1 month,
    14 days service, Ranger Muster Roll.
WEBB, William, 3rd Sgt., Comm. Off: COVINGTON, William B., and
    TRAVIS, C.E., Capt., Organ: Texas Mounted Volunteers, Co. E,
    Enlist: Nov. 1, 1854, Disc: Feb. 1, 1855, Place of Birth: Aus-
    tin, Texas, 3 months service, Ranger Muster Roll.
WEBB, William, 3rd Sgt., Comm. Off: TRAVIS, C.E., Capt.,
    Organ: Texas Volunteers, Company E, Enlist: 1854, Disc: 1855,
    3 months service, Ranger Muster Roll.
WEAVER, George W.L., Pvt., Comm. Off: SANSOM, John W., Capt.,
    Organ: Mtd. Rangers, Enlist: April 19, 1856, Age: 29, Place of
    Birth: Comal County, Ranger Muster Roll.
WEBB, William, Pvt., Comm. Off: SANSOM, John W,, Organ: Frontier
    Forces, Enlist: Aug. 25, 1870, Disc: May 31, 1871, Place of
    Birth: Shackleford County, Ranger Muster Roll.
WEBSTER, Silas, Pvt., Comm. Off: DAVENPORT, John M., Organ: Mtd.
    Vol. Minute Men, Enlist: March 13, 1856, Disc: June 1, 1857,
    Place of Birth: Uvalde County, 3 months service, Ranger Muster
    Roll.
WEDDELL, A.J., Pvt., Comm. Off: HUNTER, R.L., Organ: Rangers, Par-
    ker County, Enlist: Dec. 24, 1873, Disc: March 29, 1874, Place
    of Birth: Parker County, 96 days service, Ranger Muster Roll.

WEED, T.A., 2nd Sgt., (Pvt.), Comm. Off: PERRY, C.R., and ROBERTS, D.W., Organ: Co. D, Frontier Battalion, Enlist: May 2, 1874, Disc: May 31, 1878, Place of Birth: Blanco County, 19 months, 8 days service, Ranger Muster Roll.

WEEKES, Nicholas, Capt., Comm. Off: WEEKES, Nicholas, Organ: Star Rifles, Enlist: Sept. 21, 1874, Disc: Sept. 27, 1874, Place of Birth: Galveston County, 7 days service, Ranger Muster Roll.

WEEMS, James L., Pvt., Comm. Off: CALLAHAN, James H., Organ: Mtd. Rangers, Enlist: July 20, 1855, Disc: Oct. 19, 1855, Place of Birth: Seguin, 2 months, 29 days service, Ranger Muster Roll.

WEHICKLIN, Geo., Pvt., Comm. Off: KLEID, Peter, Organ: Co. G, Frontier Forces, Enlist: Oct. 31, 1879, Disc: May 31, 1871, Place of Birth: Camp Rio Frio, Ranger Muster Roll.

WEHMEYER, H., Corp., Comm. Off: FRANDTZEN, Erasmus, Organ: Detached, Mounted Rangers, Enlist: March 24, 1860, Disc: June 19, 1860, Appt. Corp. May 21, 1860, Ranger Muster Roll.

WEIDENMUELLER, Chas., Pvt., Comm. Off: LOVENSKIOLD, Charles, Organ: Walker Mtd. Rifles, Cortinas War, Enlist: Nov. 22, 1859, Place of Birth: Corpus Christi, Ranger Muster Roll.

WEIR, Robert W., Pvt., Comm. Off: CALLAHAN, James H., Organ: Mtd. Rangers, Enlist: July 20, 1855, Disc: Oct. 19, 1855, Place of Birth: Prairie Lee, 3 months, 29 days service, Ranger Muster Roll.

WEIR, Wm., Pvt., Comm. Off: CONNELL, J.G., Organ: Brown and San Saba Counties Rangers, Enlist: Jan. 6, 1874, Disc: March 26, 1874, Place of Birth: Brown and San Saba Counties, 2 months, 20 days service, Ranger Muster Roll.

WEIRS, Louis, Pvt., Comm. Off: INGRAM, James, GRAY, S.B., Organ: Minute Men, Enlist: Feb. 19, 1872, Disc: Nov. 17, 1872, Place of Birth: Blanco County, 71 days service, Ranger Muster Roll.

WEIZE, Morits, 1st Sgt., Comm. Off: SANSOM, John W., Capt., Organ: Rangers, Enlist: Aug. 31, 1859, Disc: Nov. 30, 1859, 3 months service, Ranger Muster Roll.

WELBORNE, James, Pvt., Comm. Off: DONELSON, John, Organ: Rangers for Cortinas War, Enlist: Nov. 5, 1859, Disc: Dec. 10, 1859, Age: 28, Place of Birth: Live Oak County, Ranger Muster Roll. Service: 1 mo. 6 days at $12--$14.40; $3 allowed for clothing & $14.40 for hire of horse--total pay $31.80.

WELBOURN, J.J., 2nd Lt., Comm. Off: HAMPTON, G.J., Organ: Mounted Volunteers, Enlist: Nov. 12, 1859, Disc: Jan. 1, 1860, Place of Birth: Hellena, Resigned Dec. 12, 1859, Ranger Muster Roll.

WELCH, Charles, Pvt., Comm. Off: WOOD, J.D., Organ: Prov. Mounted State Troops, Enlist: Oct. 9, 1871, Disc: Nov. 13, 1871, Place of Birth: Limestone County, Ranger Muster Roll.

WELCH, James, Pvt., Comm. Off: SCHWETHELM, H., Organ: Co. E, Min. Men, Enlist: April 7, 1872, Disc: March 15, 1873, Place of Birth: Kerr County, 230 days of service, Ranger Muster Roll.

WELCH, James, Pvt., Comm. Off: WOODS, William M., Organ: Mounted Rangers, Enlist: April 10, 1860, Disc: Oct. 16, 1860, Place of Birth: Bonham, Ranger Muster Roll.

WELCH, James, Pvt., Comm. Off: WRIGHT, J.A., Organ: Co. D, Minute Men, Enlist: May 25, 1872, Disc: June 1, 1873, Place of Birth: Comanche County, 70 days service, Ranger Muster Roll.

WELCH, Joshua, Pvt., Comm. Off: SANSOM, John W., Organ: Frontier Forces, Enlist: Aug. 25, 1870, Disc: Feb. 6, 1871, Place of Birth: Shackleford County, Ranger Muster Roll. Peoria, Maricopa Co., Arizona.

WELCH, W., Pvt., Comm. Off: SCHWETHELM, H., Organ: Co. E, Minute Men, Kerr County, Enlist: April 10, 1873, Disc: April 10, 1874, Place of Birth: Kerr County, 130 days of service, Ranger Muster Roll. Barksdale, Texas.

WELCH, W.D., Pvt., Comm. Off: MCNELLY, L.H., Organ: Washington Co. Vol. Militia, Enlist: Feb. 1, 1875, Disc: Nov.22, 1876, Place of Birth: Austin, Texas, 19 months, 27 days service, Ranger Muster Roll.

WELCKER, D.H., Pvt., Comm. Off: HUNTER, James M., Organ: Co. I, Frontier Forces, Enlist: Sept. 12, 1870, Disc: Jan. 24, 1871, Place of Birth: Austin, Texas, 4 months, 12 days service, Ranger Muster Roll.

WELDER, G.W., Pvt., Comm. Off: HAYNIE, Geo. E., Organ: Co. M, Minute Men, Lampasas Co., Enlist: Oct. 2, 1873, Disc: March 10, 1874, Place of Birth: Lampasas County, 40 days of service, Ranger Muster Roll.

WELDON, Jno. W., Pvt., Comm. Off: HARRISON, Thos., Capt., Organ: Tex. Rangers, Enlist: Jan. 10, 61 at Waco for 6 mos; unless sooner discharged, Age: 29. R&F 51; Thos. HARRISON, En. Off; J.C. NEWLON, Mus. Off; S.P. ROSS & D.R. LINSLEY, apprs. H: $150; HE: $30; Gun: $30; Pistol: $30. Co. sta. at camp near Waco Jan. 8, 61. Called into service of State by Gov. Sam HOUSTON. 1 Muster Roll Jan. 10, 61.

WELLBORN, H.F., Pvt., Comm. Off: COLDWELL, Neal, Organ: Co. F, Frontier Battalion, Enlist: April 1, 1876, Disc: Aug. 31, 1876, Place of Birth: Kerr County, 5 months service, Ranger Muster Roll.

WELLBROOK, J.J., Pvt., Comm. Off: GILLESPIE, J.T., Organ: Co. E, Frontier Battalion, Enlist: June 1, 1883, Disc: July 21, 1883, Place of Birth: Camp King, Texas, 1 month, 21 days service, Ranger Muster Roll.

WELLS, D.F., Pvt., Comm. Off: DONELSON, John, Organ: Rangers for Cortinas War, Enlist: Nov. 5, 1869, Disc: Dec. 10, 1859, Age: 32, Place of Birth: Live Oak County, Ranger Muster Roll. Service: 1 mo. 6 days at $12--$14.40; $3 allowed for clothing & $14.40 for hire of horse--total pay $31.80.

WELLS, D.F., Pvt., Comm. Off: CURETON, J.J., Capt., Organ: Rangers, Enlist: Dec. 5, 1860, See Newspaper Clippings. Ranger Muster Roll.

WELLS, D.W., Sgt., Comm. Off: JONES, Stephen F., Organ: Minute Men, Enlist: July 1, 1860, Disc: Aug. 29, 1860, Place of Birth: Palo Pinto County, Ranger Muster Roll.

WELLS, F.W., Pvt., Comm. Off: SPARKS, J.C., Organ: Co. C, Frontier Battalion, Enlist: Dec. 15, 1876, Disc: Aug. 31, 1877, Place of Birth: Clay County, 8 months, 16 days service, Ranger Muster Roll.

WELLS, L.B., Pvt., Comm. Off: GILLISPIE, J.T., Organ: Co. E, Frontier Battalion, Enlist: June 1, 1883, Disc: Nov. 30, 1883, Place of Birth: Camp King, Texas, 6 months service, Ranger Muster Roll.

WELLS, L.B., Pvt., Comm. Off: NEVILL, C.L., Organ: Co. E, Fron-
    tier Battalion, Enlist: Sept. 1, 1881, Disc: Aug. 31, 1882,
    Age: 26, 5'8", dark, brown hair, brown eyes, CowBoy, Place of
    Birth: Gordon, Ga., 12 months service, Ranger Muster Roll..
WELLS, R.H., Pvt., Comm. Off: MCNELLY, L.H., Organ: Washington
    Co. Vol. Militia, Enlist: Feb. 1, 1875, Disc: May 31, 1875,
    Place of Birth: Austin, Texas, 4 months service, Ranger Mus-
    ter Roll.
WENSTON, T., Pvt., Comm. Off: MCNELLY, L.H., Organ: Washington
    Co. Vol. Militia, Enlist: Oct. 1, 1876, Disc: Jan. 20, 1877,
    Place of Birth: Austin, Texas, 3 months, 20 days service,
    Ranger Muster Roll.
WENTZ, Jacob, Pvt., Comm. Off: KLEID, Peter, Organ: Co. G, Fron-
    tier Forces, Enlist: Oct. 31, 1870, Disc: May 31, 1871, Place
    of Birth: Camp Rio Frio, Ranger Muster Roll.
WERNER, August, Burler, Comm. Off: JONES, Franklin, Organ: Co. A,
    Frontier Battalion, Enlist: Aug. 25, 1870, Disc: Oct. 31, 1870,
    Place of Birth: Fort Mason, Texas, Ranger Muster Roll.
WERNER, August, Bugler, Comm. Off: JONES, Franklin, Organ: Co. A,
    Frontier Forces, Enlist: Aug. 25, 1870, Disc: Nov. 11, 1870,
    Place of Birth: Fort Mason, Texas, 2 months, 17 days service,
    Ranger Muster Roll.
WERNER, Christian, 4th Corp., Comm. Off: KLEID, Peter, Organ: Co.
    O, Frontier Forces, Enlist: Oct. 31, 1870, Disc: May 31, 1871,
    Place of Birth: Camp Rio Frio, Ranger Muster Roll.
WERNER, Frederick, Pvt., Comm. Off: BERRY, Henry W., Organ: Mtd.
    Vol. for Cortinas War, Enlist: Nov. 10, 1859, Disc: Dec. 20,
    1859, Age: 30, Place of Birth: Brownsville, Ranger Muster
    Roll.
WESLEY, Jacob, Pvt., Comm. Off: SANSOM, John W., Organ: Frontier
    Forces, Enlist: Aug. 25, 1870, Disc: May 31, 1871, Place of
    Birth: Shackleford County, Ranger Muster Roll.
WEST, A., Pvt., Comm. Off: SWISHER, Jas. M., Organ: Co. P, Fron-
    tier Forces, Enlist: Sept. 6, 1870, Disc: Nov. 27, 1870, Place
    of Birth: Camp Colorado, Ranger Muster Roll.
WEST, Benjamin, Pvt., Comm. Off: DARNELL, N.H., Organ: Mounted
    Rangers, Enlist: April 14, 1860, Disc: Aug. 13, 1860, Place of
    Birth: Dallas, Ranger Muster Roll.
WEST, B.T., 4th Corp., Comm. Off: EASTIN, S.W., Organ: Jack Cty.
    Rangers, Enlist: Dec. 3, 1873, Disc: April 3, 1874, Place of
    Birth: Jack County, 4 months service, Ranger Muster Roll.
WEST, Gustave, Pvt., Comm. Off: SWISHER, Jas. M., Organ: Co. P,
    Frontier Forces, Enlist: Sept. 6, 1870, Disc: Nov. 28, 1870,
    Place of Birth: Camp Colorado, Ranger Muster Roll.
WEST, Isaac, Pvt., Comm. Off: MCCULLOCH, Henry E., Capt.,
    Organ: Texas Volunteers, Enlist: Oct. 25, 1848, Disc: Dec. 5,
    1848, Age: 18, 1 month, 13 days service, Ranger Muster Roll.
WEST, James, Pvt., Comm. Off: TUMLINSON, Peter, Capt., Organ: Mtd.
    Vols., Enlist: Nov. 12, 1859, Disc: Feb. 10, 1860, 2 months,
    29 days service, Ranger Muster Roll.
WEST, James, Pvt., Comm. Off: TOMLINSON, Peter, Organ: Mounted
    Vols., Enlist: Jan. 2, 1860, Ranger Muster Roll.
WEST, Philip G., Pvt., Comm. Off: TOBIN, Wm. G., Organ: Mounted
    Volunteers, Enlist: Oct. 20, 1859, Disc: Nov. 3, 1859, Place

WEST, Philip G., Pvt., (Continued)
of Birth: San Antonio, Ranger Muster Roll.

WEST, W.A., Pvt., Comm. Off: THOMPSON, H.J., Capt., Organ: Min. Men, Parker County, Enlist: May 25, 61 at Veal Sta., Parker County, 20 days regular scout. R&F 40; Co. organized under Act of the Legislature Feb. 7, 61; Election cert. with roll; 1 Muster Roll dated May 27, 61; 6 Scout Reports dated Je.8-Je.23-61, Je.24-Jy.7-61, Jy.8-Jy.26-61, Jy.27-Aug.4-61, Aug.4-Aug.14-61 & Aug.17-S.22-61.

WEST, W.P., Pvt., Comm. Off: CAMPBELL, G.W., Organ: Co. B, Frontier Battalion, Enlist: Sept. 1, 1876, Disc: May 28, 1877, Place of Birth: Camp Throckmorton, 8 months, 27 days--deserted, Ranger Muster Roll.

WEST, William, Pvt., Comm. Off: WALKER, Joseph, Organ: Rangers for Cortinas War, Enlist: Nov. 30, 1859, Disc: Jan. 20, 1860, Age: 25, Place of Birth: Goliad, Ranger Muster Roll.

WEST, William, 4th Sgt., Comm. Off: FORD, John J., Organ: 3rd Co. of Rangers, Enlist: Jan. 20, 1860, Disc: May 17, 1860, Age: 25, Place of Birth: Brownsville, Deserted Feb. 11, Ranger Muster Roll.

WESTBROOK, Nathaniel, Pvt., Comm. Off: WALKER, Joseph, Organ: Rangers for Cortinas War, Enlist: Nov. 30, 1859, Disc: Jan. 20, 1860, Age: 23, Place of Birth: Banquete, Ranger Muster Roll.

WESTBROOK, Nathaniel, 2nd Sgt., Comm. Off: FORD, John J., Organ: 3rd Co. of Rangers, Enlist: Jan. 20, 1860, Disc: May 17, 1860, Age: 23, Place of Birth: Brownsville, Ranger Muster Roll.

WESTER, George W., Pvt., Comm. Off: FITZHUGH, Wm., Organ: Texas Militia, Mtd. Vol., Enlist: Nov. 2, 1854, Disc: Feb. 2, 1854, Age: 20, Place of Birth: McKinney, Texas, 3 months service, Ranger Muster Roll.

WESTERFIELD, Wm. E., 1st Sgt., Comm. Off: BALLENTYNE, Robert, Enlist: Co. K, Minute Men, Bandera Co., Enlist: Aug. 13, 1872, Disc: June 20, 1873, Place of Birth: Bandera County, 99 days of service, Ranger Muster Roll.

WETHERSBEE, Darling, Pvt., Comm. Off: WOODS, Wm. M., Organ: Mtd. Rangers, Enlist: April 10, 1860, Disc: Oct. 16, 1860, Age: 23, Place of Birth: Bonham, Ranger Muster Roll.

WETHERS, Robt., Pvt., Comm. Off: TUMLINSON, J.J., Organ: Tumlinson's Spy, 1 Rgt. Mtd. Gunmen, Enlist: Oct. 15, 1839, Disc: Nov. 22, 1839, 1 month, 9 days service, Ranger Muster Roll.

WEYMILLER, T., Pvt., Comm. Off: COLDWELL, Neal, Organ: Co. F, Frontier Battalion, Enlist: June 4, 1874, Disc: June 4, 1875, Place of Birth: Kerr County, 12 months, 1 day service, Ranger Muster Roll.

WEYRICH, Mich., 3rd Sgt., Comm. Off: CAMERON, Ewen, Capt., Organ: Co. Of Texas Rangers, Enlist: Mar. 20, 61 at Fredericksburg for 3 months, Mus. out Je.5-61 at Camp Mason by Lt. S.G. RAGSDALE, Age: 21. R&F 31; En. & Mus. Off: W. WAHRMMUND; Appraisers; F.V.D. STUCKEN & Louis WEISS; Val. H: $50; HE: $18; Gun: $18; Pistol: $30; $3.45 deducted from pay; no corn or forage issued, Co. entitled to commutation in money; 45 miles travelled from place of discharge

WEYRICH, Mich., 3rd Sgt., (Continued)
    home; Co. called into service by Gov. HOUSTON; Co. sta. on
    South Fork of Llano River, Mar. 20, 61; 1 Muster Roll.
WEYRICK, Michel, Pvt., Comm. Off: FRANDTZEN, Erasmus, Organ: De-
    tached Mounted Rangers, Enlist: April 2, 1860, Disc: June 19,
    1860, Ranger MusterRoll.
WHALEN, Edward, Pvt., Comm. Off: SANSOM, John W., Organ: Texas
    Mounted Rangers, Enlist: April 16, 1856, Disc: July 16, 1856,
    Age: 25, Place of Birth: Comal County, 90 days service, Ranger
    Muster Roll.
WHALEN, Edward, Pvt., Comm. Off: SANSOM, John W., Capt.,
    Organ: Mtd. Rangers, Enlist: April 10, 1856, Disc: July 16,
    1856, Age: 25, Place of Birth: Comal County, 3 months service,
    Ranger Muster Roll.
WHATLEY, Ben F., Pvt., Comm. Off: HARRISON, Thos., Capt.,
    Organ: Texas Rangers, Enlist: Jan. 10, 61 at Waco for 6 mos.;
    unless sooner discharged, Age: 21. R&F 51; Thos. HARRISON, En.
    Off; J.C. NEWLON, Mus. Off; S.P. ROSS & D.R. LINSLEY, Apprs.
    H: $180; HE: $30; Gun: $25; Pistol: $30. Co. sta. at camp
    near Waco Jan. 8, 61. Called into service of State by Gov.
    Sam HOUSTON. 1 Muster Roll. Jan. 10, 61.
WHATLEY, Edwrad, Pvt., Comm. Off: ROSS, L.S., Capt., Organ: Ran-
    ger Company, Enlist: Oct. 13, 60 at Belknap for 12 months,
    Serv. from Oct. 13-60 to Feb. 5, 61; 3 mos. & 25 days at $25-
    $94.16, Age: 22. R&F 66; En. Off: Capt. ROSS; Mus. Off:
    J.M.W. HALL; Appraiser Jas. H. SWINDELLS; Val. H: $125;
    HE: $20; Gun: $10; Pistol: $30; Stoppage $18.23; Bal. Paid:
    $75.93; Elec. certif. with roll; Co. sta. at Ft. Belknap Oct.
    17 & Nov. 22, 60; 1 Muster Roll & 1 Pay Roll.
WHATLEY, Edward, Pvt., Comm. Off: ROSS, L.S., Organ: Mounted
    Rangers, Enlist: Oct. 13, 1860, Age: 22, Place of Birth: Bel-
    knap, Ranger Muster Roll. Killeen, Bell Co., Texas, R.R. 3,
    Box. 605.
WHATLEY, W.M., 2nd Corp., Comm. Off: ONEAL, C.M., Organ: Co. E,
    Minute Men, Erath Co., Enlist: Jan. 1, 1873, Disc: April 10,
    1874, Place of Birth: Erath County, 110 days of service, Ran-
    ger Muster Roll.
WHEELER, J.V., Pvt., Comm. Off: PERRY, C.R., Organ: Co. D, Fron-
    tier Battalion, Enlist: May 25, 1874, Disc: Dec. 9, 1874,
    Place of Birth: Blanco County, 6 months, 20 days service, Ran-
    ger Muster Roll. Farris, Okla.
WHEELER, J.S., Pvt., Comm. Off: MALTBY, W.J., Organ: Co. E, Fron-
    tier Battalion, Enlist: June 6, 1874, Disc: Dec. 12, 1874,
    Place of Birth: Coleman County, 6 months, 7 days service, Ran-
    ger Muster Roll.
WHEELER, J.W., Pvt., Comm. Off: TACKITT, L.L., Organ: 1 Co. Min.
    Men, Enlist: Oct. 20, 1865, Disc: June 22, 1866, Place of
    Birth: Parker County, 42 days, Ranger Muster Roll.
WHEELER, John, Pvt., Comm. Off: WOOD, J.D., Organ: Prov. Mounted
    State Troops, Enlist: Oct. 9, 1871, Disc: Nov. 13, 1871, Place
    of Birth: Limestone County, Ranger Muster Roll.
WHEELER, T.B., Pvt., Comm. Off: TUSCHINSKY, Theodore, Organ: Co.
    K, Mounted Militia, Enlist: Aug. 2, 1873, Disc: Dec. 9, 1873,
    Place of Birth: Travis County, Copied Roster; 4 months, 7 days
    service, Ranger Muster Roll.

WHEELER, W.A., Pvt., Comm. Off: TACKITT, L.L., Organ: 1 Co.
    Minute Men, Enlist: Oct. 20, 1865, Disc: June 22, 1866, Place
    of Birth: Parker County, 22 days, Ranger Muster Roll. Crawell,
    Texas.
WHEELER, W.C., Pvt., Comm. Off: BALLANTYNE, Robert, Organ: Mounted
    Rangers, Enlist: March 29, 1860, Disc: July 3, 1860, Age: 36,
    Place of Birth: Bandera City, Ranger Muster Roll.
WHELAN, Dan, Pvt., Comm. Off: WALLER, J.R., Organ: Co. A, Fron-
    tier Battalion, Enlist: May 25, 1874, Disc: April 30, 1875,
    Place of Birth: Erath County, 11 months, 11 days service,
    Ranger Muster Roll.
WHELAN, D.M., 1st Sgt., Comm. Off: GREEN, M.R., Organ: Comanche
    County Rangers, Enlist: Jan. 17, 1874, Disc: Feb. 17, 1874,
    Place of Birth: Comanche County, 1 month service, Ranger Mus-
    ter Roll.
WHELAN, D.M., Pvt., Comm. Off: FOSTER, B.S., Organ: CO. E, Fron-
    tier Battalion, Enlist: June 1, 1875, Disc: Aug. 31, 1876,
    Age: 28, 5'10", light, light hair, light eyes, carpenter,
    Place of Birth: Kentucky, 15 months service, Ranger Muster
    Roll. Waco, Texas, 23 Grace St.
WHELAN, D.M., 2nd Sgt., Comm. Off: FOSTER, B.S., Organ: Co. E,
    Frontier Battalion, Enlist: Sept. 1, 1876, Disc: Aug. 31,
    1877, Place of Birth: Coleman County, 12 months service, Ran-
    ger Muster Roll.
WHELAN, James, Pvt., Comm. Off: WALLACE, Warren, Organ: Frontier
    Company, Nueces Co., Enlist: June 29, 1874, Place of
    Birth: Nueces County, Ranger Muster Roll.
WHELAN, Thos., Pvt., Comm. Off: CHAMBERLAIN, Bland, Organ: Fron-
    tier Forces, Co. H, Enlist: Nov. 15, 1870, Disc: Feb. 28,
    1871, Place of Birth: San Antonio, Ranger Muster Roll. Corpus
    Christi, Nueces Co., Texas, Star Route.
WHETSEL, P., Pvt., Comm. Off: TEAGUE, John, Capt., Organ: Minute
    Men, Wise County, Enlist: Oct. 14, 1865, Age: 31. R&F 32;
    Arms: Rifle; 1 Muster Roll.
WHETSTINE, Jas., Pvt., Comm. Off: WOODS, Wm. M., Organ: Mounted
    Rangers, Enlist: April 14, 1860, Disc: Aug. 10, 1860, Age: 20,
    Place of Birth: Bonham, Ranger Muster Roll.
WHETZEL, P.K., Pvt., Comm. Off: TEAGUE, John, Organ: Minute Men,
    Enlist: Oct. 13, 1865, Disc: April 13, 1866, Place of
    Birth: Wise County, 13 days service, RangerMuster Roll.
WHIPLER, Philip, Pvt., Comm. Off: REED, Henry, Organ: 1 Rgt., Mtd
    Gunmen, Enlist: Oct. 10, 1839, Disc: Nov. 11, 1839, 1 month,
    2 days service, Ranger Muster Roll.
WHISENANT, R.B., Pvt., Comm. Off: FITZHUGH, G.S., Capt.,
    Organ: Ranger Co., Enlist: April 14, 60; Re-enlisted May 20,
    60, Disc: May 19, 60; Oct. 25-60; served 6 mo. & 12 days at
    $25 - Total $160. R&F 83; Stoppages: $7.95. Balance Pd:
    $152.05. 1 Pay Roll.
WHISENANT, R.B., Pvt., Comm. Off: FITZHUGH, G.S., Organ: Mounted
    Rangers, Enlist: May 20, 1860, Disc: Oct. 25, 1860, Ranger
    Muster Roll. Allen, Okla., Box 23.
WHISTLER, Louis S., Pvt., Comm. Off: TUMLINSON, Peter, Capt.,
    Organ: Mtd. Vols., Enlist: Nov. 12, 1859, Disc: Feb. 10, 60,
    2 months, 29 days service, Ranger Muster Roll.

WHISTLER, L.S., Pvt., Comm. Off: TOMLINSON, Peter, Organ: Mtd.
   Vols., Enlist: Jan. 2, 1860, Ranger Muster Roll.
WHISTLER, Ross R., Pvt., Comm. Off: TUMLINSON, Peter, Capt.,
   Organ: Mtd. Vols., Enlist: Nov. 12, 1859, Disc: Feb. 10, 1860,
   2 months, 29 days service, Ranger Muster Roll.
WHITSORE, J.S., Pvt., Comm. Off: FOSTER, B.S., Organ: Co. E,
   Frontier Battalion, Enlist: June 1, 1875 to Aug. 31, 1875,
   Age: 19, 6', light, blue eyes, light hair, farmer, Place of
   Birth: Texas, 3 months service, Ranger Muster Roll. Newlin,
   Texas.
WHITAKER, L.M., Pvt., Comm. Off: WALKER, John G., Capt.,
   Organ: Mtd. Vol., Enlist: Nov. 1854, Ranger Muster Roll.
WHITAKER, M.F., Pvt., Comm. Off: BENTON, Nat, Capt., Organ: Ran-
   gers, Enlist: Sept. 15, 1855, Disc: Oct. 15, 1855, Age: 24,
   Enlisted at: Leona River, 1 month service, Ranger Muster
   Roll.
WHITAKER, V.C., Pvt., Comm. Off: WALKER, John G., Capt.,
   Organ: Mtd. Vol., Enlist: Nov. 1854, Ranger Muster Roll.
WHITE, A., Pvt., Comm. Off: DONELSON, John, Organ: Rangers for
   Cortinas War, Enlist: Nov. 6, 1859, Disc: Dec. 10, 1859,
   Age: 36, Place of Birth: Live Oak County, Ranger Muster Roll.
WHITE, Abram L., 2nd Sgt., Comm. Off: MCCULLOCH, Henry E.,
   Organ: Texas Mounted Vol., Enlist: Oct. 25, 1847, Age: 18,
   Dark eyes, dark hair, 5'6", Place of Birth: Galveston.
WHITE, Abram L., Sgt., Comm. Off: MCCULLOCH, Henry E., Capt.,
   Organ: Texas Volunteers, Enlist: Oct. 25, 1847, Disc: Oct. 24,
   1848, Age: 18; Height: 5'6", Dark comp., dark hair, dark eyes,
   Place of Birth: Galveston, Texas, 12 months service, Ranger
   Muster Roll.
WHITE, B.S., 2nd Sgt., Comm. Off: BROWN, John Henry, Organ: Tex.
   State Troops, Enlist: July 1, 1859, Disc: Sept. 4, 1859,
   Place of Birth: Travis County, 2 months, 4 days service, Ranger
   Muster Roll.
WHITE, John B., 1st Sgt., Comm. Off: FITZHUGH, Wm., Organ: Texas
   Militia, Enlist: Nov. 2, 1854, Disc: Feb. 2, 1854, Place of
   Birth: McKinney, Texas, 3 months service, Ranger Muster Roll.
WHITE, E.T., Pvt., Comm. Off: STEVINS, G.W., Organ: Minute Men,
   Enlist: Aug. 26, 1873, Disc: Oct. 31, 1873, Place of
   Birth: Wise County, 20 days service, Ranger Muster Roll.
WHITE, Ezekiel, 4th Sgt., Comm. Off: ROGERS, P.H., Capt.,
   Organ: Texas Mtd. Vols., Enlist: Oct. 1854, Disc: Dec. 1854,
   3 months service, Ranger Muster Roll. Ex. order of Mar. 1856.
WHITE, George, Pvt., Comm. Off: SANSOM, John W., Organ: Frontier
   Forces, Enlist: March 5, 1870, Disc: May 31, 1871, Place of
   Birth: Shackleford County, Ranger Muster Roll.
WHITE, H., Pvt., Comm. Off: LACEY, J.C., Organ: Co. F, Minute
   Men of Gillispie Co., Enlist: April 18, 1872, Disc: April 23,
   1874, Place of Birth: Gillispie County, 14 days of service,
   Ranger Muster Roll.
WHITE, H.F., 3rd Corp., Pvt., Comm. Off: HAMPTON, G.J., Capt.,
   Organ: Mtd. Ranger Volunteers, Enlist: Nov. 12, 59 as Pvt.,
   Dec. 12-59 as Corp., Disc: Jan. 1, 60; served as Pvt. 1 mo. at
   $12--$12. as Corp. 20 days at $14-$9.33. Total: 1 mo. & 20
   days - $21.33. R&F 34; Allowances on: Clothing: $4.17; use of
   horse: $20; Rations: $4.50; Forage: $8.25. Total: $58.25.

WHITE, H.F., 3rd Corp., Pvt., (Continued)
    Stoppages for State Arms: $30. Balance: $28.25. Co. called
    into State Service for suppression of Cortina Rebellion by
    Gov. H.R. RUNNELS. 1 Pay Roll.
WHITE, H.F., Pvt., Comm. Off: HAMPTON, G.J., Organ: Mounted Vol.,
    Enlist: Nov. 12, 1859, Disc: Jan. 1, 1860, Place of Birth: Tex-
    ana, Elected 3rd Corp. Dec. 12, Ranger Muster Roll.
WHITE, H., Pvt., Comm. Off: COLDWELL, Neal, Organ: Co. F, Fron-
    tier Battalion, Enlist: June 4, 1874, Disc: Dec. 1, 1874,
    Place of Birth: Kerr County, 5 months, 27 days service, Ranger
    Muster Roll.
WHITE, Homer H., Pvt., Comm. Off: NELSON, Allison, Organ: Minute
    Men, Enlist: March 12, 1860, Place of Birth: Bosque County,
    Ranger Muster Roll.
WHITE, James, Pvt., Comm. Off: WALLER, J.R., Organ: Co. A, Fron-
    tier Battalion, Enlist: May 25, 1874, Disc: Sept. 13, 1874,
    Place of Birth: Erath County, 4 months, 4 days service, Ran-
    ger Muster Roll. Baird, Callahan, Texas.
WHITE, James L., Pvt., Comm. Off: EASTIN, S.W., Organ: Jack Cty.
    Rangers, Enlist: Dec. 3, 1873, Disc: April 3, 1874, Place of
    Birth: Jack County, 4 months service, Ranger Muster Roll.
WHITE, James W., Pvt., Comm. Off: BARRY, James Buck, 1st Lt.,
    Organ: Co. org. & fighting Indians interval before conv. of
    '61, Expiration of service Feb. 25, 61; Serv. 1 mo. 15 days at
    $25 - $37.50. R&F 25; 1 Pay Roll; BARRY received commission
    from Governor; Convention assumed authority while in field &
    company not mustered out.
WHITE, John, Pvt., Comm. Off: HALL, A.B., Organ: Prov. State
    Troops, Detached, Enlist: Oct. 13, 1871, Disc: Oct. 20, 1871,
    Place of Birth: Groesbeck, Texas, Ranger Muster Roll.
WHITE, Jim, Pvt., Comm. Off: SNOWBALL, James, Organ: Prov. State
    Troops, Enlist: Oct. 13, 1871, Disc: Oct. 20, 1871, Place of
    Birth: Groesbeck, Texas, Ranger Muster Roll.
WHITE, John B., Pvt., Comm. Off: FORD, John S., Organ: 3rd Co.
    of Rangers, Enlist: March 1, 1860, Disc: May 17, 1860, Age: 29,
    Place of Birth: Brownsville, Ranger Muster Roll.
WHITE, J.W., Pvt., Comm. Off: REIGER, R.T., Organ: Minute Men,
    Enlist: Sept. 1, 1872, Disc: Oct. 31, 1873, Place of Birth:
    Wise County, 15 days service, Ranger Muster Roll.
WHITE, P.A., Pvt., Comm. Off: MALTBY, W.J., Organ: Co. E, Fron-
    tier Battalion, Enlist: May 30, 1874, Disc: May 31, 1875,
    Place of Birth: Coleman County, 12 months, 1 day service, Ran-
    ger Muster Roll. Hamilton, Texas, R.R. 5.
WHITE, P.L., Pvt., Comm. Off: SPARKS, J.C., Organ: Co. C, Fron-
    tier Battalion, Enlist: Oct. 1, 1876, Disc: Feb. 28, 1878,
    Place of Birth: Clay County, 17 months service, Ranger Muster
    Roll.
WHITE, R.M., 4th Sgt., Comm. Off: COVINGTON, William B., and
    TRAVIS, C.E., Capt., Organ: Texas Mounted Volunteers, Co. E,
    Enlist: Nov. 1, 1854, Disc: Feb. 1, 1855, Place of Birth: Aus-
    tin, Texas, 3 months service, Ranger Muster Roll.
WHITE, R.M., 4th Sgt., Comm. Off: TRAVIS, C.E., Capt., Organ: Tex.
    Volunteers, Company E, Enlist: 1854, Disc: 1855, 3 months ser-
    vice, Ranger Muster Roll.

WHITE, Robt. M., 1st Lt., Comm. Off: WHITE, Robert M., 1st Lt.,
Organ: Bell Cty. Rangers, Enlist: Feb. 18, 60 at Belton for 12
mos.; Enrolled for duty Feb. 20, 60, Disbanded at Belton Je.
29,60, Age: 31. R&F 26; Enr. off: Dr. John EMBREE; Mus.
Off: J.M.W. HALL; Apprs.: John S. BLAIR, John W. SCOTT; Val.
of: H: $150; HE: $25; Service 4 mos. 10 days at $75, total
$408.50; Co. std. at Belton Feb. 20, 60; Co. called into ser-
vice by Gov. HOUSTON; State arms returned upon disbandment; 2
Muster Rolls dated Feb. 20, 60 each; 1 Pay Roll; $20 per mo.
Extra pay $86 as QM of Company.

WHITE, Robt. M., 1st Lt., Comm. Off: WHITE, Robt. M., Organ: Mtd.
Rangers, Enlist: Feb. 18, 1860, Disc: June 29, 1860, Age: 31,
Place of Birth: Belton, Ranger Muster Roll.

WHITE, Sterling C., Pvt., Comm. Off: FORD, John S., Organ: 2nd Co.
of Rangers, Enlist: Nov. 10, 1858, Disc: May 10, 1859, Age: 21,
Place of Birth: Austin, Ranger Muster Roll.

WHITE, S.F., Pvt., Comm. Off: ROBERTS, D.W., Organ: Co. D, Frontier Battalion, Enlist: April 1, 1876, Disc: Aug. 31, 1876,
5 months service, Ranger Muster Roll.

WHITE, Washington, Pvt., Comm. Off: HARRINGTON, James, Organ: Co.
A, Detached, Prov. State Troops, Enlist: Oct. 9, 1871,
Disc: Nov. 13, 1871, Place of Birth: Springfield, Texas, Ranger
Muster Roll.

WHITE, Washington, Pvt., Comm. Off: WILLIAMS, Samuel J.,
Organ: Prov. State Troops, Co. A, Enlist: Oct. 9, 1871,
Disc: Nov. 13, 1871, Place of Birth: Limestone County, Ran-
ger Muster Roll.

WHITE, W.A., 1st Corp., Comm. Off: BROWN, John Henry, Organ: Tex.
State Troops, Enlist: July 1, 1859, Disc: Sept. 4, 1859,
Place of Birth: Travis County, 2 months, 4 days service, Ran-
ger Muster Roll.

WHITE, W.A., Pvt., Comm. Off: INGRAM, James, and GRAY, S.B.,
Organ: Minute Men, Enlist: Aug. 15, 1872, Disc: Nov. 17, 1872,
Place of Birth: Blanco County, 18 days service, Ranger Muster
Roll.

WHITE, Wm. A., 2nd Sgt., Comm. Off: WHITE, Robert M., 1st Lt.,
Organ: Bell Cty. Rangers, Enlist: Feb. 18, 60 at Belton for
12 mos.; Enrolled for duty Feb. 20, 60, Disbanded at Belton
Je.29-60, Age: 25. R&F 26; Enr. Off: Dr. John EMBREE; Mus.
Off: J.M.W. HALL; Apprs.: John S. BLAIR, John W. SCOTT; Val.
of: H: $100; HE: $25; Gun: $20; Pistol: $30; service 4 mo. 10
days at $29, total $125.66; Co. std. at Belton Feb. 20, 60;
Co. called into service by Gov. HOUSTON; State arms returned
upon disbandment; 2 Muster Rolls dated Feb. 20, 60 each; 1
Pay Roll.

WHITE, Wolf, Spy, Comm. Off: ROSS, Peter F., Capt., Organ: Spy
Company, Enlist: 1860, Serv. from July 1 to Aug. 1, 60; 1 mo.
& 1 day at $25-$25.83. R&F 39; 1 Pay Roll.

WHITE, T.J., Pvt., Comm. Off: CAMPBELL, G.W., Organ: Montague
Co. Rangers, Enlist: Dec. 13, 1873, Disc: Feb. 13, 1874,
Place of Birth: Montague County, 2 months service, Ranger Mus-
ter Roll.

WHITE, T.J., Pvt., Comm. Off: IKARD, E.F., Organ: Co. C, Frontier Battalion, Enlist: May 20, 1874, Disc: Dec. 10, 1874,

WHITE, T.J., Pvt., (Continued)
Place of Birth: Clay County, 6 months, 22 days service, Ranger Muster Roll.

WHITE, Wm. A., 2nd Sgt., Comm. Off: WHITE, Robt. M., Organ: Mtd. Rangers, Enlist: Feb. 18, 1860, Disc: June 20, 1860, Age: 25, Place of Birth: Belton, Ranger Muster Roll.

WHITE, Wilson H., Bugler, Comm. Off: FORD, John S., Organ: 2nd Co. of Rangers, Enlist: Nov. 10, 1858, Disc: May 10, 1859, Age: 26, Place of Birth: Austin, Ranger MusterRoll.

WHITE, Wilson H., 1st Sgt., Comm. Off: WHITE, Robt. M., Organ: Mounted Rangers, Enlist: Feb. 18,1860, Disc: June 29, 1860, Age: 29, Place of Birth: Belton, Ranger Muster Roll.

WHITECOTTON, G.W., Pvt., Comm. Off: STEVENS, G.W., Organ: Wise County Rangers, Enlist: Nov. 26, 1873, Disc: March 26, 1874, Place of Birth: Wise County, 4 months service, Ranger Muster Roll.

WHITEHEAD, A.R., Pvt., Comm. Off: CAMPBELL, G.W., Organ: Co. B, Frontier Battalion, Enlist: Sept. 1, 1877, Disc: Feb. 28, 1878, Place of Birth: Camp Throckmorton, 6 months, Ranger Muster Roll.

WHITEHEAD, D.R., Pvt., Comm. Off: CAMPBELL, G.W., Organ: Co. B, Frontier Battalion, Enlist: Dec. 1, 1877, Disc: Feb. 28, 1878, Place of Birth: Throckmartin County, 3 months service, Ranger Muster Roll.

WHITESIDES, John, Pvt., Comm. Off: HARRELL, J.M., Organ: Co. K, Frontier Forces, Enlist: Sept. 16, 1870, Disc: Feb. 20, 1871, Place of Birth: Penal Ranch, Discharged Oct. 31, 1870, Ranger Muster Roll.

WHITING, Thos. S., Pvt., Comm. Off: LEWIS, G.K., Capt., Organ: Texas Mtd. Vol., Enlist: Sept. 28, 1852, Disc: Mar. 13, 1853, Age: 30, Place of Birth: Brownsville, Texas, Ranger Muster Roll.

WHITLEY, E.H., Pvt., Comm. Off: BURLESON, A.B., Capt., Organ: Mounted Ranger Co., Enlist: April 8, 61 at Bellville, Austin County for 12 mos.; unless sooner discharged, Mustd. out May 9, 61, Age: 24. R&F 69; Enr. Off: Capt. A.B. BURLESON; H: $125; HE: $25; Arms--Guns: $20; pistols: $22; Apprs. David THOMASON & Jno. T. EVERETT; No. of miles from place of discharge to home 160; Co. called into service by Gov. HOUSTON April 4, 60. 2 Muster Rolls, one giving date of HOUSTON's order as April 4, 60, the other Dec. 29, 60.

WHITLEY, W.C., Pvt., Comm. Off: THOMPSON, H.J., Capt., Organ: Min. Men, Parker County, Enlist: May 25, 61 at Veal sta., Parker County, 34 days regular scout. R&F 40; Co. organized under Act of the Legislature Feb. 7, 61; Election cert. with Roll; 1 Muster Roll dated May 27-61; 6 Scout Reports dated Je.8-Je.23-61, Je.24-Jy.7-61, Jy.8-Jy.26-61, Jy.27-Aug.4-61, Aug.4-Aug.14-61 & Aug.17-S.22-61.

WHITMAN, E.S., Pvt., Comm.Off: WEEKES, Nicholas, Organ: Star Rifles Militia, Enlist: Sept. 21, 1874, Disc: Sept. 27, 1874, Place of Birth: Galveston County, 7 days service, Ranger Muster Roll.

WHITMORE, Thos. S., Pvt., Comm. Off: JONES, Stephen F., Organ: Min. Men, Detached, Enlist: March 26, 1860, Disc: Aug. 29, 1860,

WHITMORE, Thos. S., Pvt., (Continued)
    Place of Birth: Palo Pinto County, Ranger Muster Roll.
WHITSETT, Wm. E., Pvt., Comm. Off: WOODS, Wm. M., Organ: Mounted
    Rangers, Enlist: April 10, 1860, Disc: Aug. 10, 1860, Age: 22,
    Place of Birth: Bonham, Ranger Muster Roll.
WHITSON, Jessie, Pvt., Comm. Off: FORD, John S., Organ: 3rd Co.
    of Rangers, Enlist: Feb. 1, 1860, Disc: May 17, 1860, Age: 31,
    Place of Birth: Brownsville, Ranger Muster Roll.
WHITSON, L.J., Pvt., Comm. Off: TACKITT, A.C., Organ: Young
    County Rangers, Enlist: Jan. 17, 1874, Disc: Feb. 14, 1874,
    Place of Birth: Young County, 28 days of service, Ranger Mus-
    ter Roll.
WHITTEY, Theo., Pvt., Comm. Off: PEAK, June, Organ: Co. B, Fron-
    tier Battalion, Enlist: Nov. 22, 1878, Disc: Nov. 30, 1878,
    Place of Birth: Runnels County, 3 months service, Ranger Mus-
    ter Roll.
WHITTEY, Theo., Pvt., Comm. Off: PEAK, June, Organ: Co. B, Fron-
    tier Battalion, Enlist: Sept. 1, 1878, Disc: Nov. 30, 1878,
    Place of Birth: Runnels County, 3 months service, Ranger Mus-
    ter Roll.
WHITTINGTON, W.A., Pvt., Comm. Off: CAMPBELL, G.W., Organ: Mon-
    tague Co. Rangers, Enlist: Dec. 13, 1873, Disc: Feb. 13, 1874,
    Place of Birth: Montague County, 2 months service, Ranger Mus-
    ter Roll.
WHITTINGTON, W.B., 1st Sgt., Comm. Off: BROWN, John Henry,
    Organ: Texas State Troops, Enlist: July 1, 1859, Disc: Sept.
    12, 1859, Place of Birth: Travis County, 2 months, 12 days
    service, Ranger Muster Roll.
WHITTLE, W.D., 3rd Corp., Comm. Off: HARRELL, J.M., Organ: Co. K,
    Frontier Forces, Enlist: Sept. 16, 1870, Disc: Feb. 20, 1871,
    Place of Birth: Austin, Apptd. Corp. Oct. 18, 1870, Ranger
    Muster Roll.
WIENER, Saul B., Pvt., Comm. Off: KELSO, John R., Organ: Frontier
    Forces, Co. D, Enlist: Sept. 10, 1870, Disc: Feb. 2, 1871,
    Place of Birth: Camp Wood, Texas, Discharged Nov. 20, 1870,
    Ranger Muster Roll.
WIENERS, Christoph, Pvt., Comm. Off: KELSO, John R., Organ: Fron-
    tier Forces, Co. D, Enlist: Sept. 10, 1870, Disc: Feb. 2, 1871,
    Place of Birth: Camp Wood, Texas, Discharged Jan. 20, 1871,
    Ranger Muster Roll.
WIER, William W., Sgt. 1, Comm. Off: FORD, John S., Organ: 3rd Co.
    of Rangers, Enlist: Jan. 20, 1860, Disc: May 17, 1860, Age: 31,
    Ranger Muster Roll.
WIER, William W., Pvt., Comm. Off: WALKER, Joseph, Organ: Rangers
    for Cortinas War, Enlist: Nov. 30, 1859, Disc: Jan. 20, 1860,
    Age: 30, Ranger Muster Roll.
WIGHT, L.L., Pvt., Comm. Off: BALLANTYNE, Robert, Organ: Mounted
    Rangers, Enlist: March 29, 1860, Disc: July 3, 1860, Age: 20,
    Place of Birth: Bandera City, Ranger Muster Roll.
WIGHT, Orange L., Pvt., Comm. Off: HENRY, William R., Organ: Co.
    C, Mounted Vol., Enlist: Dec. 14, 1854, Disc: March 14, 1855,
    Age: 31, Place of Birth: San Antonio, 3 months service, Ranger
    Muster Roll.
WILBOURN, R., Pvt., Comm. Off: MOORE, F.M., Organ: Co. D, Fron-
    tier Battalion, Enlist: Sept. 1, 1876, Disc: Nov. 30, 1876,

WILBOURN, R., Pvt., (Continued)
    5'5", black hair, blue eyes, farmer, Place of Birth: Tippa,
    Miss., 3 months service, Ranger Muster Roll.
WILBURN, F.G., Pvt., Comm. Off: WALKER, John G., Capt.,
    Organ: Mtd. Vol., Enlist: Nov. 1854, Ranger Muster Roll.
WILBURN, John D., Pvt., Comm. Off: FITZHUGH, Wm., Organ: Texas
    Militia, Mtd. Vol., Enlist: Nov. 2, 1854, Disc: Feb. 2, 1854,
    Age: 19, Place of Birth: McKinney, Texas, 3 months service,
    Ranger Muster Roll.
WILBURN, Brown, Pvt., Comm. Off: DONELSON, John, Organ: Rangers
    for Cortinas War, Enlist: Nov. 5, 1859, Disc: Dec. 10, 1859,
    Age: 21, Place of Birth: Live Oak County, Ranger Muster Roll.
    Service: 1 mo. 6 days at $12--$14.40; $3 allowed for clothing
    & $14.40 for hire of horse--total pay $31.80.
WILBURN, Tom, Pvt., Comm. Off: SNOWBALL, James, Organ: Prov.
    State Troops, Enlist: Oct. 13, 1871, Disc: Oct. 20, 1871,
    Place of Birth: Groesbeck, Texas, Ranger Muster Roll.
WILCOCKS, John B., Pvt., Comm. Off: CALLAHAN, James H.,
    Organ: Mounted Rangers, Enlist: July 20, 1855, Disc: Oct. 19,
    1855, Place of Birth: Lockhart, 2 monts, 29 days service,
    Ranger Muster Roll.
WILCOX, A.J., 2nd Sgt., Comm. Off: WALLACE, Warren, Organ: Fron-
    tier Company Nueces Co., Enlist: June 29, 1874, Place of
    Birth: Nueces County, Ranger Muster Roll.
WILDER, Jack, Pvt., Comm. Off: WOOD, J.D., Organ: Prov. Mounted
    State Troops, Enlist: Oct. 9, 1871, Disc: Nov. 13, 1871,
    Place of Birth: Limestone County, Ranger Muster Roll.
WILES, Joel B.G., Pvt., Comm. Off: WALKER, John G., Capt.,
    Organ: Mtd. Vol., Enlist: Nov. 1854, Ranger Muster Roll.
WILEY, Adams, Pvt., Comm. Off: WILLIAMs, Samuel J., Organ: Prov.
    State Troops, Co. A, Enlist: Oct. 9, 1871, Disc: Nov. 13,
    1871, Place of Birth: Limestone County, Ranger Muster Roll.
WILEY, W.W., Pvt., Comm. Off: FOSTER, B.S., Organ: Co. B, Fron-
    tier Battalion, Enlist: April 1, 1876, Disc: Aug. 31, 1876,
    Place of Birth: Coleman County, Ranger Muster Roll.
WILEY, W.W., Pvt., Comm. Off: SPARKS, J.C., Organ: Co. C, Fron-
    tier Battalion, Enlist: Aug. 31, 1877, Disc: Feb. 28, 1878,
    Place of Birth: Coleman County, 6 months service, Ranger
    Muster Roll.
WILHOIT, A.J., Pvt., Comm. Off: BAKER, D.P., Organ: Frontier
    Forces, Co. F, Enlist: Nov. 5, 1870, Disc: June 15, 1871,
    Place of Birth: Decatur, Wise County, Ranger Muster Roll.
WILHOIT, A.J., Pvt., Comm. Off: STEVENS, G.W., Organ: Co. B,
    Frontier Battalion, Enlist: May 16, 1874, Disc: Dec. 12, 1874,
    Place of Birth: Lost Valley, 6 months, 28 days, Ranger Mus-
    ter Roll.
WILKERSON, James, Pvt., Comm. Off: WILLIAMS, Samuel J.,
    Organ: Prov. State Troops, Co. A, Enlist: Oct. 9, 1871,
    Disc: Nov. 13, 1871, Place of Birth: Limestone County, Ranger
    Muster Roll.
WILKES, C.M., Pvt., Comm. Off: ROBERTS, D.W., Organ: Co. D, Fron-
    tier Battalion, Enlist: March 1, 1877, Disc: May 31, 1878, 3
    months service, Ranger Muster Roll.
WILKES, U.E.T., Pvt., Comm. Off: HALL, A.L.,Organ: Special State

WILKES, U.E.T., Pvt., (Continued)
   Troops, Enlist: May 1, 1877, Disc: Feb. 28, 1878, Place of
   Birth: Clinton, Texas, 10 months service, Ranger Muster Roll.
WILKINS, Mathew D., Pvt., Comm. Off: HENRY, W.R., Organ: Rangers,
   Enlist: June 19, 1859, Place of Birth: Frio River, Ranger
   Muster Roll.
WILKINSON, S.H., Pvt., Comm. Off: MCNELLY, L.H., Organ: Washing-
   ton Co. Vol. Militia, Enlist: Aug. 20, 1874, Disc: Sept. 12,
   1874, Place of Birth: Austin, Texas, 22 days service, Ranger
   MusterRoll.
WILKS, B.T., Pvt., Comm. Off: MCNELLY, L.H., Organ: Washington Co.
   Vol. Militia, Enlist: June 22, 1875, Disc: Dec. 31, 1875, Place
   of Birth: Austin, Texas, 6 months, 9 days service, Ranger Mus-
   ter Roll.
WILKS, H.P., Pvt., Comm. Off: MCADAMS, W.C., Organ: Palo Pinto
   County, Enlist: Dec. 13, 1873, Disc: April 13, 1874, Place of
   Birth: Palo Pinto County, 4 months service, Ranger Muster
   Roll.
WILKS, H.M., Pvt., Comm. Off: ROBERTS, D.W., Organ: Co. D, Fron-
   tier Battalion, Enlist: Dec. 1, 1877, Disc: Feb. 28, 1877, 3
   months, Ranger Muster Roll.
WILLET, Aldwin, 2nd Corp., Comm. Off: CAMPBELL, G.W., Organ: Mon-
   tague Co. Rangers, Enlist: Dec. 13, 1873, Disc: Feb. 13, 1874,
   Place of Birth: Montague County, 2 months service, Ranger Mus-
   ter Roll.
WILLEY, Ira L., Pvt., Comm. Off: JOHNSON, Thomas J., Organ: Mtd.
   Rangers, Enlist: April 21, 1860, Disc: Nov. 10, 1860, Place
   of Birth: Fort Worth, Due B. MONROE 30. for pistol, Ranger
   Muster Roll.
WILLIAM, Spy, Comm. Off: ROSS, Peter F., Capt., Organ: Spy Com-
   pany, Enlist: 1860, Serv. from July 1 to Aug. 26, 60: 1 mo. &
   26 days at $25--$46.66. R&F 39; 1 Pay Roll.
WILLIAM, Fields SEE FIELDS, William.
WILLIAM, Henry, Pvt., Comm. Off: FISHER, J.C., Organ: Prov. State
   Troops, Co. C, 3 Regt., Enlist: Oct. 9, 1871, Disc: Nov. 18,
   1871, Place of Birth: Springfield, Texas, Ranger Muster Roll.
WILLIAMS, Alfred N., Pvt., Comm. Off: MCCULLOCH, Henry E., Capt.,
   Organ: Texas Vols., Enlist: Oct. 25, 1848, Disc: Dec. 8, 1848,
   Age: 21, 1 month, 12 days service, Ranger Muster Roll.
WILLIAM, Allen A., Bugler, Comm. Off: MCCULLOCH, Henry E.,
   Organ: Texas Mounted Vol., Enlist: Oct. 25, 1847, Age: 20,
   light eyes, light hair, 5'11", Place of Birth: Seguin.
WILLIAM, Allen A., (Alfred), Bugler, Comm. Off: MCCULLOCH, Henry
   E., Capt., Organ: Texas Volunteers, Enlist: Oct. 25, 1847,
   Disc: Oct. 24, 1848, Age: 20; Height: 5'7", light comp., light
   eyes, light hair, Place of Birth: Seguin, Texas, 12 months of
   service, Ranger Muster Roll.
WILLIAMS, Allen, Pvt., Comm. Off: WOOD, J.D., Organ: Prov. Mtd.
   State Troops, Enlist: Oct. 9, 1871, Disc: Nov. 13, 1871,
   Place of Birth: Limestone County, Ranger Muster Roll.
WILLIAMS, Albert, Pvt., Comm. Off: HALL, A.B., Organ: Prov. State
   Troops, Detached, Enlist: Oct. 13, 1871, Disc: Oct. 20, 1871,
   Place of Birth: Groesbeck, Texas, Ranger Muster Roll.
WILLIAMS, Charles, Pvt., Comm. Off: FITZHGUH, Wm., Organ: Texas

WILLIAMS, Charles, Pvt., (Continued)
Militia, Mtd. Vol., Enlist: Nov. 2, 1854, Disc: Feb. 2, 1854,
Place of Birth: McKinney, Texas, Age: 22, 3 months service,
Ranger Muster Roll.

WILLIAMS, Charles, Pvt., Comm. Off: SUBLETT, David L., Capt.,
Organ: Co. of Texas Rangers, Enlist: Feb. 4, 61 at Elm Creek
for 3 mos., Killed, supposedly by CURLEY, Age: 23, R&F 57;
En. Off: D.L. SUBLETT; Mus. Off: D.L. SUBLETT; Val. H: $130;
HE: $30; Guns: $20; Pistols: $35; Serv. 1 mo. 23 days at $25-
Amt. of pay $44.16, less stoppages to F.C. DOWNS of $57.24;
called into serv. of state by Gov. Sam HOUSTON from Feb. 7, 61
for 3 months; 1 Muster Roll & 1 Pay Roll; Ammunition stores,
pack mules, etc. turned over to Capt. J.M. KNIGHT's Co.. Men
residing in vicinity of station may be discharged before marching.

WILLIAMS, Charles, Pvt., Comm. Off: ROSS, L.S., Capt.,
Organ: Ranger Company, Enlist: Sept. 22, 60 at Waco for 12
mos., Serv. from Sept. 22, 60 to Feb. 5, 61; 4 mos. & 14 days
at $25-$111.66, Age: 23. R&F 66; En. Off: Capt. ROSS; Mus.
Off: J.M.W. HALL; Appraiser Jas. H. SWINDELLS; Val. H: $150;
HE: $25; Gun: $30; Pistol: $30; elec. certif. with roll; Co.
sta. at Ft. Belknap Oct. 17 & Nov. 22, 60; 1 Muster & 1 Pay
Roll. E.F. SANDIFER, Power Atty. $160.

WILLIAMS, Charles, Pvt., Comm. Off: ROSS, L.S., Organ: Mounted
Rangers, Enlist: Sept. 22, 1860, Age: 23, Place of Birth: Waco,
Ranger Muster Roll.

WILLIAMS, Charles, Pvt., Comm. Off: ROBERTS, D.W., Organ: Co. D,
Frontier Battalion, Enlist: June 1, 1875, Disc: Nov. 30, 1875,
Age: 18, 5'8", fair, blue eyes, dark hair, farmer, Place of
Birth: Parker County, Texas, 6 months, Ranger Muster Roll.

WILLIAMS, Charles A., Pvt., Comm. Off: FITZHUGH, Wm., Organ: Tex.
Militia, Mtd. Vol., Enlist: Nov. 2, 1854, Disc: Feb. 2, 1854,
Age: 22, Place of Birth: McKinney, Texas, 3 months service,
Ranger Muster Roll.

WILLIAMS, D.K., Dishcarged, Pvt., Comm. Off: WILLIAMS, John,
Organ: Second Co. of Texas Rangers, Enlist: Oct. 30, 1858, 6
months, 20 days, Ranger Muster Roll.

WILLIAMS, D.S., Pvt., Comm. Off: CONNELL, J.G., Organ: Brown and
San Saba Co. Rangers, Enlist: Jan. 6, 1874, Disc: March 26,
1874, Place of Birth: Brown and San Saba Counties, 2 months,
20 days service, Ranger Muster Roll.

WILLIAMS, Daniel W., Pvt., Comm. Off: ENGLISH, Levi, Organ: Mtd.
Volunteers, Enlist: Aug. 6, 1855, Disc: Nov. 13, 1855, Place
of Birth: Bexar County, 3 months, 6 days service, Ranger Muster Roll.

WILLIAMS, David, Sgt., Comm. Off: NELSON, G.H., Capt., Organ: Tex.
Mtd. Vols., Enlist: Oct. 10, 1857, Disc: Dec. 8, 1857, Place
of Birth: Attascosa, 2 months service, Ranger Muster Roll.

WILLIAMS, Eli, 2nd Corp., Comm. Off: WILLIAMS, Samuel J.,
Organ: Prov. State Troops, Co. A, Enlist: Oct. 9, 1871,
Disc: Nov. 13, 1871, Place of Birth: Limestone County, Ranger
Muster Roll.

WILLIAMS, E.H., 1st Sgt., Comm. Off: SNOWBALL, James, Organ: Prov.
State Troops, Enlist: Oct. 13, 1871, Disc: Oct. 20, 1871,

WILLIAMS, E.H., 1st Sgt., (Continued)
   Place of Birth: Groesbeck, Texas, Ranger Muster Roll.
WILLIAMS, Frank, Pvt., Comm. Off: SNOWBALL, James, Organ: Prov.
   State Troops, Enlist: Oct. 13, 1871, Disc: Oct.20, 1871, Place
   of Birth: Groesbeck, Texas, Ranger Muster Roll.
WILLIAMS, G., Pvt., Comm. Off: DOLAN, Pat, Organ: Co. F, Frontier
   Battalion, Enlist: April 1, 1877, Disc: Sept. 18, 1877, Place
   of Birth: Kerr County, 5 months, 18 days service, Ranger Mus-
   ter Roll.
WILLIAMS, Geo., Pvt., Comm. Off: CURETON, J.J., Organ: Rangers,
   Enlist: Dec. 5, 1860, See Newspaper Clippings, Ranger Muster
   Roll.
WILLIAMS, George, Pvt., Comm. Off: JONES, Stephen F., Organ: Min.
   Men, Detached, Enlist: March 26, 1860, Disc: Aug. 29, 1860,
   Place of Birth: Palo Pinto, Honorably discharged June 30, 1860,
   Ranger Muster Roll.
WILLIAMS, J.G.W., Pvt., Comm. Off: WADE, J.M., Organ: Co. I, Min.
   Men, Cook County, Enlist: July 24, 1872, Disc: July 6, 1873,
   Place of Birth: Cook County, 17 days of service, Ranger Muster
   Roll.
WILLIAMS, George W., Pvt., Comm. Off: DALRYMPLE, W.C., Organ: Mtd
   Rangers, Enlist: Jan. 14, 1860, Disc: Oct. 13, 1860, Age: 37,
   Place of Birth: Liberty Hill, Ranger MusterRoll.
WILLIAMS, Goin H., Farrier, Comm. Off: BOURLAND, James,
   Organ: Texas Mounted Rangers, Enlist: Oct. 28, 1858,
   Disc: Jan. 11, 1859, Place of Birth: Gainesville, Texas, 2
   months, 14 days service, Ranger Muster Roll.
WILLIAMS, H., Pvt., Comm. Off: CURETON, J.J., Capt., Organ: Ran-
   gers, Enlist: Dec. 5, 1860, See Newspaper Clippings, Ranger
   Muster Roll.
WILLIAMS, H.A., Pvt., Comm.Off: HAMNER, H.A., Capt.,
   Organ: Rangers, Enlist: Jan. 14, 60 at Jacksboro for 12 mos.;
   R&F 86; Citizens of Wise, Parker, Montague, Young & Jack
   Counties in public meeting at Jacksboro org. Co. for protection
   of Frontier; 1 Muster Roll.
WILLIAMS, Hensford B., Pvt., Comm. Off: HENRY, William R.,
   Organ: Co. C, Mounted Volunteers, Enlist: Dec. 14, 1854,
   Disc: March 14, 1855, Age: 25, Place of Birth: San Antonio, 3
   months service, Ranger Muster Roll.
WILLIAMS, Hezekiel, Pvt., Comm. Off: CALLAHAN, James H.,
   Organ: Mounted Rangers, Enlist: July 20, 1855, Disc: Oct.19,
   1855, Place of Birth: Prairie Lee, 2 months, 29 days service,
   Ranger Muster Roll.
WILLIAMS, James, Pvt., Comm. Off: WALKER, Joseph, Organ: Rangers
   for Cortinas War, Enlist: Nov. 30, 1859, Disc: Jan. 20, 1860,
   Age: 25, Place of Birth: Banquete, Ranger Muster Roll.
WILLIAMS, James, 1st Sgt., Comm. Off: WILLIAMS, John, Organ: 2nd
   Co. of Texas Rangers, Enlist: Nov. 2, 1858, 3 months, 14 days
   Ranger Muster Roll.
WILLIAMS, J., Pvt., Comm. Off: MCNELLY, L.H., Organ: Washington
   Co. Vol. Militia, Enlist: May 20, 1875, Disc: June 25, 1875,
   Place of Birth: Austin, Texas, 1 month, 5 days service, Deser-
   ted, Ranger Muster Roll.
WILLIAMS, J.C., Pvt., Comm. Off: HOLT, John T., Capt., Organ: Ft.

WILLIAMS, J.C., Pvt., (Continued)
Bend Rifles, Mtd. Riflemen (Rangers), Enlist: Jan. 14, 60 at Richmond, R&F 64; 1 Muster Roll dated Jan. 16, 60.

WILLIAMS, James, Pvt., Comm. Off: MCNELLY, L.H., Organ: Washington Co. Vol. Militia, Enlist: Dec. 20, 1875, Disc: May 31, 1876, Place of Birth: Austin, Texas, 5 months, 10 days service, Ranger Muster Roll.

WILLIAMS, Jas. J., Pvt., Comm. Off: HILL, A.C., Sgt., Organ: Min. Men, Enlist: Jan. 19, 60 at Brownsville, for 12 months; unless sooner discharged, Age: 25. R&F 21; A.C. HILL, En. & Mus. Off; W.B. WRATHER & Louis COWEN, Apprs.; H: $200; HE: $35; Gun: $35; Pistol: $30; Co. sta. at Austin Dec. 30, 59; at Brownsville Feb. 1, 60. Co. called into service of state by Gov. HOUSTON Dec. 30, 59. 1 Muster Roll.

WILLIAMS, James J., Pvt., Comm. Off: HILL, A.C., Organ: Mounted Vol. for Cortinas War, Enlist: Jan. 19, 1860, Disc: Feb. 1, 1860, Ranger Muster Roll.

WILLIAMS, J.H., Pvt., Comm. Off: MCCLURE, D.H., Organ: Co. T, Min. Men, Palo Pinto Co., Enlist: Sept. 5, 1872, Disc: Aug. 12, 1873, Place of Birth: Palo Pinto County, 120 days of service, Ranger Muster Roll.

WILLIAMS, James, Teamster, Comm. Off: MCNELLY, L.H., Organ: Washington Co. Vol. Militia, Enlist: Nov. 1, 1876, Disc: Feb., 1877, Place of Birth: Austing, Texas, No record of pay, Ranger Muster Roll.

WILLIAMS, John, Pvt., Comm. Off: MCNELLY, L.H., Organ: Washington Co. Vol. Militia, Enlist: Dec. 1, 1875, Disc: Feb. 5, 1876, Place of Birth: Austin, Texas, 2 months, 5 days service, Ranger Muster Roll.

WILLIAMS, John, Pvt., Comm. Off: WALKER, Joseph, Organ: Rangers for Cortinas War, Enlist: Nov. 30, 1859, Disc: Jan. 20, 1860, Age: 19, Place of Birth: Banquete, Ranger Muster Roll.

WILLIAMS, John, Pvt., Comm. Off: LEWIS, G.K., Capt., Organ: Texas Mtd. Vol., Enlist: Sept. 10, 1852, Disc: Mar. 13, 1853, Age: 30, Place of Birth: Brownsville, Texas, Ranger Muster Roll.

WILLIAMS, Joseph, Pvt., Comm. Off: ENGLISH, Levi, Organ: Mounted Volunteers, Enlist: Aug. 6, 1855, Disc: Nov. 13, 1855, Place of Birth: Bexar County, 3 months, 8 days service, Ranger Muster Roll.

WILLIAMS, John S., Pvt., Comm. Off: WALKER, Dixon, Lt., Organ: Mtd. Vols., Enlist: Feb. 25, 1860, Disc: May 18, 1860, 2 months, 24 days service, Ranger Muster Roll.

WILLIAMS, John, Capt., Comm. Off: WILLIAMS, John, Organ: Second Co. of Texas Rangers, Enlist: Oct. 1858, 8 months service, Ranger Muster Roll.

WILLIAMS, John A., Pvt., Comm. Off: TOBIN, Wm. G., Organ: Mtd. Volunteers, Enlist: Oct. 18, 1859, Disc: Nov. 3, 1859, Place of Birth: San Marcos, Ranger Muster Roll.

WILLIAMS, John H., Pvt., Comm. Off: BURLESON, Ed, Organ: Mounted Rangers, Enlist: Jan. 20, 1860, Disc: Sept. 7, 1860, Age: 30, Place of Birth: San Marcos, Ranger Muster Roll.

WILLIAMS, Joseph, Pvt., Comm. Off: HALL, A.B., Organ: Prov. State Troops, Detached, Enlist: Oct. 13, 1871, Disc: Oct. 20, 1871, Place of Birth: Groesbeck, Texas, Ranger Muster Roll.

WILLIAMS, Joseph H., Pvt., Comm. Off: FORD, John S., Organ: 3rd
    Company of Rangers, Enlist: Feb. 11, 1860, Disc: May 17, 1860,
    Age: 20, Place of Birth: Brownsville, Ranger Muster Roll.
WILLIAMS, J.M., Pvt., Comm. Off: WILLIAMS, John, Organ: Second Co
    of Texas Rangers, Enlist: Oct. 20, 1858, 3 months, 8 days of
    service, Ranger Muster Roll.
WILLIAMS, John, Lt., Comm. Off: WILLIAMS, John, Lt., Organ: Un-
    known, Enlist: May 24, 1858, Disc: July 24, 1858, 2 months of
    service, Ranger Muster Roll.
WILLIAMS, John S., Pvt., Comm. Off: FORD, John S., Organ: 3rd Co.
    of Rangers, Enlist: March 1, 1860, Disc: May 17, 1860, Age: 22,
    Place of Birth: Brownsville, Ranger Muster Roll.
WILLIAMS, John T., Pvt., Comm. Off: DALRYMPLE, W.C., Organ: Mtd.
    Rangers, Enlist: Jan. 14, 1860, Disc: Oct. 13, 1860, Age: 25,
    Place of Birth: Liberty Hill, Ranger Muster Roll.
WILLIAMS, J.W., Pvt., Comm. Off: PATTON, C.A., Organ: Kendall
    County Min. Men, Co. C, Enlist: July, 1873, Disc: July 6, 1873,
    Place of Birth: Kendall County, 2 days of service, Ranger Mus-
    ter Roll.
WILLIAMS, John W., Pvt., Comm. Off: FORD, John S., Organ: 3rd Co.
    of Rangers, Enlist: Jan. 20, 1860, Disc: May 17, 1860, Age: 20,
    Place of Birth: Brownsville, Ranger Muster Roll.
WILLIAMS, Kelsey, Pvt., Comm. Off: WILLIAMS, John, Lt.,
    Organ: Rangers, Enlist: May 24, 1858, Disc: July 24, 1858,
    2 months service, Ranger Muster Roll.
WILLIAMS, L.L., Pvt., Comm. Off: SELF, William B., Capt.,
    Organ: Minute Men for Young Co., Enlist: Jan. 1, 66 in Tarrant
    Co. R&F 47; En. Off: W.B. SELF; Co. raised by authority of
    A.J. HAMILTON, Provisional Governor, for service on frontier;
    1 Muster Roll, Dated Jan. 1, 66.
WILLIAMS, Lee, Pvt., Comm. Off: WOOD, J.D., Organ: Prov. Mounted
    State Troops, Enlist: Oct. 9, 1871, Disc: Nov. 13, 1871, Place
    of Birth: Limestone County, Ranger Muster Roll.
WILLIAMS, L. E., Pvt., Comm. Off: TACKITT, A.C., Organ: Young Co.
    Rangers, enlist: Jan. 6, 1874, Disc: Jan. 17, 1874, Place of
    Birth: Young County, 11 days of service, Ranger Muster Roll.
WILLIAMS, M., 2nd Corp., Comm. Off: WADE, J.M., Organ: Co. I, Min.
    Men, Cook County, Enlist: July 24, 1872, Disc: July 6, 1873,
    Place of Birth: Cook County, 8 days of service, Ranger Muster
    Roll.
WILLIAMS, M.A., Pvt., Comm. Off: WALKER, John G., Capt.,
    Organ: Mounted Volunteers, Enlist: Nov. 1854, Ranger Muster
    Roll.
WILLIAMS, M.H., Pvt., Comm. Off: MCNELLY, L.H., Organ: Washington
    Co. Vol. Militia, Enlist: April 1, 1875, Disc: Feb. 1, 1877,
    Place of Birth: Austin, Texas, 20 months, 5 days service, Ran-
    ger Muster Roll.
WILLIAMS, Peter W., Pvt., Comm. Off: CALLAHAN, James H.,
    Organ: Mounted Rangers, Enlist: July 20, 1855, Disc: Oct. 19,
    1855, 2 months, 29 days service, Ranger Muster Roll.
WILLIAMS, R.C., Pvt., Comm. Off: WILLIAMS, John, Organ: Second
    Co. of Texas Rangers, Enlist: Oct. 20, 1858, 3 months, 8 days,
    Ranger Muster Roll.
WILLIAMS, R.E., Pvt., Comm. Off: PEAK, June, Organ: Co. B, Fron-

WILLIAMS, R.E., Pvt., (Continued)
    tier Battalion, Enlist: Sept. 1, 1878, Disc: Oct. 15, 1878,
    Place of Birth: Runnels County, 1 month, 15 days service,
    Ranger Muster Roll.
WILLIAMS, R.Y., Pvt., Comm. Off: TOMLINSON, Peter, Organ: Mtd.
    Vols., Enlist: Jan. 2, 1860, Ranger Muster Roll.
WILLIAMS, R.Y., Pvt., Comm. Off: HAMPTON, G.J., Capt., Organ: Mtd.
    Ranger Volunteers, Enlist: Nov. 12, 59, Disc: Jan. 1, 60; ser-
    ved 1 mo. & 20 days at $12--$20. R&F 34; Allowances on clo-
    thing: $4.17; use of horse: $20; Rations: $4.50; Forage: $8.25;
    Total: $56.92. Co. called into State Service for suppression
    of Cortina Rebellion on Rio Grande Frontier by
    Gov. H.R. RUNNELS. 1 Pay Roll. This name is deleted on roll.
    Paid on LITTLETON's 1st Copy.
WILLIAMS, Richard, Pvt., Comm. Off: KELSO, John R., Organ: Fron-
    tier Forces, Enlist: Sept. 10, 1870, Disc: Feb. 2, 1871, Place
    of Birth: Camp Wood, Texas, Discharged Jan. 20, 1871, Ranger
    Muster Roll.
WILLIAMS, Robert Y., Pvt., Comm. Off: TOBIN, Wm. G., Organ: Mtd.
    Volunteers, Enlist: Nov. 20, 1859, Disc: Nov. 3, 1859, Place
    of Birth: Camp Runnels, Ranger Muster Roll.
WILLIAMS, Robert Y., Pvt., Comm. Off: TUMLINSON, Peter, Capt.,
    Organ: Mtd. Vols., Enlist: Jan. 1, 1860, Disc: Feb. 10, 1860,
    1 month, 10 days service, Ranger Muster Roll.
WILLIAMS, Rufus P., 2nd Corp., Comm. Off: MCCULLOCH, Henry E.,
    Organ: Texas Mounted Vol., Enlist: Oct. 25, 1847, Age: 20,
    Dark eyes, dark hair, 5'8", Place of Birth: Seguin.
WILLIAMS, Rufus P., Corp., Comm. Off: MCCULLOCH, Henry E., Capt.,
    Organ: Texas Volunteers, Enlist: Oct. 25, 1847, Disc: Oct. 24,
    1848, Age: 20; Height: 5'8", dark comp., dark eyes, dark hair,
    Place of Birth: Seguin, Texas, 12 months service, Ranger Mus-
    ter Roll.
WILLIAMS, S.B., Pvt., Comm. Off: COLDWELL, Neal, Organ: Co. F,
    Frontier Battalion, Enlist: June 25, 1875, Disc: Aug. 31, 1875,
    Age: 24, 5'11", brown hair, gray eyes, fair, Engineer, Place
    of Birth: Bourbon, Kentucky, 2 months, 6 days service, Ranger
    Muster Roll.
WILLIAMS, Samuel J., Capt., Organ: WILLIAMS, Samuel J.,
    Organ: Prov. State Troops, Co. A, Enlist: Oct. 9, 1871,
    Disc: Nov. 13, 1871, Place of Birth: Limestone County, Ranger
    Muster Roll.
WILLIAMS, Solomon, Pvt., Comm. Off: ROGERS, P.H., Capt.,
    Organ: Mtd. Vols., Enlist: Oct. 1856, Disc: Dec. 1856, 3 mos.
    service, Ranger Muster Roll. Ex. order of March, 1856.
WILLIAMS, T.F.J., Pvt., Comm. Off: MCNELLY, L.H., Organ: Washing-
    ton Co. Vol. Militia, Enlist: April 10, 1876, Disc: May 31,
    1876, Place of Birth: Austin, Texas, 1 month, 21 days service,
    Ranger Muster Roll.
WILLIAMS, Thos. M., Pvt., Comm. Off: WALKER,John G., Capt.,
    Organ: Mtd. Vol., Enlist: Nov. 1854, Ranger Muster Roll.
WILLIAMS, W.L.,Pvt., Comm. Off: CONNER, J.H., Organ: Mounted Men,
    Enlist: Dec. 2, 1857, Disc: March 2, 1858, Place of Birth: San
    Saba County, 3 months of service, Ranger Muster Roll.
WILLIAMS, W.L., Pvt., Comm. Off: JONES, John S., Organ: Texas

WILLIAMS, W.L., Pvt., (Continued)
  Rangers, Enlist: April 7, 1858, Disc: Aug. 5, 1858, Age: 25,
  Place of Birth: Comanche County, 3 months, 28 days service,
  Ranger Muster Roll.
WILLIAMS, W.S., Pvt., Comm. Off: ELKINS, J.M., Organ: Co. L, Min.
  Men, Coleman Co., Enlist: Oct. 15, 1873, Disc: Feb. 1, 1874,
  Place of Birth: Coleman County, 20 days of service, Ranger
  Muster Roll.
WILLIAMS, W.S., Pvt., Comm.Off: MALTBY, W.J., Organ: Co. E, Fron-
  tier Battalion, Enlist: June 6, 1874, Disc: May 31, 1875,
  Place of Birth: Coleman County, 11 months, 25 days service,
  Ranger Muster Roll.
WILLIAMS, W.S., 1st Corp., Comm. Off: FOSTER, B.S., Organ: Co. E,
  Frontier Battalion, Enlist: June 1, 1875, Disc: Aug. 31, 1876,
  Age: 42, 6', light, blue eyes, light hair, farmer, Place of
  Birth: North Carolina, 15 months service, Ranger Muster Roll.
WILLIAMS, W.S., Pvt., Comm. Off: CONNELL, J.G., Organ: Brown and
  San Saba County Rangers, Enlist: Jan. 6, 1874, Disc: Mar. 26,
  1874, Place of Birth: Brown and San Saba counties, 2 months,
  20 days service, Ranger Muster Roll.
WILLIAMS, W.S., Pvt., Comm. Off: ADAMS, Geroge H., Organ: Co. G,
  Minute Men, Brown Co., Enlist: June 10, 1872, Disc: Aug. 21,
  1872, Place of Birth: Brown County, 35 days service, Ranger
  Muster Roll.
WILLIAMS, W.T., 4th Sgt., Comm. Off: SANSOM, John W., Capt.,
  Organ: Rangers, Enlist: Aug. 31, 1859, Disc: Nov. 30, 1859,
  3 months service, Ranger Muster Roll.
WILLIAMS, Wash., Pvt., Comm. Off: SNOWBALL, James, Organ: Prov.
  State Troops, Enlist: Oct. 13, 1871, Disc: Oct. 20, 1871,
  Place of Birth: Groesbeck, Texas, Ranger Muster Roll.
WILLIAMS, Wm., Pvt., Comm. Off: SMITY, C.C., Organ: Co. R, Min.
  Men, Mason County, Enlist: Dec. 9, 1873, Disc: Jan. 16, 1874,
  Place of Birth: Mason County, 5 days of service, Ranger Mus-
  ter Roll.
WILLIAMS, William, Pvt., Comm. Off: MCCULLOCH, Henry E., Capt.,
  Organ: Texas Vols., Enlist: Oct. 25, 1847, Disc: Dec. 6, 1848,
  Age: 39; Height: 5'7", dk. comp., blue eyes, dk. hair, Place
  of Birth: Bastrop, Texas, 13 months, 15 days service, Ranger
  Muster Roll.
WILLIAMS, William, Pvt., Comm. Off: MCCULLOCH, Henry E., Capt.,
  Organ: Tex. Mtd. Vols., Enlist: Nov. 5, 1850, Disc: Nov. 5,
  1851, Age: 38, Enlisted at: Austin, Texas, 12 months service,
  Ranger Muster Roll.
WILLIAMS, William, Pvt., Comm. Off: MCCULLOCH, Henry E.,
  Organ: Texas Mounted Vol., Enlist: Oct. 25, 1847, Age: 39, blue
  eys, dark hair, 5'7", Place of Birth: Bastrop.
WILLIAMS, William, 1st Corp., Comm. Off: FISHER, J.C.,
  Organ: Prov. State Troops, Co. C, 3rd Regt., Enlist: Oct. 9,
  1871, Disc: Nov. 18, 1871, Place of Birth: Springfield, Tex.,
  Ranger Muster Roll.
WILLIAMS, William D., Pvt., Comm. Off: LEWIS, W. Charles, 1st Lt.,
  Organ: Detachment of Minute Men, Mason County, Enlist: May,
  1860, Served 31 days. R&F 15; On Scout on Llano River & near
  Ft. Mason, May 11--28; 1 Scout Report, May, 1860.

WILLIAMS, Wm. D.,Pvt., Comm. Off: LEWIS, W. Charles, Organ: Min.
    Men, Enlist: April 4, 1860, Disc: June 15, 1860, Age: 19,
    Place of Birth: Mason, Ranger Muster Roll.
WILLIAMS, Wm. H., Pvt., Comm. Off: DARNELL, N.H., Organ: Mounted
    Rangers, Enlist: April 14, 1860, Disc: Aug. 13, 1860, Place
    of Birth: Dallas, Ranger Muster Roll.
WILLIAMS, William L., Pvt., Comm. Off: DALRYMPLE, W.C.,
    Organ: Mounted Rangers, Enlist: Jan. 14, 1860, Disc: Oct. 13,
    1860, Age: 29, Place of Birth: Liberty Hill, Ranger Muster
    Roll.
WILLIAMS, William D., Pvt., Comm. Off: LEWIS, W. Charles, Lt.,
    Organ: Minute Men, Mason County, Enlist: April 4, 1860,
    Disc: June 15, 1860, 73 days service, Ranger Muster Roll.
WILLIAMSON, L.E., Pvt., Comm. Off: MALTBY, W.J., Organ: Co. E,
    Frontier Battalion, Enlist: June 6, 1874, Disc: Dec. 12, 1874,
    Place of Birth: Coleman County, 6 months, 7 days service,
    Ranger Muster Roll. Los Angeles, California, Soldiers Home.
WILLIAMSON, L.E., Pvt., Comm. Off: CONNELL, J.G., Organ: Brown
    and San Saba Co. Rangers, Enlist: Jan. 6, 1874, Disc: Mar. 26,
    1874, Place of Birth: Brown and San Saba Counties, 2 months,
    20 days service, Ranger Muster Roll.
WILLIAMSON, John, Pvt., Comm. Off: TOBIN, Wm. G., Organ: Mounted
    Volunteers, Enlist: Oct. 30, 1859, Disc: Nov. 3, 1859, Place
    of Birth: Helena, Ranger Muster Roll.
WILLIE, Frederick, Pvt., Comm. Off: CONNER, John H., Organ: Mtd.
    Rangers, Enlist: Jan. 20, 1860, 12 months, Age: 25, Place of
    Birth: Austin, Ranger Muster Roll.
WILLIE, Frederic, Pvt., Comm. Off: FORD,John S., Organ: 2nd Co.
    of Rangers, Enlist: Nov. 10, 1858, Disc: May 10, 1859, Age: 24,
    Place of Birth: Austin, Ranger Muster Roll.
WILLIFORD, B.F.,Pvt., Comm. Off: TACKITT, A.C., Organ: Youny Co.
    Rangers, Enlist: Jan. 6, 1874, Disc: Feb. 14, 1874, Place of
    Birth: Young County, 39 days of service, Ranger Muster Roll.
WILLINGHAM, G.S., Pvt., Comm. Off: LEDBETTER, Wm. H., Organ: Co.
    N, Minute Men, San Saba Co., Enlist: Sept. 13, 1872, Disc: Oct.
    26, 1872, Place of Birth: San Saba County, No service recorded,
    Ranger Muster Roll.
WILLINGHAM, Deloney, Pvt., Comm. Off: WILLINGHAM, John,
    Organ: Co. U, Minute Men, Montague Co., Enlist: April 20, 1872,
    Place of Birth: Dec. 21, 1873, Place of Birth: Montague County,
    98 days of service, Ranger Muster Roll.
WILLINGHAM, John, Lt., Comm. Off: WILLINGHAM, John, Organ: Co. U,
    Minute Men, Montague Co., Enlist: April 20, 1872, Disc: Dec.
    21, 1873, Place of Birth: Montague County, 167 days of service,
    Ranger Muster Roll.
WILLINGHAM, W.B., Pvt., Comm. Off: WILLINGHAM, John, Organ: Co. U,
    Minute Men, Montague Co., Enlist: April 20, 1872, Disc: Dec.
    21, 1873, Place of Birth: Montague County, 90 days service,
    Ranger Muster Roll.
WILLINGHAM, W.C., Pvt., Comm. Off: BOURLAND,James, Organ: Texas
    Mounted Rangers, Enlist: Oct. 28, 1858, Disc: Jan. 28, 1858,
    Place of Birth: Gainesville, Texas, 3 months service, Ranger
    Muster Roll.
WILLIS, Henry, Pvt., Comm. Off: SNOWBALL, James, Organ: Prov.

WILLIS, Henry, Pvt., (Continued)
    State Troops, Enlist: Oct. 13, 1871, Disc: Oct. 20, 1871,
    Place of Birth: Groesbeck, Texas, Ranger Muster Roll.
WILLIS, Henry J., Pvt., Comm. Off: MCCULLOCH, Henry E., Capt.,
    Organ: Texas Mtd. Vols., Enlist: Nov. 5, 1850, Disc: Sept.
    15, 1851, Age: 35, Died Sept. 15, 1851, Enlisted: Austin, Tex.,
    Ranger Muster Roll.
WILLIS, John, Pvt., Comm. Off: WILLIAMS, John, Organ: Second Co.
    of Texas Rangers, Enlist: Oct. 13, 1859, 1 month, 17 days,
    Ranger Muster Roll.
WILLS, Benjamin N., Pvt., Comm. Off: SUBLETT, David L., Capt.,
    Organ: Co. of Texas Rangers, Enlist: Jan. 19, 61 at Waco for
    3 mos., Mus. out May 14, 61 at Waco, Age: 24. R&F 57; En.
    Off: L.S. ROSS; Mus. Off: D.L. SUBLETT; Val. H: $100 (?),
    HE: $25; Guns: $30; Pistols: $35; Serv. 3 mos. 26 days at
    $25-Amt. of pay $96.66, less stoppages of: $27.19 to
    F.C. DOWNS, and to J. THOMASON $41.38 - Total stoppages
    $68.53-Bal. Paid $28.09; Mus. Roll gives stoppages to
    J. tHOMASON as $28.25; Called into serv. of state by Gov.
    Sam HOUSTON from Feb. 7, 61 for 3 mos.; 1 muster Roll & 1
    Pay Roll; Ammunition stores, pack mules, etc. turned to
    Capt. J.M. KNIGHT's Co.. Men residing in vicinity of station
    may be discharged before marching.
WILLS, Levi, Pvt., Comm. Off: ROGERS, P.H., Capt., Organ: Mtd.
    Vol., Enlist: Oct. 1854, Disc: Dec. 1854, 3 months service,
    Ranger Muster Rolls. Ex. order of March, 1856.
WILLIS, O.J., 1st Sgt., Comm. Off: TACKITT, A.C., Organ: Young
    County Rangers, Enlist: Jan. 6, 1874, Disc: Feb. 14, 1874,
    Place of Birth: Young County Rangers, 39 days of service,
    Ranger Muster Roll.
WILLSE, George, 2nd Sgt., Comm. Off: LEWIS, G.K., Capt.,
    Organ: Texas Mtd. Vol., Enlist: Sept. 10, 1852, Disc: March
    13, 1853, Age: 23, Place of Birth: Brownsville, Texas, Ranger
    Muster Roll.
WILLSON, Alphonse, Pvt., Comm. Off: FORD, John S., Organ: 3rd Co.
    of Rangers, Enlist: Mar. 1, 1860, Disc: May 17, 1860, Age: 28,
    Place of Birth: Brownsville, Ranger Muster Roll.
WILLSON, Edward, Pvt., Comm. Off: FISHER, J.C., Organ: Prov. State
    Troops, Co. C, 3 Regt., Enlist: Oct. 9, 1871, Disc: Nov. 18,
    1871, Place of Birth: Springfield, Texas, Ranger Muster Roll.
WILLSON, Thomas C., Pvt., Comm. Off: DALRYMPLE, W.C., Organ: Mtd.
    Rangers, Enlist: Jan. 14, 1860, Disc: Oct. 13, 1860, Age: 18,
    Place of Birth: Liberty Hill, Ranger Muster Roll.
WILLSON, Wm., Pvt., Comm. Off: SNOWBALL, James, Organ: Prov.
    State Troops, Enlist: Oct. 13, 1871, Disc: Oct. 20, 1871,
    Place of Birth: Groesbeck, Texas, Ranger Muster Roll.
WILMETH, W.C., Pvt., Comm. Off: SUBLETT, David L., Capt.,
    Organ: Co. of Texas Rangers, Enlist: Feb. 4, 61 at Elm Creek
    for 3 months, Mus. out May 14, 61 at Waco, R&F 57; En. Off:
    D.L. SUBLETT; Mus. Off: D.L. SUBLETT; Val. H: $180; HE: $20;
    Guns: $20; Pistols: $30; Serv. 3 mos. 11 days at $25- Amt. of
    pay $84.16, less stoppages of $26.90 to F.C. DOWNS - Bal. pd.
    $57.26; Called into serv. of state by Gov. Sam HOUSTON from
    Feb. 7, 61 for 3 months; 1 Muster Roll & 1 Pay Roll; Ammuni-

WILMETH, W.C., Pvt., (Continued)
tion stores, pack mules, etc. turned over to Capt. J.M. KNIGHT
Co.. Men residing in vicinity of station may be discharged before marching.

WILTAN, W.T., Pvt., Comm. Off: JOHNSON, T.J., Capt., Organ: Ran-
ger Company, Enlist: April 21, 1860, Serv. to Nov. 10, 60, 6
mos. & 20 days at $25-Total $166.66; less stoppages:
J.M. GIBBINS $17.10, State $30, RATLIFF & BUCHANAN $10.80,
G.W. NEWMAN $10.65, TURNER & DAGGETT $100, WOODS $7.50,
GOODLET & Co. $2. R&F 99; 1 Pay Roll.

WILTON, W.T., Pvt., Comm. Off: JOHNSON, Thomas J., Organ: Mounted
Rangers, Enlist: April 21, 1860, Disc: Nov. 10, 1860, Place of
Birth: Fort Worth, Due B. MONROE 30. for pistol, Ranger Muster
Roll.

WIMBERLEY, Jas., Pvt., Comm. Off: INGRAM, James, and GRAY, S.B.,
Organ: Minute Men, Enlist: Feb. 19, 1872, Disc: April, 1872,
Place of Birth: Blanco County, 23 days service, Ranger Muster
Roll.

WIMBERLY, G.C., Pvt., Comm. Off: FORD, John S., Organ: 3rd Co. of
Rangers, Enlist: Mar. 1, 1860, Disc: May, 17, 1860, Age: 32,
Place of Birth: Brownsville, Stop for wages $15, Ranger Muster
Roll.

WIMBERLY, J.B., Pvt., Comm. Off: HARRELL, J.M., Organ: Co. K,
Frontier Forces, Enlist: Sept. 16, 1870, Disc: Feb. 20, 1871,
Place of Birth: Penal Ranch, Died March 11, 1922. Discharged
Feb. 16, 1870, Ranger Muster Roll.

WIMBERLY, Joseph (James), Pvt., Comm. Off: MCCULLOCH, Henry E.,
Capt., Organ: Tex. Mtd. Vols., Enlist: Nov. 5, 1850, Disc: Nov.
5, 1851, Age: 25, Enlisted at: Austin, Texas, 12 months service, Ranger Muster Roll.

WINCOTHE, W.B., Pvt., Comm. Off: CARMACK, Thos. K., Organ: Mtd.
Rangers, Enlist: Dec. 14, 1857, Disc: Mar. 14, 1858, Place of
Birth: Travis County, 3 months service, Ranger Muster Roll.

WINDERS, L., Pvt., Comm. Off: EASTIN, S.W., Organ: Jack County
Rangers, Enlist: Dec. 3, 1873, Disc: April 3, 1874, Place of
Birth: Jack County, 4 months service, Ranger Muster Roll.

WINDHAM, C., Pvt., Comm. Off: ADAMS, George H., Organ: Co. G,
Minute Men, Enlist: June 10, 1872, Disc: Aug. 21, 1872, Place
of Birth: Brown County, 52 days of service, Ranger Muster Roll.

WINDHAM, Cal, Pvt., Comm. Off: CONNELL, J.G., Organ: Brown and
San Saba Co. Rangers, Enlist: Jan. 6, 1874, Disc: March 26,
1874, Place of Birth: Brown and San Saba Counties, 2 months,
20 days service, Ranger Muster Roll.

WINDHAM, C., Pvt., Comm. Off: JONES, J.W., Organ: Co. No. 4, Min.
Men, Callahan, Enlist: Oct. 30, 1873, Disc: March 30, 1874,
Place of Birth: Callahan County, 30 days of service, Ranger
Muster Roll.

WINDHAM, J.L., Pvt., Comm. Off: JONES, J.W., Organ: Co. No. 4,
Minute Men, Callahan, Enlist: Oct. 30, 1873, Disc: March 30,
1874, Place of Birth: Callahan County, 37 days of service,
Ranger Muster Roll.

WINDHAM, P.S., Pvt., Comm. Off: FOSTER, B.S., Organ: Co. E, Frontier Battalion, Enlist: Sept. 1, 1876, Disc: Dec. 1, 1876,
Place of Birth: Coleman County, 3 months service, Transferred
to Co. A, Dec. 1, 76, Ranger Muster Roll. Steeple Rock, New
Mex.

WINDHAM, P.S., Pvt., Comm. Off: FOSTER, B.S., Organ: Co. E, Frontier Battalion, Enlist: April 1, 1876, Disc: Aug. 31, 1876, Place of Birth: Coleman County, 5 months service, Ranger Muster Roll.

WINDHAM, P.S., Pvt., Comm. Off: DENTON, J.M., Organ: Co. A, Frontier Battalion, Enlist: Dec. 1, 1876, Disc: May 17, 1877, Place of Birth: Frio County, 5 months, 17 days service, Ranger Muster Roll.

WING, A., Pvt., Comm. Off: IKARD, E.F., Organ: Co. C, Frontier Battalion, Enlist: May 20, 1874, Disc: Oct. 11, 1874, Place of Birth: Clay County, 4 months, 22 days service, Ranger Muster Roll.

WINKLE, Henry, Pvt., Comm. Off: DALRYMPLE, W.C., Organ: Mounted Rangers, Enlist: Aug. 27, 1860, Disc: Oct. 13, 1860, Age: 38, Place of Birth: Camp Wichita, Mustered by W.C. DALEY, Aug. 1, Ranger Muster Roll.

WINKLER, (?).A., Pvt., Comm. Off: KLEID, Peter, Organ: Co. O, Frontier Forces, Enlist: Oct. 31, 1870, Disc: May 31, 1871, Place of Birth: Camp Rio Frio, Ranger Muster Roll.

WINN, Thomas, Pvt., Comm. Off: HERRON, Andrew, Organ: Mounted Vol. for Cortinas War, Enlist: Nov. 18, 1859, Disc: Jan. 1, 1860, Place of Birth: Seguine, Ranger Muster Roll.

WINSHIP, James, Pvt., Comm. Off: HALL, J.L., Organ: Special State Troops, Enlist: Feb. 1, 1878, Disc: Feb. 28, 1878, Place of Birth: Clinton, Texas, 1 month service, Ranger Muster Roll.

WINSTON, B.A., Pvt., Comm. Off: PEAK, June, Organ: Co. B, Frontier Battalion, Enlist: Sept. 1, 1878.

WINSTON, B.A., Pvt., Comm. Off: PEAK, June, Organ: Co. B, Frontier Battalion, Enlist: Nov. 22, 1878, Disc: Nov. 30, 1878, Place of Birth: Runnels County, 9 days service, Ranger Muster Roll.

WINSTON, J.E., Pvt., Comm. Off: HOLT, John T., Capt., Organ: Ft. Bend Rifles, Mtd. Riflemen (Rangers), Enlist: Jan. 14, 60 at Richmond. R&F 64; 1 Muster Roll dated Jan. 16, 60.

WINSTON, M., Pvt., Comm. Off: MOORE, D.D., Capt., Organ: Moscow Guards, Cav. Co., Polk Co., TST, Enlist: Nov. 1860 at Moscow, Tex. R&F 76; Co. org. with 64 volunteers who agreed to meet not less than 6 or more than 7 times a year; unless called out on special duty; 1 Muster Roll.

WINSTON, Wisby, Pvt., Comm. Off: FISHER, J.C., Organ: Prov. State Troops, Co. C, 3 Regt., Enlist: Oct. 9, 1871, Disc: Nov. 18, 1871, Place of Birth: Springfield, Texas, Ranger Muster Roll.

WINTERS, Josephus, Pvt., Comm. Off: DONELSON, John, Organ: Rangers for Cortinas War, Enlist: Nov. 5, 1859, Disc: Dec. 10, 1859, Age: 19, Place of Birth: Live Oak County, Ranger Muster Roll. Service: 1 mo. 6 days at $12--$14.40; $3 allowed for clothing & $14.40 for hire of horse--total pay $31.80.

WILMITH, W.C., Pvt., Comm. Off: FITZHUGH, G.S., Capt., Organ: Ranger Co., Enlist: April 14, 60, Disc: Oct. 25, 60; served 6 mo. & 12 days at $25 - Total: $160. R&F 83; 1 Pay Roll.

WILMORE, T.N., Pvt., Comm. Off: FOSTER, B.S., Organ: Co. B, Frontier Battalion, Enlist: June 1, 1875, Disc: Nov. 30, 1875, Age: 25, 6', light hair, light eyes, light, farmer, Place of Birth: Texas, 6 months service, Ranger Muster Roll.

WILMORE, T.N., Pvt., Comm. Off: MALTBY, W.J., Organ: Co. E, Frontier Battalion, Enlist: June 6, 1874, Disc: May 31, 1875, Place of Birth: Coleman County, 11 months, 25 days service, Ranger Muster Roll.

WILMOTH, D.J., Pvt., Comm. Off: HUNTER, R.L., Organ: Rangers, Parker County, Enlist: Dec. 24, 1873, Disc: March 29, 1874, Place of Birth: Parker County, 96 days of service, Ranger Muster Roll.

WILMOTH, T.J., Pvt., Comm. Off: GILLILAND, J.C., Organ: Co. P, Minute Men, Parker County, Enlist: Sept. 12, 1872, Disc: Aug. 18, 1873, Place of Birth: Parker County, 98 days of service, Ranger Muster Roll.

WILSON, A., 4th Sgt., Comm. Off: BENTON, Nat, Capt., Organ: Rangers, Enlist: Sept. 15, 1855, Disc: Oct. 15, 1855, Age: 20, Enlisted at: Leona River, 1 month service, Ranger Muster Roll.

WILSON, A., Pvt., Comm. Off: PERRY, C.R., Organ: Co. D, Frontier Battalion, Enlist: May 25, 1874, Disc: Aug. 31, 1876, Place of Birth: Blanco County, 27 months service, Ranger Muster Roll.

WILSON, A.J., Pvt., Comm. Off: SANSOM, John W., Organ: Frontier Forces, Enlist: Aug. 25, 1870, Disc: May 31, 1871, Place of Birth: Shackleford County, Ranger Muster Roll.

WILSON, B.J., Pvt., Comm. Off: BROWN, John Henry, Organ: Texas State Troops, Enlist: July 4, 1859, Disc: Sept. 1, 1859, Place of Birth: Travis County, 1 month, 27 days service, Ranger Muster Roll..

WILSON, C., 1st Corp., Pvt., Comm. Off: HAMPTON, G.J., Capt., Organ: Mtd. Ranger Volunteers, Enlist: Nov. 12, 59 as Pvt., Dec. 12, 59 as Corp., Disc: Jan. 1, 60; served 1 mo. as Pvt. at $12-$12. 20 days as Corp. at $14-$9.33. Total 1 mo. & 20 days-$21.33. R&F 34; Allowances on: Clothing: $4.17; use of horse: $20; Rations: $4.50; Forage: $8.25. Total: $58.25. Co. called into State service for suppression of Cortina Rebellion on Rio Grande Frontier by Gov. H.R. RUNNELS. 1 Pay Roll.

WILSON, C., 4th Corp., Comm. Off: IKARD, E.F., Organ: Co. C, Frontier Battalion, Enlist: May 20, 1874, Place of Birth: Clay County, 5 months, 6 days service, Ranger Muster Roll.

WILSON, C., Pvt., Comm. Off: HAMPTON, G.J., Organ: Mounted Vol., Enlist: Nov. 12, 1859, Disc: Jan. 1, 1860, Place of Birth: Victoria, Elected 1st Corp., Dec. 12, Ranger Muster Roll.

WILSON, Cyrus M., Pvt., Comm. Off: JONES, Franklin, Organ: Co. A, Frontier Battalion, Enlist: Sept. 1, 1870, Disc: Nov. 11, 1870, Place of Birth: San Antonio, Texas, 2 months, 11 days service, Ranger Muster Roll.

WILSON, Cyrus M., Pvt., Comm. Off: JONES, Franklin, Organ: Co. A, Frontier Battalion, Enlist: Sept. 1, 1870, Disc: Oct. 31, 1870, Place of Birth: Mason, Texas, Ranger Muster Roll.

WILSON, Elsie, Pvt., Comm. Off: SNOWBALL, James, Organ: Prov. State Troops, Enlist: Oct. 13, 1871, Disc: Oct. 20, 1871, Place of Birth: Groesbeck, Texas, Ranger Muster Roll.

WILSON, Ed, Pvt., Comm. Off: EASTIN, S.W., Organ: Jack County Rangers, Enlist: Dec. 3, 1873, Disc: April 3, 1874, Place of Birth: Jack County, 4 months service, Ranger Muster Roll.

WILSON, Frank, Pvt., Comm. Off: YOUNT, Andrew J., Capt., Organ: Ranger Company, Enlist: Nov. 26, 66 at Denton, Texas.

WILSON, Frank, Pvt., (Continued)
  R&F 71; Co. org. in conformity to instructions from Gov.
  THROCKMORTON. 1 Muster Roll.
WILSON, Green, Pvt., Comm. Off: DONELSON, John, Organ: Rangers
  for Cortinas War, Enlist: Nov. 5, 1859, Disc: Dec. 10, 1859,
  Age: 37, Place of Birth: Live Oak County, Ranger Muster Roll.
WILSON, H.C., Pvt., Comm. Off: HALL, J.L., Organ: Special State
  Troops, Enlist: March 24, 1877, Disc: Feb. 28, 1878, Place of
  Birth: Clinton, Texas, 8 months, 7 days service, Ranger Muster
  Roll.
WILSON, Hiram, Pvt., Comm. Off: ROSS, L.S., Capt., Organ: Ranger
  Co., Enlist: Oct. 3, 60 at Waco for 12 mos., Serv. from Oct.
  3,60 to Feb. 5,61; 4 mos. & 3 days at $25-$102.50, Age: 29,
  R&F 66; En. Off: Capt. ROSS; Mus. Off: J.M.W. HALL; Appraiser:
  Jas. H. SWINDELLS; Val. H: $80; HE: $20; Gun: $20; Pistol: $30;
  Stoppage $32.76; Bal. Paid: $69.74; elec. certif. with roll;
  Co. sta. at Ft. Belknap Oct. 17 & Nov. 22, 60; 1 Muster Roll
  & 1 Pay Roll.
WILSON, I.N., Sgt., Comm. Off: YOUNT, Andrew J., Capt.,
  Organ: Ranger Comapny, Enlist: Nov. 26, 66 at Denton, Texas.
  R&F 71; Co. org. in conformity to instructions from Governor
  THROCKMORTON. 1 Muster Roll.
WILSON, J.M., Pvt., Comm. Off: BOURLAND, J., Capt., Organ: Mtd.
  Vol. TR, Enlist: Jan. 28, 59, Place of Birth: Gainesville,
  Disc: April 28, 59, R&F 43, 1 Muster Roll, April 28, 59.
WILSON, Jackson, Pvt., Comm. Off: WOOD, J.D., Organ: Prov. Mtd.
  State Troops, Enlist: Oct. 9, 1871, Disc: Nov. 13, 1871,
  Place of Birth: Limestone County, Ranger Muster Roll.
WILSON, Jaco, Pvt., Comm. Off: SANSOM, John W., Capt.,
  Organ: Rangers, Enlist: Aug. 31, 1859, Disc: Nov. 30, 1859,
  3 months service, Ranger Muster Roll.
WILSON, Jaco, Pvt., Comm. Off: BURLESON, Ed, Organ: Mounted Ran-
  gers, Enlist: Jan. 20, 1860, Disc: Sept. 7, 1860, Age:18,
  Place of Birth: San Marcos, Ranger Muster Roll.
WILSON, James, Pvt., Comm. Off: KLEID, Peter, Organ: Co. G,
  Frontier Forces, Enlist: Oct. 31, 1870, Disc: May 31, 1871,
  Place of Birth: Camp Rio Frio, Ranger Muster Roll.
WILSON, J.P.H., Pvt., Comm. Off: DOLAN, Pat, Organ: Co. F, Fron-
  tier Battalion, Enlist: Aug. 1, 1877, Disc: Feb. 28, 1878,
  Place of Birth: Kerr County, 7 months service, Ranger Muster
  Roll.
WILSON, James, Pvt., Comm. Off: MCCULLOCH, Henry E., Capt.,
  Organ: Texas Vols., Enlist: Oct. 25, 1848, Disc: Dec. 8, 1848,
  Age: 22, 1 month, 13 days service, Ranger Muster Roll.
WILSON, John, Pvt., Comm. Off: WOOD, J.D., Organ: Prov. Mounted
  State Troops, Enlist: Oct. 9, 1871, Disc: Nov. 13, 1871,
  Place of Birth: Limestone County, Ranger Muster Roll.
WILSON, John, Pvt., Comm. Off: MCCULLOCH, Henry E., Organ: Texas
  Mounted Vol., Enlist: Oct. 25, 1847, Age: 26, Grey Eyes, light
  hair, 5'7", Place of Birth: Gonzales.
WILSON, John, Pvt., Comm. Off: MCCULLOCH, Henry E., Capt.,
  Organ: Texas Vols., Enlist: Oct. 25, 1847, Disc: Dec. 8, 1848,
  Age: 26; Height: 5'7", dk. comp., grey eyes, light hair, Place
  of Birth: Gonzales, Tex., 13 mos., 15 days service, Ranger Mus-
  ter Roll.

WILSON, J.P.H., Pvt., Comm. Off: COLDWELL, Neal, Organ: Co. F,
    Frontier Battalion, Enlist: June 4, 1874, Disc: June 4, 1875,
    Place of Birth: Kerr County, 12 months, 1 day service, Ranger
    Muster Roll.
WILSON, James M., 3rd Corp., Comm. Off: ROBERTS, D.W., Organ: Co.
    D, Frontier Battalion, Enlist: June 1, 1875, Disc: Nov. 30,
    1875, Age: 24, 5'6", fair, gray eyes, dark hair, farmer, Place
    of Birth: Wayne, Indiana, 4 months, 18 days service, Ranger
    Muster Roll.
WILSON, J.M., Pvt., Comm. Off: BOURLAND, James, Organ: Texas Mtd.
    Rangers, Enlist: Feb. 28, 1859, Disc: April 28, 1859, Place
    of Birth: Gainesville, Texas, 3 months service, Ranger Muster
    Roll.
WILSON, J.L., Pvt., Comm. Off: ONEAL, C.M., Organ: Co. Z, Minute
    Men, Erath Co., Enlist: Jan. 1, 1873, Disc: March 31, 1873,
    Place of Birth: Erath County, 70 days of service, Ranger Mus-
    ter Roll.
WILSON, John H.B., 1st Lt., Comm. Off: WILLIAMS, Samuel J.,
    Organ: Prov. State Troops, Co. A, Enlist: Oct. 9, 1871,
    Disc: Nov. 13, 1871, Place of Birth: Limestone County, Ranger
    Muster Roll.
WILSON, J.T., 2nd Lt., Comm. Off: WALLER, J.R., Organ: Co. A,
    Frontier Battalion, Enlist: May 25, 1874, Disc: April 30, 1875,
    Place of Birth: Stephens, 11 months, 11 days service, Ranger
    Muster Roll.
WILSON,J.T., 1st Lt., Comm. Off: MCADAMS, W.C., Organ: Palo Pinto
    County Rangers, Enlist: Dec. 13, 1873, Disc: April 13, 1874,
    Place of Birth: Palo Pinto County, 4 months service, Ranger
    Muster Roll.
WILSON, Hyram, Pvt., Comm. Off: ROSS, L.S., Organ: Mounted Ran-
    gers, Enlist: Oct. 3, 1860, Age: 29, Place of Birth: Waco,
    Ranger Muster Roll.
WILSON, L.C., Pvt., Comm. Off: WOODS, Wm. M., Organ: Mounted Ran-
    gers, Enlist: April 10, 1860, Disc: Aug. 10, 1860, Age: 22,
    Place of Birth: Bonham, Ranger Muster Roll.
WILSON, N.D., Pvt., Comm. Off: SANSOM, John W., Organ: Frontier
    Forces, Enlist: Aug. 25, 1870, Disc: Feb. 7, 1871, Place of
    Birth: Shackleford County, Ranger Muster Roll.
WILSON, Riley, Pvt., Comm. Off: WOOD, J.D., Organ: Prov. Mounted
    State Troops, Enlist: Oct. 9, 1871, Disc: Nov. 13, 1871, Place
    of Birth: Limestone County, Ranger Muster Roll.
WILSON, R.B., Pvt., Comm. Off: ADAMS, George H., Organ: Co. G,
    Min. Men, Brown Co., Enlist: Nov. 14, 1872, Disc: Feb. 25, 1874,
    Place of Birth: Brown County, 14 days of service, Ranger Muster
    Roll.
WILSON, R.J., 1st Sgt., Comm. Off: BOURLAND, James, Organ: Texas
    Mounted Rangers, Enlist: Oct. 28, 1858, Disc: Jan. 28, 1859,
    Place of Birth: Gainesville, Texas, 3 months service, Ranger
    Muster Roll.
WILSON, Robert, Pvt., Comm. Off: SANSOM, John W., Organ: Frontier
    Forces, Enlist: Aug. 25, 1870, Dsic: May 31, 1871, Place of
    Birth: Shackleford County, Ranger Muster Roll.
WILSON, Robert, Pvt., Comm. Off: MCCULLOCH, Henry E., Capt.,
    Organ: Texas Vols., Enlist: Oct. 25, 1848, Disc: Dec. 8, 1848,

WILSON, Robert, Pvt., (Continued)
   Age: 21, 1 month, 13 days service, Ranger Muster Roll.
WILSON, S.W., 1st Corp., Comm. Off: BAYLOR, G.W., Organ: Co. A,
   Frontier Battalion, Enlist: Dec. 1, 1882, Disc: Feb. 28, 1883,
   3 months service, Ranger Muster Roll.
WILSON, Solomon, Pvt., Comm. Off: HARRISON, Thos., Capt.,
   Organ: Texas Rangers, Enlist: Jan. 10, 61 at Waco for 6 months
   unless sooner discharged, Age: 23. R&F 51; Thos. HARRISON, En.
   Off; J.C. NEWLON, Mus. Off; S.P. ROSS & D.R. LINSLEY, Apprs.
   H: $175; HE: $30; Gun: $30; Pistol: $30. Co. sta. at camp
   near Waco Jan. 8, 61. Called into service of State by Gov.
   Sam HOUSTON. 1 Muster Roll; Jan. 10, 61.
WILSON, V.C., Pvt., Comm. Off: DENTON, J.M., Organ: Co. A, Fron-
   tier Battalion, Enlist: Sept. 23, 1876, Disc: Feb. 28, 1878,
   Age: 19, 5'11", brown hair, brown eyes, fair, clerk, Place of
   Birth: Va., 20 months, 7 days service, Ranger Muster Roll.
WILSON, Valentine, Pvt., Comm. Off: JONES, John S., Organ: Texas
   Rangers, Enlist: Feb. 23, 1858, Disc: Aug. 5, 1858, Age: 24,
   Place of Birth: Comanche County, 5 months, 12 days service,
   Ranger Muster Roll.
WILSON, W.A., Pvt., Comm. Off: ARRINGTON, G.W., Capt.,
   Organ: Frontier Battalion Co. C, Enlist: Feb. 14, 1882, Aug.
   15, 1882, Disc: Aug. 31, 1882, Made Corp. on June 1. Reduced
   to Pvt. on Aug. 15, 1882, 4 months service, Photostat: orig.
   in A.G. Office.
WILSON, W.A., 2nd Corp., Comm. Off: ARRINGTON, G.W., Capt.,
   Organ: Frontier Battalion, Co. C, Enlist: Feb. 14, 1882,
   Disc: Aug. 31, 1882, Made Corp. June 1 to Aug. 15, 82, 2 mos.
   15 days service as Corp., Photostat: Orig. in A.G. Office.
WILSON, W.C., Pvt., Comm. Off: MCADAMS, W.C., Organ: Palo Pinto
   County Rangers, Enlist: Dec. 13, 1873, Disc: April 13, 1874,
   Place of Birth: Palo Pinto County, 4 months service, Ranger
   Muster Roll.
WILSON, W.D., Pvt., Comm. Off: SANSOM, John W., Organ: Frontier
   Forces, Enlist: Feb. 7, 1871, Disc: May 31, 1871, Place of
   Birth: Shackleford County, Ranger Muster Roll. Bonneville,
   Logan (?) Co., Ark., 101 Wilson Ave.
WILSON, W.D., 1st Sgt., Comm. Off: HUNTER, James M., Organ: Co.
   I, Frontier Forces, Enlist: Sept. 12, 1870, Disc: January 24,
   1871, Place of Birth: Austin, Texas, 4 months, 12 days service,
   Ranger Muster Roll.
WILSON, W.J., 1st Sgt., Comm. Off: BOURLAND, J., Capt.,
   Organ: Mtd. Vol. TR, Enlist: Oct. 28, 58, Disc: Jan. 28, 59,
   Place of Birth: Gainesville, R&F 77, 2 Muster Rolls, Jan. 28,
   59.
WILSON, W.L., Pvt., Comm. Off: TAYA, J.B., Organ: Co. C, Vol.
   Battalion, Enlist: Jan. 15, 1878, Disc: Feb. 28, 1878, Place
   of Birth: El Paso County, 1 month, 15 days service, Ranger Mus-
   ter Roll.
WILSON, W.L., Pvt., Comm. Off: TAY, J.B., Lt., Organ: Vol. Batta-
   lion Co. C, Enlist: Jan. 15, 1878, Disc: Feb. 2-, 1878, 1 month
   15 days service, Ranger Muster Roll.
WILSON, White H., 1st Lt., Comm. Off: BROWN, John Henry,
   Organ: Texas State Troops, Enlist: July 1, 1859, Disc: Sept.

WILSON, White H., 1st Lt., (Continued)
1859, Place of Birth: Travis County, 2 months, 12 days service,
Ranger Muster Roll.
WILSON, William, Pvt., Comm. Off: YOUNT, Andrew J., Pvt.,
Organ: Ranger Company, Enlist: Nov. 26, 66 at Denton, Texas.
R&F 71; Co. org. in conformity to instructions from Governor
THROCKMORTON. 1 Muster Roll.
WILSON, William C., Pvt., Comm. Off: FORD, John S., Organ: 2nd Co.
of Rangers, Enlist: Nov. 10, 1858, Disc: May 10, 1858, Age: 25,
Place of Birth: Austin, Ranger Muster Roll.
WILSON, Z., Pvt., Comm. Off: DONELSON, John, Organ: Rangers for
Cortinas War, Enlist: Nov. 5, 1859, Disc: Dec. 10, 1859,
Age: 21, Place of Birth: Live Oak County, Ranger Muster Roll.
Service: 1 mo. 6 days at $12--$14.40; $3 allowed for clothing
& $14.40 for hire of horse--total pay $31.80.
WINTERS, B.F., Pvt., Comm. Off: WINTERS, James W., Capt.,
Organ: Reserve Co., Oakville Pr., Live Oak Co., TM, H.P. BEE,
Brig. Gen., Enlist: Aug. 5, 61. R&F 70; Company had no arms
worth mentioning; 1 roll dated Aug. 5, 61; from Photostat, ori-
ginal in AGO.
WINTERS, Ben F., Pvt., Comm. Off: GUSSETT, N., Capt., Organ: Co.
for Live Oak County, 3rd Frontier Dist. TST, Gen. J.D. MCADOO
Commdg. Enlist: Feb. 23, 64 in Live Oak County, Serv. 24 days
at $2-Total $48.00; only 1/4 time calculated, Age: 43.
R&F 85; En. & Mus. Off: Wm. GAMBEL; Co. org. under Act D. 15-
63; 1 Muster Roll dated Feb. 23, 64; 1 Muster & Pay Roll from
Feb. 23, to Je. 1, 64.
WINTERS, James W., Capt., Comm. Off: WINTERS, James W., Capt.,
Organ: Reserve Co., Oakville Pr., Live Oak Co., TM, H.P. BEE,
Brig. Gen., Enlist: Aug. 5, 61. R&F 70; Company had no arms
worth mentioning; 1 roll dated Aug. 5, 61. From Photostat:
Original in AGO.
WINTERS, James W., Capt., Comm. Off: WINTERS, James W., Capt.,
Organ: Co. Live Oak & MCMullen Counties, 29th Brig., TST,
Enlist: Jan. 63, Age: 45. R&F 91; Arms--2 rifles, 1 shot gun,
1 pistol; 1 Muster Roll dated Jan. 63. 5 names illegible on
roll.
WINTERS, Terrel, Pvt., Comm. Off: ELKINS, J.M., Organ: Co. L, Min.
Men, Coleman Co., Enlist: April 5, 1873, Disc: June 20, 1873,
Place of Birth: Coleman County, 20 days of service, Ranger
Muster Roll.
WISDOM, Andrew J., 2nd Bugler, Comm. Off. Off: FITZHUGH, Wm.,
Organ: Texas Militia, Enlist: Nov. 2, 1854, Disc: Feb. 2, 1854,
Age: 24, Place of Birth: McKinney, Texas, 3 months service,
Ranger Muster Roll.
WISDOM, J.L., Pvt., Comm. Off: IKARD, E.F., Organ: Co. C, Fron-
tier Battalion, Enlist: May 20, 1874, Disc: Sept. 20, 1874,
Place of Birth: Clay County, 4 months, 2 days service, Ranger
Muster Roll.
WISE, Henry, Pvt., Comm. Off:HOLT, John T., Capt., Organ: Fort
Bend Rifles, Mtd. Riflemen (Rangers), Enlist: Jan. 14, 60 at
Richmond. R&F 64; 1 Muster Roll dated Jan. 16, 60.
WISEMAN, Wm., Pvt., Comm. Off: MCADAMS, W.C., Organ: Palo Pinto
County Rangers, Enlist: Dec. 13, 1873, Disc: April 13, 1874,

WISEMAN, Wm., Pvt., (Continued)
    Place of Birth: Palo Pinto County, 4 months service, Ranger
    Muster Roll.
WISH, Jasper, Pvt., Comm. Off: HENRY, W.R., Organ: Rangers,
    Enlist: June 19, 1859, Place of Birth: Sabinal Canyon, Ranger
    Muster Roll.
WISMAR, R., Pvt., Comm. Off: CAMERON, Ewen, Capt., Organ: Co. of
    Texas Rangers, Enlist: Mar. 20, 61 at Fredericksburg for 3
    months, Mus. out Je. 5, 61 at Camp Mason by Lt. S.G. RAGSDALE,
    Age: 36. R&F 31; En & Mus Off: W. WAHRMMUND; Appraisers:
    F.V.D. STUCKEN & Louis WEISS; Val. H: $36; HE: $20; Gun: $15;
    Pistols: $25; $11.90 deducted from pay; no corn or forage
    issued. Co. entitled to commutation in money; 45 miles
    travelled from place of discharge home; Co. called into service
    by Gov. HOUSTON; Co. sta. on South Fork of Llano River Mar. 20
    61; 1 Muster Roll.
WITCHER, Adam, SEE WICTKER, Adam, Pvt.
WITCHER, Adam, Pvt., Comm. Off: GENTRY, F.B., Organ: Minute Men,
    Enlist: March 20, 1860, Disc: June 20, 1860, Age: 19, Place
    of Birth: Hamilton, Ranger Muster Roll.
WITCHER, J., SEE WITCKER, J., Corp.
WITCHER, J.W., 1st Corp., Comm. Off: GENTRY, F.B., 1st Corp.,
    Organ: Minute Men, Enlist: March 20, 1860, Disc: June 20, 1860,
    Age: 22, Place of Birth: Hamilton, Ranger Muster Roll.
WITCKER, Adam, Pvt., Comm. Off: GENTRY, F.B., Lt., Organ: Ranger
    Company, Enlist: Mar. 20, 60, disc: Je. 21, 60; served 3 mo. &
    1 day at $25 - Total: $75.83. R&F 14; 2 Pay Rolls.
WITCKER, J., Corp., Comm. Off: GENTRY, F.B., Lt., Organ: Ranger
    Company, Enlist: Mar. 20, 60, Disc: Je. 21, 60; served 3 mo. &
    1 day at $28-Total $84.93. R&F 14; 2 Pay Rolls.
WITHERS, W.T., Pvt., Comm. Off: PERRY, C.R., Organ: Co. D, Fron-
    tier Battalion, Enlist: May 25, 1874, Disc: Sept. 17, 1874,
    Place of Birth: Blanco County, 6 months, 20 days service, Ran-
    ger Muster Roll.
WITHERS, W.T., Pvt., Comm. Off: SWISHER, Jas. M., Organ: Co. P,
    Frontier Forces, Enlist: Sept. 6, 1870, Disc: Feb. 6, 1871,
    Place of Birth: Camp Colorado, Ranger Muster Roll.
WITHOT, Frederick, Pvt., Comm. Off: KLEID, Peter, Organ: Co. O,
    Frontier Forces, Enlist: Oct. 31, 1870, Disc: May 31, 1871,
    Place of Birth: Camp Rio Frio, Ranger Muster Roll.
WITNEY, Stanislaus, Pvt., Comm. Off: RICHARZ, H.J., Organ: Co. E,
    Frontier Forces, Enlist: Sept. 9, 1870, Disc: June 15, 1871,
    Place of Birth: Uvalde County, Ranger Muster Roll.
WITT, Jeremiah C., Pvt., Comm. Off: SUBLETT, David L., Capt.,
    Organ: Co. of Texas Rangers, Enlist: Feb. 15, 61 at McKinney
    for 3 mos., Mus. out May 14, 61 at Waco. R&F 57; En. Off:
    MCGARAH; Mus. Off: D.L. SUBLETT; Val. H: $150; HE: $25;
    Guns: $25; Pistols: $35; Serv. 3 mos. at $25-Amt. of pay $75.00,
    Less stoppages of: $10.45 to F.C. DOWNS and $40.00 to J. HUNTER
    Total stoppages $50.45; Called into service of state by Gov.
    HOUSTON from Feb. 7, 61 for 3 mos.; 1 Muster Roll & 1 Pay Roll;
    Ammunition stores pack mules, etc. turned over to
    Capt. J.M. KNIGHT's Co.- Men residing in vicinity of station
    may be discharged before marching.

WITT, N.B., 2nd Lt., Comm. Off: CONNELL, J.G., Organ: Brown and San Saba Counties, Enlist: Jan. 6, 1874, Disc: March 26, 1874, Place of Birth: Brown and San Saba Counties, 2 months, 20 days service, Ranger Muster Roll.

WITT, W.H., 2nd Corp., Comm. Off: COLDWELL, Neal, Organ: Co. F, Frontier Battalion, Enlist: Sept. 1, 1875, Disc: Aug. 31, 1876, Age: 21, 6', black hair, blue eyes, fair, farmer, Place of Birth: Weekly, Tenn., 12 months service, Ranger Muster Roll.

WITT, J.C., Pvt., Comm. Off: MOORE, F.M., & ROBERTS, D.W., Organ: Co. D, Frontier Battalion, Enlist: March 1, 1877, Disc: May 31, 1878, Age: 23, 5'8", light brown hair, light, grey eyes, farmer, Place of Birth: Kerr County. 15 months service, Ranger Muster Roll. So. San Antonio, Texas, Biddel Ave.

WITT, W.H., Pvt., Comm. Off: MOORE, F.M., Organ: Co. D, Frontier Battalion, Enlist: Sept. 1, 1876, Disc: Nov. 30, 1876, 6', light hair, blue eyes, farmer, Place of Birth: Weekly, Tenn., 9 months service, Ranger Muster Roll. Center Point, Texas.

WITT, W.H., Pvt., Comm. Off: COLDWELL, Neal, Organ: Co. F, Frontier Battalion, Enlist: June 4, 1874, Disc: June 4, 1875, Place of Birth: Kerr County, 12 months, 1 day service, Ranger Muster Roll.

WOFFORD, J.R., Pvt., Comm. Off: MCNELLY, L.H., Organ: Washington Co. Vol. Militia, Enlist: April 6, 1875, Disc: Aug. 8, 1875, Place of Birth: Austin, Texas, 4 months, 2 days service, Ranger Muster Roll.

WOLDERP, Ed, Pvt., Comm. Off: WALKER, John G., Capt., Organ: Mtd. Vol., Enlist: Nov. 1854, Ranger Muster Rolls.

WOLF, A.H., 2nd Corp., Comm. Off: ALEXANDER, John, Organ: Co. O, Minute Men, Burnet Co., Enlist: Sept. 11, 1872, Disc: Aug. 13, 1873, Place of Birth: Burnet County, 10 days of service, Ranger Muster Roll.

WOLF, E.N., Pvt., Comm. Off: ALEXANDER, John, Organ: Co. O, Min. Men, Burnet Co., Enlist: Sept. 11, 1872, Disc: Aug. 13, 1873, Place of Birth: Burnet County, 20 days of service, Ranger Muster Roll.

WOLF, T.R., Pvt., Comm. Off: ALEXANDER, John, Organ: Co. O, Min. Men, Burnet Co., Enlist: Jan. 10, 1873, Disc: Aug. 13, 1873, Place of Birth: Burnet County, 21 days of service, Ranger Muster Roll.

WOLF, Monroe J., Pvt., Sgt., Comm. Off: LEE, A.P., Organ: Co. M, Minute Men, Lampasas Co., Enlist: Aug. 6, 1873, Disc: March 20, 1874, Place of Birth: Lampasas County, 25 days of service, Ranger Muster Roll.

WOLTER, John, Pvt., Comm. Off: BURLESON, A.B., Capt., Organ: Mtd. Ranger Co., Enlist: Dec. 29, 60 at Austin for 12 mos.; unless sooner discharged. Mustd. out May 9, 61, Age: 21. R&F 69; Enr. Off: Capt. A.B. BURLESON; H: $105; HE: $22; Arms--guns: $13; Pistols: $22; No. of miles from place of discharge to home 70; Apprs. David THOMASON & Jno. T. EVERETT; Co. called into service by Gov. Sam HOUSTON April 4, 60. 1 crupper. These last received at Ft. Chadbourne thru services of Henry E. MCCULLOCH, Com of Secession Convention these articles had been used by U.S. Regulars, except hats & shoes, & were old & worn. 2 Muster Rolls; one giving date of HOUSTON's order as April 4, 60, the other Dec. 29, 60.

WOLTERS, N.H., Pvt., Comm. Off: SCHWETHELM, H., Organ: Co. E, Minute Men, Enlist: April 7, 1872, Disc: March 15, 1873, Place of Birth: Kerr County, 110 days service, Ranger Muster Roll.

WOMACK, E.W., Pvt., Comm. Off: MOORE, D.D., Capt., Organ: Moscow Guards, Cav. Co., Polk Co., TST, Enlist: Nov. 1860, at Moscow, Tex. R&F 76; Co. org. with 64 volunteers who agreed to meet not less than 6 or more than 7 times a year; unless called out on special duty; 1 Muster Roll.

WOMACK, Jasper N., Comm. Off: CONNELL, J.G., Capt., Organ: Co. C, Texas Rangers, Enlist: Jan. 6, 1874, Disc: March 6, 1874, Place of Birth: Brownwood, Texas, Gen. Del., Dept. of the Interior--Pensions, N.H. NICHOLSON, Inspector.

WOMACK, William, Pvt., Comm. Off: TRAVIS, C.E., Capt., Organ: Tex. Volunteers, Company E, Enlist: 1854, Disc: 1855, 3 months of service, Ranger Muster Roll.

WOMMICK, J.L., Pvt., Comm. Off: WOODS, Wm. M., Organ: Mounted Rangers, Enlist: April 16, 1860, Disc: Aug. 10, 1860, Age: 18, Place of Birth: Bonham, Ranger Muster Roll.

WONSLEY, David W., Comm. Off: COX, A.H., Organ: Frontier Forces, Co. B, Enlist: Sept. 8, 1870, Disc: May 31, 1871, Place of Birth: Henly, Hays Co., Texas, Dept. of the Interior--Pensions, N.H. NICHOLSON, Inspector.

WOODALL, J.A., 2nd Sgt., Comm. Off: HUNTER, W.L., Organ: Rangers, Parker County, Enlist: Dec. 24, 1873, Disc: March 29, 1874, Place of Birth: Parker County, 96 days of service, Ranger Muster Roll.

WOODBRIDGE, J.L., Pvt., Comm. Off: LOWE, John C., 1st Lt., Organ: Ranger Company, Enlist: March 26, 60, Disc: Dec. 24, 60, R&F 43; Serv. 2 mos. 7 days at $25-$55.83; less stoppages of $25 to state - Bal. paid $28.83; 1 Pay Roll.

WOODBRIDGE, S.E., Surgeon, Comm. Off: RICHARZ, H.J., Organ: Co. L, Frontier Forces, Enlist: Sept. 10, 1870, Disc: June 15, 1871, Place of Birth: Uvalde County, Ranger Muster Roll.

WOODDY, Sam, Pvt., Comm. Off: TEAGUE, John, Capt., Organ: Minute Men, Wise County, Enlist: Oct. 14, 1865, Age: 45, R&F 32; Arms; rifles; 1 Muster Roll.

WOODRUFF, D.G., Corp., Comm. Off: BAKER, D.P., Organ: Frontier Forces, Co. F, Enlist: Nov. 5, 1870, Disc: June 15, 1871, Place of Birth: Decatur, Wise County, Ranger Muster Roll.

WOODRUFF, E.B., Pvt., Comm. Off: BAKER, D.P., Organ: Frontier Forces, Co. F, Enlist: Nov. 5, 1870, Disc: June 15, 1871, Place of Birth: Decatur, Wise County, Ranger Muster Roll.

WOODRUFF, Fountain B., Pvt., Comm. Off: WALKER, Joseph, Organ: Rangers for Cortinas War, Enlist: Nov. 30, 1859, Disc: Jan. 20, 1860, Age: 22, Place of Birth: Banquete, Ranger Muster Roll.

WOODRUFF, Fountain B., Pvt., Comm. Off: FORD, John S., Organ: 3rd Company of Rangers, Enlist: Jan. 20, 1860, Disc: Mar. 17, 1860, Age: 22, Place of Birth: Brownsville, Ranger Muster Roll.

WOOD, C.P., Pvt., Comm. Off: BROWN, John Henry, Organ: Texas State Troops, Enlist: July 1, 1859, Disc: Sept. 4, 1859, Place of Birth: Travis County, 2 months, 4 days service, Ranger Muster Roll.

WOOD, C.P., Pvt., Comm. Off: DAVIDSON, S.G., Lt., Organ: Ranger

WOOD, C.P., Pvt., (Continued)
Co., Enlist: March 20, 1860, April 14, 60; Served 25 days.
R&F 15; Rate of pay $25-Amt. pay $20.83. One payroll.

WOOD, G.W., Pvt., Comm. Off: LEDBETTER, Wm. H., Organ: Co. N, Min.
Men, San Saba County, Enlist: Sept. 13, 1872, Disc: April 5,
1874, Place of Birth: San Saba County, 71 days of service,
Ranger Muster Roll.

WOOD, George W., Pvt., Comm.Off: WOOD, W.R., Organ: Minute Men,
Enlist: March 5, 1860, Disc: June 4, 1860, Age: 17, Place of
Birth: San Saba, Ranger Muster Roll.

WOOD, H.N., Pvt., Comm. Off: BROWN, John Henry, Organ: Texas
Troops, Enlist: July 1, 1859, Disc: Sept. 4, 1859, Place of
Birth: Travis County, 2 months, 4 days service, Ranger Muster
Roll.

WOOD, Henry, 2nd Sgt., Comm. Off: WOOD, W.R., Organ: Minute Men,
Enlist: March 5, 1860, Disc: June 4, 1860, Age: 27, Place of
Birth: San Saba, Ranger Muster Roll.

WOOD, Jacob, Pvt., Comm. Off: JONES, Franklin, Organ: Co. A, Fron-
tier Battalion, Enlist: Aug. 25, 1870, Disc: Nov. 11, 1870,
Place of Birth: Ft. Mason, Texas, 2 months, 17 days service,
RAnger Muster Roll. Tucson, Pima (?) Co., Arizona, R.R. 2,
Box 42.

WOOD, Jasp. P., Pvt., Comm. Off: DAVIDSON, S.C., Lt., Organ: Ranger Co., Enlist: March 20, 1860, Disc: April 14, 60; Served 25
days. R&F 15; Rate of pay $25; Amt. of pay $20.83. One Pay
Roll.

WOOD, J., Pvt., Comm. Off: FOSTER, B.S., Organ: Co. E, Frontier
Battalion, Enlist: Sept. 1, 1876, Disc: Aug. 31, 1877, Place
of Birth: Coleman County, 12 months service, Ranger Muster
Roll.

WOOD, Joseph, Pvt., Comm. Off: STEVENS, G.W., Organ: Wise County
Rangers, Enlist: Nov. 26, 1873, Disc: March 26, 1874, Place
of Birth: Wise County, 4 months service, Ranger Muster Roll.

WOOD, J., Pvt., Comm. Off: FOSTER, B.S., Organ: Co. E, Frontier
Battalion, Enlist: April 1, 1876, Disc: Aug. 31, 1876, Place
of Birth: Coleman County, 5 months service, Ranger Muster Roll.

WOOD, Jacob, Pvt., Comm. Off: JONES, Franklin, Organ: Co. A, Frontier Battalion, Enlist: Aug. 25, 1870, Disc: Oct. 31, 1870,
Place of Birth: Mason, Texas, Ranger Muster Roll.

WOOD, J.R., Pvt., Comm. Off: MCCLURE, D.H., Organ: CO. T, Min.
Men, Palo Pinto Co., Enlist: Sept. 5, 1872, Disc: Aug. 12,
1873, Place of Birth: Palo Pinto County, 120 days of service,
Ranger Muster Roll. Seymour, Texas, Box 356.

WOOD, Samuel D., Pvt., Comm. Off: SALMON, John, Lt., Organ: Ranger Company, Enlist: Feb. 28, 1860, Disc: May 21, 1860,
R&F 20; Serv. 2 mos. 24 days at $25 per mo. - Amt. of pay $70,
plus allowances of $4.65 - Total amt. due & paid $74.65; Each
member entitled to 10 days rations, 1/2 lb. of powder, 2 lbs.
of lead & 250 percussion caps; 1 Pay Roll.

WOOD, Jeff T., Pvt., Comm. Off: SMITH, C.C., Organ: Co. R, Min.
Men, Mason County, Enlist: Dec. 9, 1873, Disc: Jan. 21, 1874,
Place of Birth: Mason County, 10 days of service, Ranger Mus-
ter Roll.

WOOD, Joe, Pvt., Comm. Off: WALLER, J.R., Organ: Co. A, Frontier

WOOD, Joe, Pvt., (Continued)
  Battalion, Enlist: May 25, 1874, Disc: April 30, 1875, Place
  of Birth: Erath County, 11 months, 11 days, Ranger Muster Roll.
WOOD, J.D., Capt., Comm. Off: WOOD, J.D., Organ: Prov. State
  Troops, Mounted, Enlist: Oct. 9, 1871, Disc: Nov. 13, 1871,
  Place of Birth: Limestone County, Ranger Muster Roll.
WOOD, J.H., Farrier, Comm. Off: BAKER, D.P., Organ: Frontier For-
  ces Co. F, Enlist: Nov. 5, 1870, Disc: June 15, 1871, Place of
  Birth: Decatur, Wise County, Ranger Muster Roll.
WOOD, John M., 1st Sgt., Comm. Off: DALRYMPLE, W.C., Organ: Mtd.
  Rangers, Enlist: Jan. 14, 1860, Disc: Oct. 13, 1860, Age: 23,
  Place of Birth: Liberty Hill, Discharged Aug. 27, 60-family
  sick, Ranger Muster Roll.
WOOD, L.B., Pvt., Comm. Off: MOORE, D.D., Capt., Organ: Moscow
  Guards, Cav. Co., Polk Co., TST, Enlist: Nov. 1860, at Moscow,
  Texas. R&F 76; Co. org. with 64 volunteers who agreed to meet
  not less than 6 or more than 7 times a year; unless called out
  on special duty; 1 Muster Roll.
WOOD, L.B., 4th Sgt., Comm. Off: WALKER, John G., Capt.,
  Organ: Mtd. Vol., Enlist: Nov. 1854, Ranger Muster Roll.
WOOD, P.P., Pvt., Comm. Off: WEEKES, Nicholas, Organ: Star Rifles
  Militia, Enlist: Sept. 21, 1874, Disc: Sept. 27, 1874, Place
  of Birth: Galveston County, 7 days service, Ranger Muster Roll.
WOOD, Robert, Pvt., Comm. Off: CURETON, J.J., Capt.,
  Organ: Rangers, Enlist: Dec. 5, 1860, See Newspaper Clippings,
  Ranger Muster Roll.
WOOD, Rufus, Pvt., Comm. Off: WOOD, J.D., Organ: Prov. Mounted
  State Troops, Enlist: Oct. 9, 1871, Disc: Nov. 13, 1871, Place
  of Birth: Limestone County, Ranger Muster Roll.
WOOD, Samuel, Pvt., Comm. Off: DALRYMPLE, W.C., Organ: Mounted
  Rangers, Enlist: May 1, 1860, Disc: Oct. 13, 1860, Place of
  Birth: Belknap, Substitute for L.H. HUNGEFARD, Ranger Muster
  Roll.
WOOD, Samuel D., Pvt., Comm. Off: SALMON, John, Organ: Mounted
  Rangers, Enlist: April 12, 1860, Disc: May 12, 1860, Place of
  Birth: Erath County in camp, Ranger Muster Roll.
WOOD, Saml. J., Pvt., Comm. Off: WALKER, John G., Capt.,
  Organ: Mtd. Vol., Enlist: Nov. 1854, Ranger Muster Roll.
WOOD, Spencer, Pvt., Comm. Off: MCCULLOCH, Henry E., Organ: Texas
  Mounted Vol., Enlist: Oct. 25, 1847, Age: 23, Grey eyes, dark
  hair, 5'8", Place of Birth: Bastrop.
WOOD, Spencer, Pvt., Comm. Off: MCCULLOCH, Henry E., Capt.,
  Organ: Texas Vols., Enlist: Oct. 25, 1847, Disc: Oct. 24,
  1848, Age: 23; Height: 5'8", dk. comp., grey eyes, dk. hair,
  Place of Birth: Bastrop, Texas, 12 months service, Ranger Mus-
  ter Roll.
WOOD, T.J., Pvt., Comm. Off: LEDBETTER, Wm. H., Organ: Co. N, Min.
  Men, San Saba Co., Enlist: Sept. 19, 1873, Disc: April 5, 1874,
  Place of Birth: San Saba County, 18 days of service, Ranger
  Muster Roll.
WOOD, W.R., 1st Lt., Comm. Off: WOOD, W.R., Organ: Minute Men,
  Enlist: June 4, 1860, Age: 35, Place of Birth: San Saba, Ran-
  ger Muster Roll.
WOODS, Cary, Pvt., Comm. Off: MCCULLOCH, Henry E., Organ: Texas

WOODS, Cary, Pvt., (Continued)
    Mounted Vol., Enlist: Oct. 25, 1847, Age: 24, Blue eyes, light
    hair, 5'10", Place of Birth: Washington County.
WOODS, Cary, Pvt., Comm. Off: FROST, Thomas C., Lt., Organ: Mtd.
    Rangers, Enlist: Dec. 21, 1857, Disc: Mar. 21, 1858, 3 months
    service, Ranger Muster Roll.
WOODS, Carey, Pvt., Comm. Off: MCCULLOCH, Henry E., Capt.,
    Organ: Texas Vols., Enlist: Oct. 25, 1847, Disc: Oct. 24, 1848,
    Age: 24; Height: 5'10", light comp., blue eyes, light hair,
    Place of Birth: Washington County, 12 months service, Ranger
    Muster Roll.
WOODS, Gilman S., 1st Lt., Comm. Off: LEWIS, G.K., Capt.,
    Organ: Texas Mtd. Vol., hnlist: Sept. 6, 1852, Disc: March
    13, 1853, Age: 39, Place of Birth: Salt Lake, Texas, Stationed
    at: Brownsville, Ranger Muster Roll.
WOODS, Joe, Pvt., Comm. Off: SPARKS, J.C., Organ: Co. C, Frontier
    Battalion, Enlist: Aug. 31, 1877, Disc: Feb. 28, 1878, Place
    of Birth: Coleman County, 6 months service, Ranger Muster Roll.
WOODS, Jos., Pvt., Comm. Off: PEAK, June, Organ: Co. B, Frontier
    Battalion, Enlist: Sept. 1, 1878, Disc: Nov. 30, 1878, Place
    of Birth: Runnels County, 3 months service, Ranger Muster Roll.
WOODS, Jno., Pvt., Comm. Off: LONG, Ira, Organ: Co. A, Frontier
    Battalion, Enlist: Sept. 8, 1875, Disc: July 15, 1876,
    Age: 33, 5'10", fair, blue eyes, light hair, carpenter, Place
    of Birth: Missouri, 10 months, 18 days service, Ranger Muster
    Roll.
WOODS, Joseph, Pvt., Comm. Off: STEVENS, G.W., Organ: Co. B, Fron-
    tier Battalion, Enlist: May 16, 1874, Disc: Dec. 10, 1874,
    Place of Birth: Lost Valley, 6 months, 26 days, Ranger Muster
    Roll.
WOODS, W.E., Pvt., Comm. Off: GREEN, M.R., Organ: Comanche County
    Rangers, Enlist: Jan. 17, 1874, Disc: Feb. 17, 1874, Place of
    Birth: Comanche County, 1 month service, Ranger Muster Roll.
WOODS, Wm. P., Pvt., Comm. Off: MCCULLOCH, Henry E., Capt.,
    Organ: Texas Vols., Enlist: Oct. 25, 1847, Disc: Oct. 24,
    1848, Age: 31; Height: 5'7", dk. comp., black eyes, dk. hair,
    Place of Birth: Rusk County, 12 months service, Ranger Muster
    Roll.
WOODS, W.E., Pvt., Comm. Off: WALLER, J.R., Organ: Co. A, Fron-
    tier Battalion, Enlist: May 25, 1874, Disc: Dec. 23, 1874,
    Place of Birth: Erath County, 7 months, 4 days service, Ranger
    Muster Roll.
WOOD, William M., Pvt., Comm. Off: SALMON, John, Lt., Organ: Ran-
    ger Company, Enlist: Feb. 28, 1860, Disc: May 21, 1860,
    R&F 20; Serv. 2 mos. 24 days at $25 per mo. - Amt. of pay $70,
    plus allowances of $4.65 - Total amt. due & paid $74.65; Each
    member entitled to 10 days rations, 1/2 lb. of powder, 2 lbs.
    of lead & 250 percussion caps; 1 Pay Roll.
WOOD, Wm. W., Pvt., Comm. Off: SALMON, John, Organ: Mounted Ran-
    gers, Enlist: April 12, 1860, Disc: May 12, 1860, Place of
    Birth: Erath County in camp, Ranger Muster Roll.
WOODS, Ham, Pvt., Comm. Off: SNOWBALL, James, Organ: Prov. State
    Troops, Enlist: Oct. 13, 1871, Disc: Oct. 20, 1871, Place of
    Birth: Groesbeck, Texas, Ranger Muster Roll.

WOODS, Pinckney, Pvt., Comm. Off: BURLESON, Edward, Capt.,
    Organ: State Guards, Enlist: July 15, 65 at Austin. Mustd. in
    July 15, 65 at Austin, Disc: Aug. 4, 65, 21 days service -
    $16.00. R&F 41; Mus. off: Capt. Ed BURLESON; Amt. of pay -
    $11.20 plus subsistence $15.75, forage $5.60 & use of horse -
    $8.40--total $40.95. Co. org. for protection of prop. belong-
    ing to state in Travis County under authority from
    Gen. G. GRANGER. Co. stationed at Austin, Aug. 4, 65. 1 Mus-
    ter Roll & 1 Pay Roll dated Aug. 4, 65.
WOODS, Robert, Pvt., Comm. Off: ROGERS, P.H., Capt., Organ: Mtd.
    Vol., Enlist: Oct. 1854, Disc: Dec. 1854, 3 months service,
    Ranger Muster Roll. Ex. order of March, 1856.
WOODS, Robert E., Pvt., Comm. Off: WOOD, W.R., Organ: Minute Men,
    Enlist: March 5, 1860, Disc: June 4, 1860, Age: 20, Place of
    Birth: San Saba, Ranger Muster Roll.
WOODS, Thos. W., Pvt., Comm. Off: WOODS, Wm. M., Organ: Mounted
    Rangers, Enlist: April 10, 1860, Disc: Aug. 10, 1860, Age:22,
    Place of Birth: Bonham, Ranger Muster Roll.
WOODS, Wm. M., Pvt., Comm. Off: LOWE, John C., 1st Lt.,
    Organ: Ranger Company, Enlist: Mar. 26, 60, Disc: Dec. 24, 60,
    R&F 43; Serv. 10 days at $25 per mo. = $8.33-total amount paid;
    1 Pay Roll.
WOODS, William M., Capt., Organ: Mounted Rangers, Enlist: April
    10, 1860, Disc: Oct. 16, 1860, Age: 24, Place of Birth: Bonham,
    Ranger Muster Roll.
WOODS, Wm. P., Pvt., Comm. Off: MCCULLOCH, Henry E., Organ: Texas
    Mounted Vol., Enlist: Oct. 25, 1847, Age: 31, black eyes,
    dark hair, 5'7", Place of Birth: Rusk County.
WOODVILLE, L.C., Pvt., Comm. Off: FORSHEY, J.M., Organ: Washing-
    ton Guards, Enlist: Sept. 21, 1874, Disc: Sept. 27, 1874,
    Place of Birth: Galveston County, 7 days service, Ranger Mus-
    ter Roll.
WOODWORTH, S.F., Pvt., Comm. Off: STEWART, F.C., Organ: Co. Q,
    Minute Men, Llano County, Enlist: Sept. 8, 1872, Disc: Aug. 9,
    1873, Place of Birth: Llano County, 81 days of service, Ranger
    Muster Roll.
WOODWARD, J.W., Pvt., Comm. Off: WOOD, J.D., Organ: Prov. Mounted
    State Troops, Enlist: Oct. 9, 1871, Disc: Nov. 13, 1871, Place
    of Birth: Limestone County, Ranger Muster Roll.
WOODWARD, W.H., Jr., Pvt., Comm. Off: WALLACE, Warren,
    Organ: Frontier Company, Nueces Co., Enlist: June 29, 1874,
    Place of Birth: Nueces County, Ranger Muster Roll.
WOODWARD, W.H., Sr., Pvt., Comm. Off: WALLACE, Warren,
    Organ: Frontier Company Nueces Co., Enlist: June 29, 1874,
    Place of Birth: Nueces County, Ranger Muster Roll.
WOODWARD, Wm. H., Pvt., Comm. Off: DALRYMPLE, W.C., Organ: Mtd.
    Rangers, Enlist: Jan. 14, 1860, Disc: Oct. 13, 1860, Age: 29,
    Place of Birth: Liberty Hill, Ranger Muster Roll.
WOODY, Brice, Pvt., Comm. Off: THOMPSON, H.J., Capt.,
    Organ: Minute Men, Parker County, Enlist: May 25, 61 at Veal
    Sta., Parker County, 47 days regular scout. R&F 40; Co. org.
    under act of the Legislature Feb. 7, 61; Election cert. with
    Roll; 1 Muster Roll dated May 27, 61; 6 scout reports dated
    Je. 8-Je.23-61, Je.24-Jy.7,61, Jy.8-Jy.26-61, Jy.27-Aug.4,61,
    Aug.4-Aug.14-61 & Aug.17-S.22-61.

WOODY, John, 2nd Lt., Comm. Off: THOMPSON, H.J., Capt.,
Organ: Minute Men, Parker County, Enlist: May 25, 61 at Veal
Sta., Parker County, 20 days regular scout. R&F 40; Co. orga-
nized under Act of the Legislatrue Feb. 7, 61; Election cert.
with Roll; 1 Muster Roll dated May 27-61; 6 Scout Reports dtd.
Je.8-Je.23-61, Je.24-Jy.7-61, Jy.8-Jy.26-61, Jy.27-Aug.4-61,
Aug.4-Aug.14-61 & Aug.17-S.22-61.
WOODY, John, Pvt., Comm. Off: JOHNSON, T.J., Capt., Organ: Ran-
ger Company, Enlist: April 21, 1860, Serv. to Nov. 10, 60; 6
mos. & 20 days at $25-Total $166.66; Less stoppages:
J.M. GIBBINS $3.80, State $30, RATLIFF & BUCHANAN $6.80 -
Total $40.60; Bal. Paid: $126.06. R&F 99; 1 Pay Roll; Capt.
T.J. JOHNSON, General Power of Attorney.
WOODY, John, Pvt., Comm. Off: JOHNSON, Thomas J., Organ: Mounted
Rangers, Enlist: April 21, 1860, Disc: Nov. 10, 1860, Place
of Birth: Fort Worth, Due B. MONROE 30. for pistol, Ranger
Muster Roll.
WOODY, Samuel, Pvt., Comm. Off: TEAGUE, John, Organ: Minute Men,
Enlist: Oct. 13, 1865, Disc: April 3, 1866, Age: 45, Place of
Birth: Wise County, 25 days service, Ranger Muster Roll.
WOOLDRIDGE, Charles A., 2nd Sgt., Comm. Off: SHAW, Owen,
Organ: Texas Militia Volunteers, Enlist: Aug. 18, 1852,
Disc: Aug. 28, 1852, Place of Birth: Austin, 10 days service,
Ranger Muster Roll.
WOOLDRIDGE, Charles A., 2nd Sgt., Comm. Off: SHAW, Owen, Capt.,
Organ: Mounted Vol., Enlist: Aug. 18, 1852, Disc: Aug. 28,
1852, Age: 18, Discharged. Enlisted at: Austin, TExas, 10
days service, Ranger Muster Roll.
WOOLDRIDGE, Charles A., Pvt., Comm. Off: DALRYMPLE, W.C.,
Organ: Mounted Rangers, Enlist: Jan. 14, 1860, Disc: Oct. 13,
1860, Age: 27, Place of Birth: Liberty Hill, Ranger Muster
Roll.
WOOLDRIDGE, J.R., Pvt., Comm. Off: HUGHS, Moses, Lt.,
Organ: Min. Men, Lampasas County, Enlist: Mar. 21, 1860,
Disc: June 24, 1860, 2 months, 1 day service, Ranger Muster
Roll.
WOOLDRIDGE, J.R., Pvt., Comm. Off: HUGHS, Moses, Organ: Minute
Men, Enlist: March 21, 1860, 6 months service, Place of
Birth: Lampasas, Ranger Muster Roll.
WOOLF, Wm., Pvt., Comm. Off: WOODS, Wm. M., Organ: Mounted Ran-
gers, Enlist: April 10, 1860, Disc: Aug. 10, 1860, Age: 26,
Place of Birth: Bonham, Ranger Muster Roll.
WOOLFOLK, J.A., Pvt., Comm. Off: HAMNER, H.A., Capt.,
Organ: Rangers, Enlist: Jan. 14, 60 at Jacksboro for 12 mos.,
R&F 86; citizens of Wise, Parker, Montague, Young & Jack
counties in public meeting at Jacksboro org. Co. for protec-
tion of frontier; 1 Muster Roll.
WOOLIVER, John, Pvt., Comm. Off: DALRYMPLE, W.C., Organ: Mounted
Rangers, Enlist: Jan. 14, 1860, Disc: Oct. 13, 1860, Age: 22,
Place of Birth: Liberty Hill, Ranger Muster Roll.
WOOTEN, John A., Pvt., Comm. Off: CONNER, John H., Organ: Mounted
Rangers, Enlist: Jan. 20, 1860, 12 months service, Age: 25,
Place of Birth: Austin, Ranger Muster Roll.
WOOTON, H.B., Pvt., Comm. Off: HAMNER, H.A., Capt., Organ: Ran-
gers, Enlist: Jan. 14, 60 at Jacksboro for 12 months,

WOOTON, H.B., Pvt., (Continued)
   R&F 86; Citizens of Wise, Parker, Montague, Young & Jack
   counties in public meeting at Jacksboro org. Co. for protec-
   tion of frontier; 1 Muster Roll.
WORCESTER, W.W., 1st Sgt., Comm. Off: ROBERTS, D.W., & MOORE, F.M.
   Organ: Co. D, Frontier Battalion, Enlist: April 16, 1877,
   Disc: Aug. 31, 1878, Age: 28, 5'8", brown hair, grey eyes,
   Place of Birth: Kendall County, farmer, 14 months, 16 days
   Service, Ranger Muster Roll.
WORCESTER, W.W., 1st Sgt., Comm. Off: ROBERTS, D.W. & MOORE, F.M.
   Organ: Co. D, Frontier Battalion, Enlist: April 16, 1877,
   Disc: May 31, 1878, Age: 28, 5'8", brown hair, grey eyes,
   Place of Birth: Kendall County, farmer, 1 month, 16 days ser-
   vice.
WORCESTER, W.W., Pvt., Comm. Off: MOORE, F.M., Organ: Co. D, Fron-
   tier Battalion, Enlist: April 16, 1877, 5 months, 16 days of
   service, Ranger Muster Roll.
WORCESTER, W.W., 1st Sgt., Comm. Off: ROBERTS, D.W., Organ: Co. D,
   Frontier Battalion, Enlist: Sept. 1, 1877, Disc: May 31, 1878,
   Age: 28, 5'8", brown hair, grey eyes, farmer, Place of
   Birth: Kendall County, 9 months service, Ranger Muster Roll.
WORCESTER, W.W., Pvt., Comm. Off: SANSOM, John W., Organ: Fron-
   tier Forces, Enlist: Aug. 25, 1870, Disc: May 31, 1871, Place
   of Birth: Shackleford County, Ranger Muster Roll. Seacliff,
   Baldwin Co., Okla.
WORCESTER, W.W., 1st Sgt., Comm. Off: PATTON, C.A., Organ: Ken-
   dal Co. Minute Men, Co. C, Enlist: Feb. 4, 1872, Disc: Mar. 1,
   1874, Place of Birth: Kendal County, 132 days of service,
   Ranger Muster Roll.
WORD, W.H., 3rd Corp., Comm. Off: COVINGTON, William B., and
   TRAVIS, C.E., Capt., Organ: Texas Mounted Volunteer, Co. E,
   Enlist: Nov. 1, 1854, Disc: Feb. 1, 1855, Place of Birth: Aus-
   tin, Texas, 3 months service, Ranger Muster Roll.
WORD, W.H., 3rd Corp., Comm. Off: TRAVIS, C.E., Capt.,
   Organ: Texas Volunteers, Company E, Enlist: 1854, Disc: 1855,
   3 months service, Ranger Muster Roll.
WORK, John Dr., Surgeon, Comm. Off: WALKER, John G., Capt.,
   Organ: Mtd. Vol., Enlist: Nov. 1854, Ranger Muster Roll.
WORK, Philip H., 1st Sgt., Comm. Off: WALKER, John G., Capt.,
   Organ: Mtd. Vol., Enlist: Mtd. Vol., Enlist: Nov. 1854, Ran-
   ger Muster Roll.
WORD, William H., 2nd Sgt., Comm. Off: CALLAHAN, James H.,
   Organ: Mounted Rangers, Enlist: July 20, 1855, Disc: Oct. 19,
   1855, Place of Birth: San Marcos, 2 months, 29 days service,
   Ranger Muster Roll.
WORMACK, J.N., 1st Sgt., Comm. Off: CONNELL, J.G., Organ: Brown
   and San Saba County Rangers, Enlist: Jan. 6, 1874, Disc: Mar.
   26, 1874, Place of Birth: Brown and San Saba Counties, 2 mos.
   20 days service, Ranger Muster Roll.
WORMWOOD, H.R., Pvt., Comm. Off: STEVENS, G.W., Organ: Co. B,
   Frontier Battalion, Enlist: Aug. 8, 1874, Disc: Aug. 31, 1876,
   Place of Birth: Lost Valley, 24 months, 29 days service, Ran-
   ger Muster Roll.
WORRELL, J.R., Surgeon, Comm. Off: HAMNER, H.A., Capt.,
   Organ: Rangers, Enlist: Jan. 14, 60 at Jacksboro for 12 mos.;

WORRELL, J.R., Surgeon, (Continued)
R&F 86; citizens of Wise, Parker, Montague, Young & Jack
counties in public meeting at Jacksboro org. Co. for protection of frontier; 1 Muster Roll.

WORSHAM, Edward S., Pvt., Comm. Off: FORD, John S., Organ: 2nd Co.
of Rangers, Enlist: Nov. 10, 1858, Disc: May 10, 1859, Age: 20,
Place of Birth: Austin, Ranger Muster Roll.

WORTHAM, Thomas, 1st Sgt., Comm. Off: FISHER, J.C., Organ: Prov.
State Troops, Co. C, 3 Regt., Enlist: Oct. 9, 1871, Disc: Nov.
18, 1871, Place of Birth: Springfield, Texas, Ranger Muster
Roll.

WORTHINGTON, N., Pvt., Comm. Off: IKARD, E.F., Organ: Co. C,
Frontier Battalion, Enlist: May 20, 1874, Disc: Aug. 31, 1874,
Place of Birth: Clay County, 3 months, 12 days service, Ran-
ger Muster Roll.

WORTHINGTON, M.B., Pvt.,Comm. Off: EASTIN, S.W., Organ: Jack
County Rangers, Enlist: Dec. 3, 1873, Disc: April 3, 1874,
Place of Birth: Jack County, 4 months service, Ranger Muster
Roll.

WORTHINGTON, N.B., 1st Corp., Comm. Off: STEVENS, G.W., Organ: Co.
B, Frontier Battalion, Enlist: June 1, 1875, Disc: July 15,
1875, Place of Birth:Flat Top Mountain, 1 month, 15 days of
service, Deserted, Ranger Muster Roll.

WORTHY, William, Pvt., Comm. Off: FORD, John S., Organ: 3rd Co.
of Rangers, Enlist: Feb. 1, 1860, Disc: May 17, 1860, Age: 26,
Place of Birth: Coprus Christi, Died Feb. 6, 1860 from wound,
Ranger Muster Roll.

WRAY, Stephen H., Pvt., Comm. Off: FORD, John S., Organ: 2nd Co.
of Rangers, Enlist: Nov. 10, 1858, Disc: May 10, 1859, Age: 23,
Place of Birth: Austin, Ranger Muster Roll.

WREN, James A., 2nd Sgt., Comm. Off: BURLESON, Ed, Organ: Unknown,
Enlist: Jan. 20, 1860, Disc: Sept. 7, 1860, Age: 28, Place of
Birth: San Marcos, Ranger Muster Roll.

WREN, James A., 3rd Corp., Comm. Off: FORD, John S., Organ: Texas
Rangers, Enlist: Feb. 5, 1858, Disc: Aug. 5, 1858, Age: 24,
Place of Birth: Austin, Texas, 6 months service, Ranger Muster
Roll.

WREN, Thomas P., Pvt., Comm. Off: TOBIN, Wm. G., Organ: Mounted
Volunteers, Enlist: Oct. 29, 1859, Disc: Nov. 3, 1859, Place
of Birth: Oakville, Ranger Muster Roll.

WRIGHT, Andrew W.P., Pvt., Comm. Off: HENRY, William R.,
Organ: Co. C, Mounted Vol., Enlist: Dec. 14, 1854, Disc: Mar.
14, 1855, Age: 20, Place of Birth: San Antonio, 3 months of
service, Ranger Muster Roll.

WRIGHT, Armenius, Pvt., Comm. Off: MARLIN, W.N.P., Organ: Texas
Mounted Rangers, Enlist: July 15, 1858, Disc: April 5, 1859.
Place of Birth: Camp Runnels, 5 months, 10 days service, Ran-
ger Muster Roll.

WRIGHT, Armenius, Pvt., Comm. Off: MARLIN, Wm. N.P., Organ: Rangers, Enlist: July 1858, Disc: April 4, 1859, Age: 20, Place
of Birth: Camp Runnel, Ranger Muster Roll.

WRIGHT, B.F., Pvt., Comm. Off: Unknown, Organ: Co. D, Minute Men,
Enlist: May 25, 1872, Disc: April 30, 1873, Place of
Birth: Comanche County, 80 days of service, Ranger Muster Roll.

WRIGHT, Benj. T., Pvt., Comm. Off: BURLESON, Ed, Organ: Mtd. Rangers, Enlist: Jan. 20, 1860, Disc: Sept. 7, 1860, Age: 23, Place of Birth: San Marcos, Ranger Muster Roll.

WRIGHT, David, Pvt., Comm. Off: FITZHUGH, G.S., Capt., Organ: Ranger Co., Enlist: April 14, 60, Disc: Oct. 25, 60; served 6 mo. & 12 days at $25. Total: $160. R&F 83; 1 Pay Roll.

WRIGHT, David, Comm. Off: FITZHUGH;s G.S., Capt., Organ: Mounted Rangers, Enlist: April 14, 1860, Disc: Oct. 25, 1860, Place of Birth: Confederate Home, Austin, Texas, Dept. of the Interior, N.H. NICHOLSON, Inspector.

WRIGHT, Geo. M., Comm. Off: Unknown, Organ: Co. B, Frontier Battalion, Place of Birth: Granbury, Texas, Dept. of the Interior-Pensions, N.H. NICHOLSON, Inspector.

WRIGHT, William J., Pvt., Comm. Off: DALRYMPLE, W.C., Organ: Mtd. Rangers, Enlist: Jan. 14, 1860, Disc: Oct. 13, 1860, Age: 22, Place of Birth: Liberty Hill, Ranger Muster Roll. Lampasas, Texas.

WRIGHT, (RIGHT), E.B., Pvt., Comm. Off: ALEXANDER, John, Organ: Co. O, Minute Men, Enlist: Sept. 11, 1872, Disc: Aug. 13, 1873, Place of Birth: Burnet County, 67 days of service, RAnger Muster Roll.

WRIGHT, E.M., Lt., Comm. Off: WOODS, William M., Organ: Mounted Rangers, Enlist: April 10, 1860, Disc: Aug. 10, 1860, Age: 23, Place of Birth: Bonham, Ranger Muster Roll.

WRIGHT, E.M., Pvt., Comm. Off: WOODS, Wm. M., Organ: Mounted Rangers, Enlist: April 10, 1860, Disc: Aug. 10, 1860, Age: 23, Place of Birth: Bonham, Ranger Muster Roll.

WRIGHT, Ewel M., Pvt., Comm. Off: CALLAHAN, James H., Organ: Mtd. Rangers, Enlist: July 20, 1855, Disc: Oct. 19, 1855, Place of Birth: Prairie Lee, 2 months, 29 days service, Ranger Muster Roll.

WRIGHT, George W.S., Pvt., Comm. Off: MCCULLOCH, Henry E., Capt., Organ: Texas Mtd. Vols., Enlist: Nov. 5, 1850, Disc: May 5, 1851, Age: 25, Enlisted at: Austin, Texas, 6 months service, Ranger Muster Roll.

WRIGHT, Hall, Pvt., Comm. Off: FISHER, J.C., Organ: Prov. State Troops, Co. C, 3, Regt., Enlist: Oct. 9, 1871, Disc: Nov. 18, 1871, Place of Birth: Springfield, Texas, Ranger Muster Roll.

WRIGHT, Harry, Pvt., Comm. Off: HALL, J.L., Organ: Special State Troops, Enlist: Jan. 1, 1878, Disc: Feb. 28, 1878, Place of Birth: Clinton, Texas, 2 months service, Ranger Muster Roll.

WRIGHT, Henry, Pvt., Comm. Off: SNOWBALL, James, Organ: Prov. State Troops, Enlist: Oct. 13, 1871, Disc: Oct. 20, 1871, Place of Birth: Groesbeck, Texas, Ranger Muster Roll.

WRIGHT, James F., Pvt., Comm. Off: MCCULLOCH, Henry E., Capt., Organ: Texas Mtd. Vols., Enlist: Nov. 5, 1850, Disc: May 5, 1851, Age: 18, Enlisted: Austin, TExas, 6 months service, Ranger Muster Roll.

WRIGHT, John, Pvt., Comm. Off: DARNELL, N.H., Organ: Mounted Rangers, Enlist: April 14, 1860, Disc: Aug. 13, 1860, Place of Birth: Dallas, Ranger Muster Roll.

WRIGHT (RIGHT), J., Pvt., Comm. Off: WILLIAMS, John,

WRIGHT (RIGHT), J., Pvt., (Continued)
Organ: 2nd Co. of Texas Rangers, Enlist: Jan. 20, 1859, Ranger Muster Roll.
WRIGHT, J.A., Lt., Comm. Off: WRIGHT, J.A., Organ: Co. D, Minute Men, Enlist: May 5, 1872, Disc: June 1, 1873, Place of Birth: Comanche County, 80 days service, Ranger Muster Roll. Comanche, Texas.
WRIGHT, James M., Pvt., Comm. Off: DALRYMPLE, W.C., Organ: Mtd. Rangers, Enlist: Jan. 14, 1860, Disc: Oct. 13, 1860, Age: 20, Place of Birth: Liberty Hill, Ranger Muster Roll.
WRIGHT, J.R., Pvt., Comm. Off: HAMPTON, G.J., Capt., Organ: Mtd. Ranger Volunteers, Enlist: Nov. 12, 59, Disc: Dec. 11, 59; served 1 mo. at $12--$12. R&F 34; Allowances on: Clothing; $2.50; use of horse: $12; Rations: $4.50; Forage: $8.25; Total: $39.25. Co. called into State service for suppression of Cortina Rebellion on Rio Grande Frontier by Gov. H.R. RUNNELS. 1 Pay Roll.
WRIGHT, J.K., Pvt., Comm. Off: HAMPTON, G.J., Organ: Mounted Volunteers, Enlist: Nov. 12, 1859, Disc: Jan. 1, 1860, Place of Birth: Mission Valley, Left on the 11 Dec., Ranger Muster Roll.
WRIGHT, Marshall, Pvt., Comm. Off: MARLIN, W.N.P., Organ: Texas Mounted Rangers, Enlist: July 15, 1858, Disc: Nov. 14, 1858, Place of Birth: Camp Runnels, 4 months service, Ranger Muster Roll.
WRIGHT, L.B., Pvt., Comm. Off: MCNELLY, L.H., Organ: Washington Co. Vol. Militia, Enlist: July 25, 1874, Disc: Feb. 1, 1877, Place of Birth: Austin, Texas, 28 months, 10 days service, Ranger Muster Roll.
WRIGHT, L.B., Pvt., Comm. Off: HALL, J.L., Organ: Special State Troops, Enlist: Feb. 1, 1878, Disc: Feb. 28, 1878, Place of Birth: Clinton, Texas, 1 month service, Ranger Muster Roll.
WRIGHT, L.L., Pvt., Comm. Off: HALL, J.L., Organ: Special State Troops, Enlist: Feb. 15, 1877, Disc: Feb. 28, 1878, Place of Birth: Clinton, Texas, 12 months, 13 days service, Ranger Muster Roll.
WRIGHT, Marshall, Pvt., Comm. Off: MARLIN, Wm. N.P., Organ: Rangers, Enlist: July, 1858, Disc: April 4, 1859, Age: 22, Place of Birth: Camp Runnel, Ranger Muster Roll.
WRIGHT, Nathan, Pvt., Comm. Off: FITZHUGH, G.S., Capt., Organ: Ranger Co., Enlist: April 14, 60, Disc: Oct. 25, 60; Served 6 mo. & 12 days at $25 - Total $160. R&F 83; Stoppages: $16.70. Balance Pd: $143.30. 1 Pay Roll.
WRIGHT, Nathan, Pvt., Comm. Off: FITZHUGH, G.S., Organ: Mounted Rangers, Enlist: May 20, 1860, Disc: Oct. 25, 1860, Ranger Muster Roll.
WRIGHT, Pleasant, 3rd Corp., Comm. Off: WALKER, John G., Capt., Organ: Mtd. Vol., Enlist: Nov. 1854, Ranger Muster Roll.
WRIGHT, L.L., Pvt., 4th Sgt., Comm. Off: MCNELLY, L.H., Organ: Washington Co. Vol. Militia, Enlist: Jan. 1, 1875, Disc: Feb. 1, 1877, Place of Birth: Austin, Texas, 23 months 5 days service, Ranger Muster Roll.
WRIGHT, T.M., Pvt., Comm. Off: HALL, J.L., Organ: Special State

WRIGHT, T.M., Pvt., (Continued)
Troops, Enlist: July 15, 1877, Disc: Aug. 31, 1877, Place of
Birth: Clinton, Texas, 1 month 15 days service, Ranger Muster
Roll.

WRIGHT, Wm., Pvt., Comm. Off: FITZHUGH, G.S., Capt., Organ: Ranger Company, Enlist: April 14, 60, Disc: Oct. 25, 60; served 6
mo. & 12 days at $25. Total: $160. R&F 83; Stoppages: $20.60;
Balance Pd: $139.40. 1 Pay Roll.

WRIGHT, Wm., Pvt., Comm. Off: WILLIAMS, John, Organ: 2nd Co. of
Texas Rangers, Enlist: Jan. 20, 1859, Ranger Muster Roll.

WRIGHT, William, 2nd Sgt., Comm. Off: TUMLINSON, J.J.,
Organ: Tumlinson's Spy, 1 Rgt., Mtd. Gunmen, Enlist: Oct. 13,
1839, Disc: Nov. 22, 1839, 1 month, 11 days service, Trans-
fered from Capt. HALLUM's Co., Ranger Muster Roll.

WRIGHT, William, Pvt., Comm. Off: BERRY, Henry W., Organ: Mounted
Vol. for Cortinas War, Enlist: Nov. 10, 1859, Disc: Dec. 20,
1859, Age: 40, Place of Birth: Brownsville, Ranger Muster Roll.

WRIGHT, Wm. G., Pvt., Comm. Off: HUNTER, R.L., Organ: Rangers,
Parker County, Enlist: Dec. 24, 1873, Disc: March 29, 1874,
Place of Birth: Parker County, 96 days of service, Ranger Mus-
ter Roll.

WURZBACH, Adolph, 2nd Sgt., Comm. Off: HABY, George, Organ: Co. V
Minute Men, Medina Co., Enlist: Sept. 1, 1872, Disc: Aug. 15,
1873, Place of Birth: Medina County, 120 days of service, Ab-
sent March 1-21, 1873. August WURZBACH served, Ranger Muster
Roll.

WURZBACH, August, Pvt., Comm. Off: HABY, George, Organ: Co. V, Min.
Men, Medina Co., Enlist: March 16, 1873, Disc: March 21, 1873,
Place of Birth: Medina County, Served for Adolph WURZBACH. 10
days service, Ranger Muster Roll. Riomedia, Texas.

WURZBACH, Emil F., Comm. Off: ROGERS, P.H., Capt., Organ: Mounted
Rangers, Enlist: Dec. 22, 1854, Disc: March 21, 1855, Place
of Birth: 1210 Gevers St., San Antonio, Texas, Dept. of the
Interior--Pensions, N.H. NICHOLSON, Inspector.

WYATT, D.H. (M.E. in signature), Pvt., Comm. Off: WATKINS, W.C.,
Organ: Co. D, Minute Men, Enlist: Nov. 16, 1873, Disc: April
30, 1873, Place of Birth: Comanche County, 15 days service,
Ranger Muster Roll.

WYATT, J.F., Pvt., Comm. Off: TOM, Wm. Capt., Organ: Texas Vols.,
Enlist: Oct. 18, 1855, Disc: Nov. 16, 1855, Withdrew and not
entitled to pay. Ranger Muster Roll.

WYATT, Miram B., Pvt., Comm. Off: MCCULLOCH, Henry E., Capt.,
Organ: Texas Mtd. Vols., Enlist: Nov. 5, 1850, Disc: May 5,
1851, Age: 22, Enlisted at: Austin, TExas, 6 months service,
Ranger Muster Roll.

WYDICK, Emanuel, Pvt., Comm. Off: CALLAHAN, James H., Organ: Mtd.
Rangers, Enlist: July 20, 1855, Disc: Oct. 19, 1855, Place of
Birth: Prairie Lee, 2 months, 29 days service, Ranger Muster
Roll.

WYLIE, S., Sgt., Comm. Off: HANNA, Wood, Capt., Organ: Ranger Co.,
Enlist: Jan. 18, 1861, Served to Feb. 29, 1861; 12 days at
$1.50 per day; $18.00. R&F 15; One Pay Roll.

WYMAN, J.B., 1st Sgt., Comm. Off: NELSON, G.H., Organ: Texas

WYMAN, J.B., 1st Sgt., (Continued)
Mounted Militia, Enlist: Oct. 10, 1857, Disc: Dec. 28, 1857,
Place of Birth: San Antonio, 2 months, 20 days service, Ranger
Muster Roll.

WYNDHAM, Jas., Pvt., Comm. Off: WALKER, John G., Capt.,
Organ: Mtd. Vol., Enlist: Nov. 1854, Ranger Muster Roll.

WYNN, Jasper, Pvt., Comm. Off: ENGLISH, Levi, Organ: Mounted Vol.,
Enlist: Aug. 6, 1855, Disc: Nov. 13, 1855, Place of Birth: Bexar County, 3 months, 8 days service, Ranger Muster Roll.

WYNN, J.P., 3rd Corp., Comm. Off: PERRY, C.R., Organ: Co. D, Frontier Battalion, Enlist: May 25, 1874, Disc: May 25, 1875,
Place of Birth: Blanco County, 12 months service, Ranger Muster Roll.

WYNN, Philip, Pvt., Comm. Off: TOM, Wm., Capt., Organ: Texas
Vol., Enlist: Oct. 18, 1855, Disc: Nov. 16, 1855, 1 month of
service, Ranger Muster Roll.

WYNN, Calvin, Pvt., Comm. Off: ENGLISH, Levi, Organ: Mounted Vol.,
Enlist: Aug. 6, 1855, Disc: Nov. 13, 1855, Place of Birth: Bexar County, 3 months, 8 days service, Ranger Muster Roll.

YANDELL, W.H., Pvt., Comm. Off: ROBERTS, D.W., Organ: Co. D,
Frontier Battalion, Enlist: June 1, 1875, Disc: Nov. 30, 1875,
Age: 19, 5'5", fair, brown eyes, dark hair, farmer, Place of
Birth: Lawrence, Ala., 9 months service, Ranger Muster Roll.

YARBOROUGH, J.B., Pvt., Comm. Off: CAMPBELL, G.W., Organ: Montague Co. Rangers, Enlist: Dec. 13, 1873, Disc: Feb. 13, 1874,
Place of Birth: Montague County, 2 months service, Ranger Muster Roll.

YARBOROUGH, William, Pvt., Comm. Off: WALKER, John G., Capt.,
Organ: Mtd. Vol., Enlist: Nov. 1854, Ranger Muster Roll.

YARBER, David M., Pvt., Comm. Off: TUMLINSON, Peter, Capt.,
Organ: Mtd. Vols., Enlist: Nov. 12, 1859, Disc: Feb. 10, 1860,
2 months, 29 days service, Ranger Muster Roll.

YARBRO, Jesse, Pvt., Comm. Off: BARRY, James Buck, 1st Lt.,
Organ: C-. org. & fighting Indians interval before conv. of
1861, Disc: Feb. 25, 61; Serv. 1 mo. 15 days at $25 - $37.50.
R&F 25; 1 Pay Roll; BARRY received commission from Governor;
Convention assumed authority while in field and company not
mustered out.

YELLON, P.S., 3rd Lt., Comm. Off: FITZHUGH, G.S., Capt.,
Organ: Ranger Company, Enlist: April 14, 1860, Disc: July 25,
1860; served 6 mo. & 12 days at $29 to $60; Total: $298.22.
R&F 83; Stoppages: $3.20; Balance Pd: $295.02. 1 Pay Roll.
Elected 3rd Lt. from 3rd Sgt. July 7, 60.

YELTON, Philip, 3rd Lt., Comm. Off: FITZHUGH, G.S., Organ: Mtd.
Rangers, Enlist: May 20, 1860, Disc: Oct. 25, 1860, Ranger
Muster Roll.

YELTON, Phillip, Pvt., Comm. Off: BOURLAND, James, Organ: Texas
Mounted Rangers, Enlist: Jan. 28, 1859, Disc: April 28, 1859,
Place of Birth: Gainesville, Texas, 3 months service, Ranger
Muster Roll.

YATES, William J., Pvt., Comm. Off: MCCULLOCH, Henry E., Capt.,
Organ: Texas Mtd. Vols., Enlist: Nov. 5, 1850, Disc: May 5,
1851, Age: 22, Enlisted at: Austin, Texas, 6 months service,
Ranger Muster Roll.

YEAREY, John, Lt., Comm. Off: BOURLAND, J.Capt., Organ: Unknown,
    Enlist: Spring 41, Ranger Muster Roll.
YELLOW-Wolf, Spy, Comm. Off: ROSS, Peter F., Capt., Organ: Spy Co.,
    Enlist: 1860, Serv. from July 1 to Aug. 26, 60; 1 mo. & 26 days
    at $25--$46.66. R&F 39; 1 Pay Roll.
YERION, Joseph R., Pvt., Comm. Off: FITZHUGH, Wm., Organ: Texas
    Militia Mtd. Vol., Enlist: Nov. 2, 1854, Disc: Feb. 2, 1854,
    Age: 26, Place of Birth: McKinney, Texas, 3 months service,
    Ranger Muster Roll.
YUFANTE, Antonio, Pvt., Comm. Off: BERRY, Henry W., Organ: Mounted
    Vol. for Cortinas War, Enlist: Nov. 10, 1859, Disc: Dec. 20,
    1859, Age: 21, Place of Birth: Brownsville, Ranger Muster Roll.
YUFANTE, Joseph N., Pvt., Comm. Off: BERRY, Henry W., Organ: Mtd.
    Vol. for Cortinas War, Enlist: Nov. 10, 1859, Disc: Dec. 20,
    1859, Age: 35, Place of Birth: Brownsville, Ranger Muster Roll.
YNN, I.L., Pvt., Comm. Off: EASTIN, S.W., Organ: Jack County
    Rangers, Enlist: Dec. 3, 1873, Disc: April 3, 1874, Place of
    Birth: Jack County, 4 months service, Ranger Muster Roll.
YELTON, Phillip, Pvt., Comm. Off: BOURAND, James, Capt.,
    Organ: Mtd. Vol., Enlist: Jan. 28, 1859, Disc: April 28, 1859,
    Place of Birth: Gainesville, 3 months service, Ranger Muster
    Roll.
UOAKUM, D., Pvt., Comm. Off: LONG, Ira, Organ: Co. A, Frontier
    Battalion, Enlist: March 1, 1876, Disc: June 1, 1876, 3 months
    service, Ranger Muster Roll.
YOAS, C.A., Pvt., Comm. Off: HAYNIE, Geo. E., Organ: Co. M. Min.
    Men, Lampasas Co., Enlist: March 9, 1873, Disc: March 10,
    1874, Place of Birth: Lampasas County, 73 days of service,
    Ranger Muster Roll. Brady, Texas.
YONKER, John, Corp., Comm. Off: KELSO, John R., Organ: Frontier
    Forces, Enlist: Sept. 10, 1870, Disc: Feb. 2, 1871, Place of
    Birth: Camp Wood, Texas, Discharged Jan. 20, 1871, Ranger Mus-
    ter Roll.
YORK, Alfred, Pvt., Comm. Off: JOHNSON, T.J., Capt., Organ: Ran-
    ger Company, Enlist: April 21, 1860, Deserted May 28, 1860,
    R&F 99; 1 Pay Roll; Stoppages: J.M. GIBBINS $7.60, State $30.
YORK, Harrison, Pvt., Comm. Off: REED, Henry, Organ: 1 Rgt., Mtd.
    Gunmen, Enlist: Oct. 10, 1839, Disc: Nov. 22, 1839, 1 month,
    14 days service, Ranger Muster Roll.
YORK, Jeremiah, Pvt., Comm. Off: BARRY, James Buck, 1st Lt.,
    Organ: Co. org. & fighting Indians interval before Conv. of
    1861, Enlist: Jan. 10, 61, Disc: Feb. 25, 61; Serv. 1 mo. 15
    days at $25 - $37.50. R&F 25; 1 Pay Roll; BARRY received
    commission from Governor; Convention assumed authority while
    in field and company not mustered out.
YORK, Jonathan, Pvt., Comm. Off: HENRY, William R., Organ: Co. C,
    Mounted Vol., Enlist: Dec. 14, 1854, Disc: March 14, 1855,
    Age: 42, Place of Birth: San Antonio, 3 months service, Ranger
    Muster Roll.
YORK, W.W., Pvt., Comm. Off: LONG, Ira, Organ: Co. A, Frontier
    Battalion, Enlist: Sept. 8, 1875, Disc: Aug. 15, 1876,
    Age: 27, 6'2", dark, black hair, black eyes, Place of
    Birth: Warren, Ken., 11 mos. 18 days service, Ranger Muster
    Roll.

YOUNG, A.B., Pvt., Comm. Off: SPARKS, J.C., Organ: Co. C, Frontier Battalion, Enlist: Oct. 1, 1876, Disc: Aug. 31, 1877, Place of Birth: Clay County, 11 months service, Ranger Muster Roll.

YOUNG, A.T., Pvt., Comm. Off: BOURLAND, James, Organ: Texas Mtd. Rangers, Enlist: Oct. 28, 1858, Disc: Jan. 28, 1858, Place of Birth: Gainesville, Texas, 3 months service, Ranger Muster Roll.

YOUNG, C.H., Pvt., Comm. Off: FOSTER, B.S., Organ: Co. E, Frontier Battalion, Enlist: June 1, 1875, Disc: Nov. 30, 1875, Age: 30, 5'8-1/2", dark, blue eyes, dark hair, farmer, Place of Birth: Canada, 6 months service, Ranger Muster Roll. San Angelo, Texas, 12015 Chadbourne St.

YOUNG, C.H., Pvt., Comm. Off: FOSTER, B.S., Organ: Co. E, Frontier Battalion, Enlist: April 1, 1876, Disc: Aug. 31, 1876, Place of Birth: Coleman County, 5 months service, Ranger Muster Roll.

YOUNG, C.H., Pvt., Comm. Off: FOSTER, B.S., Organ: Co. E, Frontier Battalion, Enlist: Sept. 1, 1876, Disc: Aug. 31, 1877, Place of Birth: Coleman County, 12 months service, Ranger Muster Roll.

YOUNG, C.H., Pvt., Comm. Off: SPARKS, J.C., Organ: Co. C, Frontier Battalion, Enlist: May 31, 1877, Disc: Aug. 31, 1877, Place of Birth: Clay County, 3 months service, Transf. from Co. E, Ranger Muster Roll.

YOUNG, Lewis, Pvt., Comm. Off: MCCULLOCH, Henry E., Capt., Organ: Texas Mtd. Vols., Enlist: Nov. 5, 1850, Disc: May 5, 1851, Age: 22, Enlisted at: Austin, Texas, 6 months service, Ranger Muster Roll.

YOUNG, R.R., Pvt., Comm. Off: MALTBY, W.J., Organ: Co. E, Frontier Battalion, Enlist: June 6, 1874, Disc: May 31, 1875, Place of Birth: Coleman County, 11 months, 25 days service, Ranger Muster Roll.

YOUNG, C.H., Pvt., Comm. Off: WALLER, J.R., Organ: Co. A, Frontier Battalion, Enlist: May 25, 1874, Disc: April 30, 1875, Place of Birth: Erath County, 11 months, 11 days, Ranger Muster Roll.

YOUNG, John, Pvt., Comm.Off: WOOD, J.D., Organ: Prov. Mounted State Troops, Enlist: Oct. 9, 1871, Disc: Nov. 13, 1871, Place of Birth: Limestone County, Ranger Muster Roll.

YOUNT, Andrew J., Capt., Comm. Off: YOUNT, Andrew J., Capt., Organ: Ranger Company, Enlist: Nov. 26, 66 at Denton, Texas. R&F 71; Co. org. in conformity to instructions from Governor THROCKMORTON. 1 Muster Roll.

YOWS, J., Pvt., Comm. Off: NAPIER, E.R., Organ: State Guards Co. H, 6 Regt., Enlist: Jan. 10, 1871, Disc: Jan. 24, 1871, Ranger Muster Roll.

ZAPETA, Jesus, Pvt., Comm. Off: HABY, George, Organ: Co. V. Min. Men, Medina County, Enlist: Sept. 1, 1872, Disc: Aug. 15, 1873, Place of Birth: Medina County, 120 days of service, Ranger Muster Roll. San Antonio, Texas, 921 Castro St.

ZICKEFOOSE, A.A., Pvt., Comm. Off: TAYS, J.B., Organ: Co. C, Frontier Battalion, Enlist: Nov. 26, 1877, Disc: Feb. 28,

ZICKEFOOSE, A.A., Pvt., (Continued)
    1878, Place of Birth: El Paso County, 3 months, 5 days service,
    Ranger Muster Roll.
ZICKEFOOSE, A.S., 5th Corp., Comm. Off: TAY, J.B., Lt.,
    Organ: Vol. Battalion Co. C, Enlist: Dec. 1, 1877, Disc: Feb.
    28, 1878, 3 months service, Ranger Muster Roll.
ZICKEFOOSE, T.A., Pvt., Comm. Off: TAYS, J.B., Organ: Co. C, Fron-
    tier Battalion, Enlist: Nov. 26, 1877, Disc: Feb. 28, 1878,
    Place of Birth: El Paso County, 3 months, 5 days service, Ran-
    ger Muster Roll.
ZICKEFOOSE, T.A., 4th Sgt., Comm. Off: TAY, J.B., Lt.,
    Organ: Vol. Battalion Co. C, Enlist: Nov. 26, 1877, Disc: Feb.
    28, 1878, Made Sgt. on Dec. 1, 1877, Served 3 months as 4th
    Sgt., Ranger Muster Roll.
ZEIGLER, August, Pvt., Comm. Off: HENRY, William R., Organ: Co.
    C, Mounted Vol., Enlist: Dec. 14, 1854, Disc: March 14, 1855,
    Age: 21, Place of Birth: San Antonio, 3 months service, Ranger
    Muster Roll.
ZIEGLER, Jacob, Bugler, Comm. Off: LOVENSKIOLD, Charles,
    Organ: Walker Mtd. Rifles, Cortinas War, Enlist: Nov. 22, 1859,
    Place of Birth: Corpus Christi, Ranger Muster Roll.
ZIMMERMAN, Geo. H., Pvt., Comm. Off: MCCULLOCH, Henry E.,
    Organ: Texas Mounted Vol., Enlist: Oct. 25, 1847, Age: 35,
    Blue eyes, sandy hair, 6'6", Place of Birth: New Braunfels.
ZIMMERMAN, George, Surgeon, Comm. Off: CAMERON, Ewen, Capt.,
    Organ: Co. of Texas Rangers, Enlist: Mar. 20, 61 at Fredericks-
    burg for 3 months, Disc: Je. 5, 61 at Camp Mason by
    Lt. S.G. RAGSDALE, Age: 30. R&F 31; En. & Mus. Off:
    W. WAHRMMUND, Appraisers: F.V.D. STUCKEN & Louis WEISS; Val.
    H: $40; HE: $20; Gun: $30; Pistol: $25; Instruments: $40;
    $9.35 deducted from pay; no corn or forage issued, Co. en-
    titled to commutation in money; 45 miles travelled from place
    of discharge home; Co. called into service by Gov. HOUSTON;
    Co. sta. on South Fork of Llano River Mar. 20, 61; 1 Muster
    Roll.
ZIMMERMAN, Geo. H., Pvt., Comm. Off: MCCULLOCH, Henry E., Capt.,
    Organ: Texas Vols., Enlist: Oct. 25, 1847, Disc: Oct. 24, 1848,
    Age: 35; Height: 6'6", light comp., blue eyes, sandy hair,
    Place of Birth: New Braunfels, Tex., 12 months service, Ran-
    ger Muster Roll.
ZIMPLEMAN, G.B., Pvt., Comm. Off: TUSCHINSKY, Theodore, Organ: Co.
    K, Mounted Militia, Enlist: Aug. 2, 1873, Disc: Dec. 9, 1873,
    Place of Birth: Travis County, Copied Roster; 4 months, 7
    days, Ranger Muster Roll.
ZORN, F.S., Pvt., Comm. Off: HALL, J.L., Organ: Special State
    Troops, Enlist: May 1, 1877, Disc: July 31, 1877, Place of
    Birth: Clinton, Texas, 3 months service, Ranger Muster Roll.
ZUMWALT, T.B., Pvt. Comm. Off: COLDWELL, Neal, Organ: Co. F, Fron-
    tier Battalion, Enlist: July 1, 1875, Disc: Aug. 31, 1875,
    Age: 22, 5'8", dark hair, gray eyes, dark, farmer, Place of
    Birth: Gonzales, Texas, 2 months service, Ranger Muster Roll.
    Nagal, New Mexico.
ZUMWALT, John, Pvt., Comm. Off: MCCULLOCH, Henry E., Capt.,

ZUMWALT, John, Pvt., (Continued)
    Organ: Texas Volunteers, Enlist: Oct. 25, 1848, Disc: Dec. 8,
    1848, Age: 20, 1 month, 13 days service, Ranger Muster Roll.
ZUNIGA, Higinio, Comm. Off: MONTES, Telesforo, Lt., Organ: Minute
    Men, Enlist: May 27, 1874, Disc: April 20, 1875, Place of
    Birth: San Elizario, Texas, Dept. of the Interior--Pensions,
    N.H. NICHOLSON.
ZURCHER, L., Pvt., Comm. Off: DOLAN, Pat, Organ: Co. F, Frontier
    Battalion, Enlist: Sept. 10, 1876, Disc: Dec. 12, 1876,
    Age: 22, 5'8", dark hair, dark eyes, dark, farmer, Place of
    Birth: Medina Co., Texas, 3 months, 2 days service, Ranger
    Muster Roll.

INDEX
NAME MAY APPEAR MORE THAN ONCE ON ANY GIVEN PAGE

A.
ADAMS, 69;72;76.
ALEXANDER, 4;34;47;50;
80;89.
ARRINGTON, 7;18;24;42;
43;77.
ATKINSON, 40.

B.
BAKER, 5;14;20;26;62;
81;82
BALLANTYNE, 19;61;54;56.
BARRY, 21;28;35;58;92;
93.
BAU, 20;30.
BAYLOR, 3;4;24;42;76.
BEE, 78.
BENTON, 39;57;74.
BERRY, 16;19;53;91;93.
BLACK, 30;34;35.
BLAIR, 31;42;43;59.
BLEVINS, 4;21.
BOURLAND, 13;15;22;23;
30;32;45;50;65;70;75;
76;77;92;93;94.
BROWN, 20;37;38;42;43;
57;59;61;74;77;81;82.
BROWNIE, 21.
BUCHANAN, 72;86.
BURLESON, 2;3;12;16;
32;33;37;40;44;60;66;
75;80;85;88;89.

C.
CALLAHAN, 3;4;18;41;49;
51;62;65;67;87;89;91.
CAMBEL, 78.
CAMERON, 40;54;79;95.
CAMPBELL, 5;6;25;27;29;
35;38;39;41;49;54;59;
60;61;63;92.
CARMACK, 11;72.
CARROLLS, 41.
CASEY, 6.
CHAMBERLAIN, 9;20;47;56.
CLAMENTS, 17.
COLDWELL, 3;8;9;18;26;40;
42;43;44;48;50;52;54;58;
58;76;80;95.
COLLIER, 22.
CONNELL, 3;4;13;14;21;23;
50;51;64;69;70;72;80;81;
87.

CONNER, 2;6;28;33;
68;70;86.
CONNOR, 17.
COVINGTON, 20;23;26;
33;38;41;50;58;87.
COWEN, 31;39;45;46;
66.
COX, 13;15;16;19;20;
31;41;49;81.
CURETON, 28;52;65;83.
CURLEY, 64.

D.
DAGGET, 24.
DAGGETT, 72.
DALEY, 73.
DALRYMPLE, 10;11;37;
42;65;67;70;71;73;83;
85;86;89;90.
DARNELL, 5;6;13;20;24;
29;50;53;70;89.
DAVENPORT, 12;20;42;
50.
DAVIDSON, 81;82.
DENTON, 11;73;77.
DOLAN, 8;18;42;43;65;
75;96.
DONELSON, 21;31;51;52;
57;62;73;75;78.
DOWNS, 1;7;64;71;79.
DUNCAN, 16.

E.
EASTIN, 9;10;12;19;32;
35;41;53;58;72;74;88;
93.
ELKINS, 69;78.
EMBREE, 31;42;43;59.
ENGLISH, 5;23;31;38;
64;66;92.
EVERETT, 16;60;80.

F.
FALCON, 17;21.
FIELDS, 63.
FISHER, 14;25;27;41;45;
47;63;69;71;73;88;89.
FITZHUGH, 5;8;11;14;21;
22;30;32;34;36;39;44;
47;48;54;56;57;62;63;
89;90;91;92;93.
FONTLEROY, 39.

FORD, 2;4;5;10;13;
17;38;39;46;49;54;
58;59;60;61;67;71;
72;78;81;88.
FORSHEY, 29;40;85.
FOSTER, 9;10;36;
37;42;43;56;62;69;
72;73;82;94.
FRANDTZEN, 51;55.
FROST, 84.

G.
GARCIA, 2;22.
GENTRY, 35;79.
GIBBENS, 24;72.
GIBBINS, 9;21;23;40;
86;93.
GILLESPIE, 10;40;42;
43;52.
GILLILAND, 1;74.
GOODLET, 72.
GRANGER, 33;44;46;85.
GRAY, 3;20;36;51;59;
72.
GREEN, 7;12;16;21;22;
49.
GUSSETT, 78.

H.
HABY, 30;91;94.
HALL, 2;13;17;25;26;
31;36;39;41;42;43;45;
48;55;58;59;62;63;
64;66;73;75;89;90;95.
HALLUM, 91.
HALLUMS, 23.
HAMILTON, 4;41;67.
HAMNER, 27;28;29;65;
86;87.
HAMPTON, 36;51;57;58;
68;74;90.
HANNA, 91.
HARRELL, 8;10;32;34;
42;43;60;61;72.
HARRINGTON, 46;57.
HARRISON, 8;9;12;26;
37;52;55;77.
HAYNIE, 24;25;52;93.
HENDRICKS, 1.
HENRY, 5;6;8;13;14;18;
23;26;33;38;42;43;48;
61;63;65;79;88;93;95.

97

Heritage Books by Frances T. Ingmire:

Arkansas Confederate Veterans and Widows Pension Applications

Citizens of Missouri Territory: 1787-1810, Grants in Present Day Missouri, Arkansas and Oklahoma, Vol. 1

Citizens of Missouri Territory: 1810-1812, Grants in Present Day Missouri, Arkansas and Oklahoma, Vol. 2

Citizens of Missouri Territory to-1835, Grants in Present Day Missouri, Arkansas and Oklahoma, Vol. 3

North Carolina Marriage Bonds and Certificates Series: Craven County, North Carolina, Marriage Records, 1780–1867

North Carolina Marriage Bonds and Certificates Series: Cumberland County, North Carolina, Marriage Records, 1803–1878

North Carolina Marriage Bonds and Certificates Series: Guilford County, North Carolina, Marriage Records, 1771–1868

North Carolina Marriage Bonds and Certificates Series: Lincoln County, North Carolina, Marriage Records, 1783–1866

North Carolina Marriage Bonds and Certificates Series: Orange County, North Carolina, Marriage Records, 1782–1868

North Carolina Marriage Bonds and Certificates Series: Randolph County, North Carolina, Marriage Records, 1785–1868

North Carolina Marriage Bonds and Certificates Series: Rowan County, North Carolina, Marriage Records, 1754–1866

North Carolina Marriage Bonds and Certificates Series: Stokes County, North Carolina, Marriage Records, 1783–1868

North Carolina Marriage Bonds and Certificates Series: Surry County, North Carolina, Marriage Records, 1783–1868

North Carolina Marriage Bonds and Certificates Series: Wake County, North Carolina, Marriage Records, 1781–1867

North Carolina Marriage Bonds and Certificates Series: Wilkes County, North Carolina, Marriage Records, 1779–1868

Texas Ranger Service Records, 1838–1846

Texas Ranger Service Records, 1847–1900, Volume 1: A-C

Texas Ranger Service Records, 1847–1900, Volume 2: D-G

Texas Ranger Service Records, 1847–1900, Volume 3: H-K

Texas Ranger Service Records, 1847–1900, Volume 4: L-N

Texas Ranger Service Records, 1847–1900, Volume 5: O-S

Texas Ranger Service Records, 1847–1900, Volume 6: T-Z

www.ingramcontent.com/pod-product-compliance
Lightning Source LLC
Chambersburg PA
CBHW080337270326
41927CB00014B/3268